D0215347

Introduction to

Career
Counselling
& Coaching

Hazel Reid

Los Angeles | London | New Delhi
Singapore | Washington DC

Los Angeles | London | New Delhi
Singapore | Washington DC

SAGE Publications Ltd
1 Oliver's Yard
55 City Road
London EC1Y 1SP

SAGE Publications Inc.
2455 Teller Road
Thousand Oaks, California 91320

SAGE Publications India Pvt Ltd
B 1/I 1 Mohan Cooperative Industrial Area
Mathura Road
New Delhi 110 044

SAGE Publications Asia-Pacific Pte Ltd
3 Church Street
#10-04 Samsung Hub
Singapore 049483

Editor: Susannah Trefgarne
Assistant editor: Laura Walmsley
Production editor: Rachel Burrows
Marketing manager: Camille Richmond
Cover design: Lisa Harper-Wells
Typeset by: C&M Digitals (P) Ltd, Chennai, India
Printed and bound by CPI Group (UK) Ltd,
Croydon, CR0 4YY

© Hazel Reid 2016

First published 2016

Apart from any fair dealing for the purposes of research or
private study, or criticism or review, as permitted under the
Copyright, Designs and Patents Act, 1988, this publication may
be reproduced, stored or transmitted in any form, or by any
means, only with the prior permission in writing of the
publishers, or in the case of reprographic reproduction, in
accordance with the terms of licences issued by the Copyright
Licensing Agency. Enquiries concerning reproduction outside
those terms should be sent to the publishers.

Library of Congress Control Number: 2015936315

British Library Cataloguing in Publication data

A catalogue record for this book is available from
the British Library

MIX
Paper from
responsible sources
FSC® C013604

ISBN 978-1-4462-6035-7
ISBN 978-1-4462-6036-4 (pbk)

At SAGE we take sustainability seriously. Most of our products are printed in the UK using FSC papers and boards.
When we print overseas we ensure sustainable papers are used as measured by the Egmont grading system.
We undertake an annual audit to monitor our sustainability.

To family – before, beside and beyond career.

Contents

List of figures   viii
About the author   ix
Acknowledgements   x

1. Introduction   1

2. What do we mean by career?   6

3. Career coaching and career mentoring   26

4. Established theories of career decision making   41

5. Counselling theories to inform career counselling and
    coaching practice   63

6. New and emerging approaches   85

7. Using narrative approaches in career counselling and
    career coaching   104

8. Working with diversity   123

9. Career development in organisations   144

10. Models for structuring career conversations   163

11. Developing skills and techniques for career counselling and coaching   182

12. Supporting career learning and development in a range of contexts   200

13. Using digital technologies and creative approaches in careers work   222

14. Becoming a critically reflective practitioner   241

Appendices   260
References   271
Index   287

List of figures

2.1   Career services: a comparison of guidance, education
and counselling   12

5.1   Client = Adaptive Child/Career Practitioner = Nurturing Parent   78

5.2   Client = Free Child/Career Practitioner = Critical Parent   79

5.3   Client = Critical Parent/Career Practitioner = Adaptive Child   79

6.1   The wheel of change   96

9.1   The seven-stage transition curve   157

10.1   Comparison of Egan and SIM   165

10.2   The three-stage model   167

12.1   The three-stage model applied to group work   212

About the author

Professor Hazel Reid has a BA (Hons) Degree in Sociology, a post-graduate diploma in Career Guidance, a Masters Degree in Psychology and a Doctorate in Education. She is Director of Research for the Faculty of Education at Canterbury Christ Church University, UK, supervises doctoral students, and until recently coordinated the auto/biography and narrative research theme group. Until August 2014, Hazel was the Director of the Centre for Career & Personal Development at Canterbury Christ Church, leading the development of education, training and research in career guidance and counselling, and youth support programmes. Hazel is a Fellow of the Career Development Institute, a Fellow of the National Institute of Careers Education and Counselling (and co-edits the NICEC journal) and a founding member of the European Society for Vocational Designing and Career Counselling. She is also a Fellow of the Higher Education Academy in the UK. She is actively involved in a number of European projects related to the work of career guidance counsellors and a member of the steering group for NICE (Network for Innovation in Career Guidance and Counselling in Europe).

Hazel has a particular interest in the development of supervision for career counsellors and in exploring narrative career counselling, and has presented her work at national and international conferences. She is also undertaking research into the lived experiences of long-term unemployed young people in an area of social and economic disadvantage in the UK. Hazel has published widely on a number of topics relating to the work of career counsellors.

Acknowledgements

I would like to thank Sage Publications for the invitation to write this book and Kate Wharton and Laura Walmsley for their support and encouragement, alongside other colleagues at Sage who prepared the manuscript for publication. A number of academic colleagues reviewed individual chapters and I am very grateful for their constructive comments. In alphabetical order, my thanks go to: Gideon Arulmani, Rebecca Corfield-Tee, Alison Fielding, Tristram Hooley and Jane Westergaard. Jane reviewed several chapters, always taking great care to question my assumptions and inconsistencies, whilst offering helpful suggestions for improvement. Finally I would like to thank my institution, Canterbury Christ Church University, for awarding me a number of days 'study leave' to help with the writing of the text.

I

Introduction

At the start

I had a dream. It happened on the night after I accepted the invitation from Sage to write a proposal for 'a single-authored book of about 100,000 words'. It did not take me long to think about whether or not I should write the book and I accepted with some excitement, and no doubt pleasure at having been asked. And then I had a dream. It went like this:

I am in a courtyard which is open to the sky and designed for people to cook food for guests. There are cooking tables, suitably equipped and provisioned. I am there with my husband John and two friends, Gideon and Sonali Arulmani who are visiting us from their home in India. We are somewhere in Europe and it could be the UK, it is late afternoon and the sun is shining. I volunteer to cook the meal – an Indian meal for friends from India. I am a competent cook but have never cooked 'Indian food'. A handful of other people arrive in this place to cook for their friends at other tables in the courtyard. John, Gideon and Sonali wander off to sit in the shade and enjoy a bottle of wine. I start cooking using ingredients and spices I am not familiar with and I am without a recipe book. I have absolutely no idea what I am doing. Other people arrive to join our meal – this is a surprise. I add more ingredients. It is now very hot and very noisy in the court-yard, with many other people cooking for their guests. The cooking table will also be serving as the eating table and I worry that it will not be big enough, so I move all my stuff to a larger table that is not yet occupied and continue cooking. Everyone is having a good time enjoying bottles of wine and telling me how much they are looking forward to the meal. I think I should taste the food, but do not have time. Finally I can do no more as all the ingredients have been used in the dish. I place the meal on the table and call people over. They sit down, but the food is in the middle of the table and no one can reach it – they cannot access it.

I then wake up. I tell Mr Freud that I do not need his analysis. I have taken on a huge task and my dream is questioning if it was wise to accept. It's clear I need a plan and I need people to sample the content, but why did I think writing this book was a good idea and why now?

Why this book – why now?

The meaning of 'career' varies according to the context, be this economic, cultural or sector-based. The concept of career has also changed over time, from its emergence as a 'discipline' in the early twentieth century to diverse meanings in the twenty-first century. The rapid changes that are taking place question established thinking about how career guidance and counselling should be theorised and implemented in practice, alongside the growth in career coaching as an alternative approach for supporting individuals in the construction of their careers. The recent upheaval in economies based on capitalism, the political changes in many countries in the Middle East and elsewhere, the expanding economies of China and India – these are just some of the events that are having a significant impact both within and between nations and the environment. The recession in countries in the Northern Atlantic has led to calls for realism and resilience in terms of career interests, but this is a prevalent discourse that requires examination. Flexibility, adaptability, recognising that jobs are rarely 'for life' are all important concepts, but what do we mean when we expect people to make 'realistic' choices – realistic on whose terms? And does this ignore or marginalise the concept of career satisfaction? There is a tendency in the call for realism and resilience to shift the 'blame' for unemployment and underemployment onto individuals, despite the wider social and economic context. And we live in a world of restricted natural resources. Decisions about future education, training and employment take place in a global context where sustainability issues lead to many wanting to make what they regard as ethical or moral choices: this could be described as a commitment to 'green careers'.

In discussing these contemporary issues and offering definitions of the terms used, the book begins by establishing the groundwork for exploring the relevant theories evolving from psychology, sociology and labour economics. Its aim, however, is to advocate for *psychosocial* understandings that work across academic disciplines in order to be relevant for current times. It cautions against individualistic accounts that pay insufficient attention to social context but at the same time recognises that career is all about biography – how individuals define themselves. That said, it acknowledges that for a large percentage of the world's population, work is about livelihood, thus multicultural or transcultural issues are appraised. As an **introductory** text then, the scope is broad: to serve the needs of the changing context for careers work.

Who is the book for?

The book is intended to be a core text aimed at courses and programmes for students and trainees undertaking university and work-based learning, who want to enter or are working in the career development, career counselling and career coaching field. As it outlines new and emerging approaches, it will also be a resource for experienced career practitioners to support continuous professional development. The field includes independent careers organisations working in the compulsory sector of education, careers counsellors working independently in schools (state and private) and other educational establishments (Further or Higher Education), and those working as career coaches, or in Human Resource departments in commercial organisations and in employment placement providers (state funded or private). The book will be useful as a modular textbook where career counselling and/or career coaching are optional modules on a programme of study within a general counselling course of training. In additional it could be viewed as a supplementary text for trainee teachers (who in their tutorial role often guide students in terms of options in education, training and work; alongside others in schools who may be offering support for career activities). The book cannot encompass the career counselling and coaching systems found across the globe, but it is mindful of taking a multicultural approach and has international relevance.

What are the aims of the book?

The book aims to provide a comprehensive text that not only explains established and emerging theory and practice, but also addresses developments in the career counselling and coaching field that are not covered in existing textbooks. For example, career coaching is a developing practice that is not yet underpinned by much supporting literature, but courses are now being offered by universities as well as commercial training organisations. More generally, there is a need for a careers text that combines (as an introductory reader) many of the shorter publications dealing with established approaches, constructivist theory and methods, career education, development and learning; and covers potential 'gaps' in the literature. These gaps include career coaching, the use of web technologies, 'green careers', multicultural career counselling, the use of innovative and creative approaches, developing and supporting careers in organisations, effective use of labour market intelligence, critical reflective practice within careers work, supervision, career counselling in groups – all within a context of change.

What is excluded would be the depth that would be required from a text that seeks to cover any one of those topics as a discrete publication. That said, the approach is critical and evaluative, drawing on research, theory and practice. The work is fully referenced, but has avoided saturating the text with citations. In summary, it is a comprehensive introductory text for those whose work roles include supporting career development and growth within education, public services, private practice and commercial organisations. Alongside explaining established theories and their application, it explores emerging and innovative perspectives relevant for current practice in a local and global economy.

What's the writing style?

Drawing on the author's practical experience, teaching and research, the book is illustrated throughout with case studies derived from practice, it pauses to encourage reflection and includes activities and further reading to aid learning and extend understanding. Throughout the book, when a concept or term is introduced an activity will help readers to pause and 'unpack' the meaning. The style is intended to be accessible for those new to the field and for those returning to the literature for a text to support their learning for new contexts. So although grounded in theory and research, the intention throughout is to illustrate ways the reader can apply the concepts to practice. As in the opening of this chapter, the first person singular 'I' will be used, alongside the use of 'we' where this is appropriate: this is not the convention in most academic texts, but is employed to engage the reader in the conversation about career counselling and coaching as 'we' progress through the text.

What's the content?

Each chapter begins with a short list of the intended outcomes and ends with a summary. It is possible to read the chapters in any order, but there is logic in the order in which they are presented. The early chapters engage with definitions and issues, before moving on to describe established theory and application. What follows are two chapters which explore new and emerging approaches for career counselling and coaching. The book then progresses by examining different contexts for careers work and then outlining models, skills and techniques to support the development of career practitioners. In the final chapters it considers the broad topic of career learning and development, the use of digital technologies and other creative practices, and it ends with the important concept of critical reflective practice for careers work.

At the end

The introduction for a book is always written at the end of the project. The writing has taken 20 months and at times has felt like a juggernaut that is approaching me at a rapid pace from an ever-diminishing horizon. I have had to remind myself constantly that the book is an **introduction** and that I cannot cover everything and work at the depth that the topics deserve. At other times it has been a completely absorbing activity that has been exciting and rewarding. Whether my 'recipe' works as an introductory text to career counselling and coaching remains to be seen; without stretching the metaphor too far, 'the proof of the pudding is in the eating', so please read on.

2

What do we mean by career?

This chapter will:

- define career, career guidance, career education, career counselling and career coaching;
- discuss how the context affects our understanding of the term career;
- describe the changing concept of career over time;
- explore the core competences and training required for effective careers work;
- question the prevalence of 'Western' approaches in a changing world.

Introduction

The meaning of 'career' will vary according to its context as discourses, or ways of thinking and talking around the concept, relate to social, historical, economic, cultural and policy contexts. Within a shifting landscape this chapter will offer general definitions of 'career', before moving on to describe career guidance, career education, career counselling and career coaching. Each of these areas will be explored in greater detail as the book develops, but initial definitions will be given here. Contextual issues will then be considered as these affect the extent and reach of careers work in relation to the 'operational' setting in which it occurs; and also influence our understanding of the purpose of careers work. Albeit that the title of this book relates to career counselling and coaching, I am using the term 'careers work' as an overarching term to incorporate the activities of both career practitioners and their clients. The chapter will also discuss how the concept of career changes over time; from its emergence as a 'discipline' in the early twentieth century to diverse meanings in the twenty-first century. These contextual issues question established thinking about how careers work should be theorised and implemented in practice, and point to the emergence of career coaching as an activity that has increasing relevance for current times. A little time will be spent considering the notion of competences for careers work, before reflecting on the Western 'world view' that underpins an understanding of career. So, this will be a chapter that engages with definitions of career in a changing context: establishing the groundwork for exploring the relevant theories evolving from psychology, sociology and labour economics.

Definitions – what's in a name?

The word career is related to the Latin *cursus*, linked to words such as running; course, voyage, journey; race; direction; march; and career. Many current definitions make reference to movement, journeys and progression through life and work. My dictionary also tells me that 'From the 2nd cent. BC there developed a standard cursus honorum (career path) followed by leading citizens of Rome. The first step was to be quaester often followed by the aedileship; this was followed by the praetorship and then the consulship' (OLD, 2005). Most of us will associate the word career with work, but there are a number of words that might substitute, all of which will vary in their meaning; to some extent depending on who is doing the interpreting. Before having a look at my definitions, take some time to engage with the activity below.

Activity 2.1

Consider the following words and note down what they mean for you:

- Work
- Job
- Livelihood
- Occupation
- Profession
- Vocation
- Career

There are similarities in these terms, but in the attempt to understand what we mean by career, differences should be considered as careers work does not take place in a politically neutral context. The success of any service dedicated to supporting individuals as they develop a career is largely dependent on the cultural, historical and policy context in which that service operates (Sultana, 2011). We will return to these changing contextual issues later. *Work*, as a noun and a verb, has a longer list of possible meanings (OED, 1992) but includes employment or occupation, especially as a way of earning income, and tasks to be undertaken, which could include unpaid work and the application of mental or physical effort. *Job* is similar but sounds more singular – a task to be done. *Livelihood* can be defined as a means for living, throughout life. *Occupation*, in the context of career, relates to employment but also to how we pass the time, 'our pastimes'; i.e. both paid and leisure activities. *Profession* has the ring of a worthy occupation, something that is governed by norms of professional conduct, implying significant training and competence. *Vocation* suggests a strong 'calling' (from the Latin 'voco') for a particular type of work; for example when associated with a career in the church this can be perceived as a divine call from God. However, it is also associated with careers dedicated to helping and evokes a selfless pursuit of caring about the needs of others.

A dictionary definition of the noun career (OED, 1992) will usually focus on a profession, with its sense of stability and progress. Interestingly, as a verb the word career also means to swerve about wildly. There is a nice dichotomy here that reflects the tensions felt by many in the world of work in the twenty-first century. The point of the activity above is to acknowledge that words are important and that our experience of the world and career is shaped by language which cannot be separated from context. To many, livelihood, the getting of one's daily bread, does not evoke notions of profession, vocation or career and these words may have 'middle class' and Western connotations that have little or no relevance to the material conditions of their lives. In our careers work it is therefore always important to combine the personal with the political (Wright Mills, 1970); this book will strive to maintain a balance between the psychological and the social – in short a *psychosocial* approach.

In Act Two, Scene Two, of Shakespeare's *Romeo and Juliet*, Juliet muses:

What's in a name? That which we call a rose

By any other word would smell as sweet.

Juliet refers here to Romeo being a Montague, the sworn enemy of Juliet's family the Capulets, and suggests that labels – what things are called – do not determine our relationship with the thing thus named, ''Tis but thy name that is my enemy'. But in this book, as is common in many texts of this nature, we are examining our understanding of terms – what things are called – in an attempt to have a shared understanding of their meaning. This is not an easy task as careers work varies between countries and within countries according to how it is provided and who is involved. The work is not simply about helping people to make career decisions, as it involves considering educational and training options, work opportunities, career development within work and managing redundancy and unemployment or under-employment (Kidd, 2006). It can encompass disengagement with the world of work at the end of a career span (King, 2010). It also includes helping people to cope with disappointment, the management of work relationships and concerns around what is now referred to as 'work–life balance'.

Careers work must also engage with the rhetoric around employability skills, resilience and adaptability. Whilst many of these tensions derive from external political and economic forces, the effects are felt by the individual when work is difficult to find. Employment opportunities remain structured by the society in which individuals live (Roberts, 2005), albeit that individuals, to varying degrees, have the ability to act upon the world – to be 'agentic'. The career practitioner needs to pay attention to the prevailing discourses about work and how these influence the nature of their own work. In other words, if the work is to be truly client-centred, the practitioner needs to be mindful of the individualistic rhetoric that surrounds much careers work.

Reflection point 2.1

What does the term client-centred mean to you? Have you come across the term before, and if so, where?

The work of Carl Rogers, from which the term client-centred derives, will be discussed in a later chapter. Within careers work a client-centred approach suggests that it is the client's needs, as they determine them, which are the focus of the work; rather than a wider agenda external to the client's expressed wishes. This approach is not, however, without contextual difficulty, as per this discussion. If our definition settles on an interpretation which suggests that career is linear, with a seamless development from initial ideas that are tested and that build towards an ultimate achievement or goal – we will be misunderstanding the realities of the lives of many. Too much focus on the individual can lead to a culture of blame if the individual does not demonstrate adaptability, flexibility and resilience; 'does not try hard enough' to locate and work towards an identified career goal. Such thinking also underestimates the impact of the instability of the contemporary working world from which the call for adaptability, flexibility and resilience stems. This can be referred to as the rise of a neoliberal agenda, which may not ignore, but certainly masks the structural constraints that can be experienced as an unremitting source of stress; rather than an impetus for creative self-determination.

Activity 2.2

What is your understanding of the term 'neoliberal agenda'? Before you read on, construct a sentence that 'unpacks' the term drawing on what you have read so far.

When I hear the term 'neoliberal', I am reminded of the policies of Thatcher's Conservative government in the UK during the 1980s. That government supported economic liberalisation, in the form of free trade and open markets. This resulted in privatisation and the deregulation of many public services and a move to increase the role of the private sector in 'delivering' public services. As a consequence, the size of the public sector decreased and the power of the trade unions was diminished. However, like many definitions, the meaning of neoliberalism shifted over the twentieth century; currently the concept of a neoliberal agenda is used critically to bring attention to laissez-faire economic policies that derive from a focus on a market economy (in other words, 'leave it alone' and the market will find the balance). The philosophy behind such an approach seems disconnected from a humanistic world view that seeks to promote social justice; and a more enabling sense of work and career being a source of life satisfaction. And we could add, this is a predominant view in the Western world and should not be viewed as universal.

Returning to definitions of career, there are a number that can be found in the literature. Collin and Young suggest:

> In the abstract, as a concept, career can refer to the individual's movement through time and space. It can also focus on the intersection of individual biography and social structures ... [it can] refer to the patterns and sequences of occupations and positions occupied by people across their working lives. (Collin and Young, 2000: 3)

Super viewed career counselling as

> the process of helping a person to develop and accept an integrated and adequate picture of himself [*sic*] and of his role in the world of work, to test this concept against reality, and to convert it into reality, with satisfactions to himself and benefit to society. (Super, 1951: 92)

In line with the previous discussion, the difficulty with both of these definitions when taken out of context is the sense of stability, whereas 'work in the 21st century leaves people feeling anxious and insecure' (Savickas, 2011: 3). The current experience of work is more fluid, with the notion of a linear career trajectory seeming outdated. Indeed Savickas goes on to state, 'The "dejobing" or "jobless work" that has accompanied the digital revolution changes long-term employment into short-term projects, making it increasingly difficult to comprehend careers with theories that emphasise stability rather than mobility' (ibid.). Theories, old and new, will be examined in a later chapter, but what the above alerts us to is a state of flux within which it is not possible to be definite about our definitions.

Before continuing, a further note is required in terms of what to call those who engage in professional careers work. By professional here I mean those who are educated, trained and qualified, and experienced, to help individuals construct their career ideas. And I am aware that we could start another discussion running at this point about the word professional, but we will come back to that later. What follows draws further on the work of Mark Savickas, in order to consider different and complementary types of career services. Depending on the context, what people call themselves will vary, but as an overarching term, when one is needed, the book will use 'career practitioner'. The chapter will now consider other terms used in careers work, but first a pause.

Reflection point 2.2

We have spent some time now engaging in definitions and have not finished yet. What are your thoughts about the time invested in this – is it useful? Why? Or why not? Clearly I think it is important to examine the language we use, but a) what do you think, and b) why do you think what you think? Time will be spent throughout the book working reflexively. Have a go with this now – it can help to note (in a style that suits you, e.g. notes, diagrams, journal writing) your immediate reactions to the questions posed here.

Career guidance, career education and career counselling

The terms career guidance, career education and career counselling are often used interchangeably but they relate to different activities. Savickas has linked the terms to the provision of career services that were evident in Western economies in the twentieth century (Figure 2.1).

Savickas states (2011) that *vocational guidance*, derived from the work of Parsons (1909), Holland (1997) and others, centred on the need to fit individuals' traits to

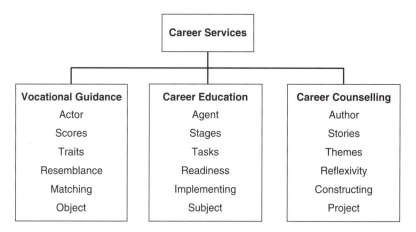

Figure 2.1   Career services: a comparison of guidance, education and counselling (Savickas, 2011: 7)

job factors. Thus, in the early twentieth century this was a scientific and objective matching approach that aimed to meet the needs of an industrial economy. Bimrose, writing about career guidance in the UK (2010), states that the 'trait/factor' matching approach remains the dominant model that can be observed in practice. An example might help to illustrate this.

Case study 2.1: Career guidance – matching in practice

Ali works with young unemployed people in an open access point in the centre of a seaside town where unemployment statistics are generally high, but do vary according to the season. A client, Jake, arrives for a pre-arranged meeting with Ali. Jake left school recently at age 16 with few qualifications, but is keen to start work and says he 'would not mind a bit of training, but does not want to go to college every day of the week'. Ali decides to use a computer career matching programme with Jake, so that they can assess his likes and dislikes and match these to a job profile. They spend time doing this together, as Ali believes that this should not be used as a 'quick fix, you know leaving them to get on with it while I go and do something else! That is not helpful in my view – if I sit alongside the client I can help with the interpretation when needed'. At the end of the session they have a list of jobs that Jake feels does match his interests, current qualification level and aspirations. Ali then says, 'In some ways, Jake, that is the easy bit, we now need to see what is available in terms of vacancies in your local area – but at least now we have a clearer idea of what you like and what might match your interests'.

The term *career education*, however, acknowledged that people (and occupations) develop over time and that learning about self and job opportunities – career education – is a subjective, rather than objective, developmental task (Super, 1957). Again an example may help to clarify this.

Case study 2.2: Career education, learning about self and career

Sienna works in a school where she is employed to arrange group work sessions to prepare students in Year 9 (age 13–14) to make their decisions about future courses, and again in Year 11 (age 15–16) for the choices that they make at the end of that year. She also sees some students in Year 11 on a one-to-one basis, if they are having difficulty making decisions about what to do next. She joined the staff 18 months ago, and is developing her knowledge about local employers, training providers and college courses. She talks about her role as a career educator.

'Yes, it is an important part of my work and an aspect that the school values. They accept, from their own experience as teachers of course, that people develop over time and their ideas about what they want to do often change. I prefer the term career learning and development to "careers education" and have recently persuaded the school to rebrand these sessions. I design the sessions to reflect the sorts of decisions that students are trying to make at particular points in time – although of course they have to be general enough for each individual to think of where they are in terms of their own individual learning. The sessions do not replace the guidance that some need later on, on a one-to-one basis, but they help in terms of preparation, as career is something you can learn about with others.

Some sessions focus on particular types of careers – job families if you like – but mostly the sessions are about the options available, thinking about what they like and are good at, considering the advantages and disadvantages of an option and how to decide, and also exploring that move from school to something else – out

(Continued)

(Continued)

there. It's relatively easy for us adults to think about that, but not so easy when all you have known is school. I'd like to think they can apply that learning later the next time they face a transition – as we know there are plenty of changes in a working life these days!'

Barnes et al. (2011) also prefer the term 'career learning and development' rather than career education or career guidance. Although others may locate career development as a term associated with career trajectories within organisations, Barnes et al. offer a different interpretation that is located in social constructionism, emphasising that knowledge about career and the self is ongoing and mediated through interactions with others in a social context. This resonates with approaches that focus on the interpersonal processes that influence an individual as they construct a career.

Career counselling, appearing in the late twentieth century, is about working with individuals to identify the meaningful life themes that can be taken into a career as part of the individual's biography. In a postmodern view of the world (at least in the West) the expectation of a biographical trajectory based on a fixed sequence of school/work/retirement is no longer tenable within employment markets that are unstable and unpredictable. Once more an example may be helpful.

Case study 2.3: Career counselling – constructing a new career story

Stuart works as a private career practitioner alongside teaching part-time on a career coaching course at a local college. Through his website he has been contacted by Dee, who says she is fed up with her job and wants to investigate alternatives. Through the email, they discuss an outline contract for the work, which clarifies the costs, and they agree to meet for an initial conversation, before deciding on whether to work together. Stuart meets his clients in their homes if local or in his office at his home; but often arranges the initial meeting in a public space if this feels right for both parties. He explains that this first meeting will take up to an hour, possibly less, and is included in the costs if they proceed. Stuart is fortunate that there is an interview room he can use occasionally at the college, although he tells Dee 'I also use the coffee lounge in that book shop on the high street, if you prefer'. Dee is happy with the college and they arrange a time to meet there. After the initial meeting, Stuart summarises their conversation.

'Dee was very fed up with her current job – I sensed some turmoil currently; although this was not the time to delve into that in any depth. She said that when she entered the financial sector after completing her qualifications, she thought she was "set for life", but now she feels "out of tune" with the values of the organisation she works for. We explored this a bit and she alluded to changes in her home life which had led her to reassess what she wants from a career. My initial assessment is that she is now in a dysfunctional career which no longer feels meaningful to her. Anyway, I outlined the type of exploration that we could do together and my approach to career counselling, the methods I might use. We agreed to meet for a career consultation next week and she is happy for me to visit her at her home. I explained the need for some privacy as we talk, but that it would be quite OK with me if there were someone else in the house – that seemed to reassure her. One session may be enough for her to begin the process of constructing a new career story."

What is important here is to acknowledge that each of the above types of careers work (i.e. career guidance, career education, career counselling) has relevance – they are not proposed as a development of services or activities where one supersedes another. And, each can be carried out in the public or private sector. That said, and it has been said earlier, contextual and cultural factors will shape the availability, usefulness and applicability of the service offered. Trait/factor matching and developmental approaches are rooted in the discipline of psychology and knowledge of structural/sociological theories is also required. It would be naïve and incorrect to state that social context is ignored in these psychological approaches, but less attention is paid to wider structural forces. It is not the intention here to polarise the disciplines of psychology and sociology, hence the use of the term psychosocial in this book. Savickas (2011), as a preface to introducing career construction theory, highlights how the social reorganisation of work in the twenty-first century compels us to think in new ways; incorporating a range of perspectives and 'world views' in order to re-vision theories that underpin careers work: 'career construction theory concentrates on self-construction *through work and relationships*' (2011: 13, *my emphasis*). Savickas views this as career *counselling,* as it involves working alongside a client in a collaborative relationship.

In the UK, practitioners working in the statutory sector (i.e. in schools and with young people) are more used to the term career guidance than career counselling. The latter is associated with therapeutic counselling which, historically, has been viewed as a separate profession (Kidd, 2006). Career guidance has been seen as broader than career counselling as, alongside one-to-one interviews, it can include interventions such as presentations and group work, supported by a range of guidance activities, identified as informing, advising, using counselling skills, assessing, enabling, advocating, feeding back, networking and referring (Reid and Fielding, 2007).

So, the distinctions between career counselling and career guidance are not as clear as a discussion on definitions or a list of activities may suggest – not only do career practitioners use counselling skills, they are often working with issues that require a knowledge of counselling models: more on this later.

Career coaching

For many working outside of the statutory sector and outside of education, Juliet's question 'What's in a name?' may be more relevant. There has been a significant interest in the growth of career and life coaching in recent years. Whereas life coaching has a broader focus, career coaching involves interventions to enhance self-development and performance (the similarities with sports coaching are obvious here) and is usually orientated to setting and achieving goals. That said the premise of this book is that career is not separate from life and needs to be viewed holistically, within a life; but definitions are only helpful if they offer some distinctiveness. There is a focus on action toward behavioural change and techniques are often underpinned by learning from cognitive behavioural therapy (CBT). CBT can be summarised as a psychotherapeutic approach, utilising both behaviourist and cognitive therapy. The approach works with dysfunctional and non-rational ideas and behaviours that are learnt and can therefore be unlearnt, through goal orientated procedures and action strategies to help address the issue. (A simplistic example, not related to career, might be helping someone to unlearn a fear of spiders or flying, by gradual exposure to the object which produces an irrational fear to change their perception of the threat it poses.) A career coach may work with a client or clients to plan the development of their career, investigate alternative careers, improve self-presentation and communication skills – alongside constructing relevant CVs and improving performance at job interviews. This work may take place with clients of varying ages and in a range of settings. Other tasks may relate to leadership skills and the management of the careers of others, or self-management in terms of balancing the demands of work and personal life and other occupational issues.

Within career coaching, as part of an action-focused approach, there is a growing number of resources available: some are work-books. For example, Mills (2011: xvii) makes reference to 'rather complicated career and psychological theory', but the focus is (understandably for a work-book) on practical 'self-help' exercises that can be undertaken without the help of a specialist. Others draw on theory whilst illustrating the approach with case studies and narratives (MacLennan, 2013). Zeus and Skiffington (2000) draw explicitly on psychology and the development of adult and constructivist learning principles as the roots of coaching. Zeus and Skiffington are clear about what coaching is not, but point to the interdisciplinarity of the process: 'coaching is sometimes seen as a style of facilitation or management and is occasionally used interchangeably with mentoring, consulting and even therapy' (2000: 3). Clarifying that in their view *Coaching at Work* (the title of their text) is about learning and is collaborative, they offer the following definition:

> Coaching is essentially a conversation – a dialogue between a coach and a coachee – within a productive, results-orientated context. Coaching involves helping individuals access what they know. They may never have asked themselves the questions, but they have the answers. A coach assists, supports and encourages individuals to find these answers. (ibid.)

With the reframing of careers work in the UK and elsewhere, the traditional distinctions around career guidance, career education/development and career counselling are breaking down. Many practitioners are beginning to operate across previous boundaries and career coaching *may* emerge as the term that becomes more inclusive. It could be argued that specialisms will then be lost, but all workers in the twenty-first century are encouraged to be flexible and adaptable, and career practitioners are not excluded from that necessity. A case study of a career coach demonstrates this.

Case study 2.4: A career coach names her practice

'What do I call myself? Well it all depends where I am working and with whom. I'll try and explain. At the moment I have three ongoing projects. I am working with a business organisation which is about to make a number of their professional workers redundant. At this stage for them I am a career consultant, advising them on how to manage this process in terms of designing a programme of activities that will help individuals prepare for new jobs outside of the company. It may be me who does the workshops with these individuals, or it may be their own human resources people – I don't know yet, although I hope they ask me to tender for this.

I am also working with someone who is very dissatisfied with their current occupation. We have met once for a half-day session and then have communicated by email as she has worked through the tasks we agreed. Our next meeting will be via Skype, but we may meet again – virtually or in reality – if we agree that is needed. Because of the

(Continued)

(Continued)

time involved and the depth of some of our conversations, I would call this work career counselling. That said many career coaches will not do this kind of work as it requires different knowledge and skills, I think. Most career coaching is very present and future focused; whereas this work needs to spend time thinking about how past experience influences present and future thoughts about work and life.

And the third project is working with a man who has been unemployed for some time due to an accident that meant he could not carry on in his previous career. We are working to assess what he can do and what he wants to do, and how he will present this to potential employers. This work I would call career coaching. What does it say on my business card? Career consultant and coach – but the website says much more!'

Location, location, location: Context and our understanding of the term career

The exploration of definitions thus far should have made clear that the word career is rather elastic and can be stretched in many different directions. This is a reflection of the complex and highly differentiated society, or societies, within which we live and work. Labour markets change, are not static and in many parts of the world they are under stress – fractured even. Career is also part of a language tradition – a discourse – that is also not fixed and not neutral, as meanings are governed by culture, history and socio-economic ideologies. Ideologies serve to discipline us – to support the status quo. An ideology is a network of ideas that can be conscious, but more often operates at the unconscious level; shaping our values, expectations and behaviours. Ideologies are upheld by the more powerful in any society, who have the power to impose their own world view; albeit where there is power there is resistance (Foucault, 1979). The more nuanced view would state that power operates at a distance, in networks through social institutions like education, health and helping services (Foucault, 1980). Governmental policy is informed by ideological viewpoints – discourses – although these are often promulgated as common-sense solutions towards a problem that we all share.

For example, there is a growing discourse around the need for flexibility for both employees and employers across Europe and North America, which also tries to acknowledge the concerns about job security. In other words this is not just a call for workers to be flexible in terms of skills, retraining and their career expectations: it suggests there is also a need for employers to be flexible in terms of job contracts within a 'free market economy' – but whose needs does this discourse serve? For instance, if an employer is flexible about my contract, what does that mean for me and my job security? In combining both aspects, the oxymoron 'flexicurity' is becoming part of the accepted language; if it becomes a common-sense way of talking about job security, it may not be contested. Sultana (2013) draws attention to this increasingly important and tricky concept by offering a critique, alongside considering the place of careers work within this discourse (more on this later).

Away from these important contextual and structural concerns, it is likely that those who enter careers work want to help, assist, facilitate, counsel and/or coach individuals or groups, in order to support people to find work that is personally meaningful within the social context of their lives. Although this book will continue to emphasise the need for a political awareness, it will also explore what can be done 'in practice', in the context of people's lives. Readers will expect as much from an introductory handbook, but here in this chapter we are still building the foundations of our understanding.

Reflection point 2.3

Moving from the political to the personal, what part has location played in the development of your career profile? What has influenced your education, training and the occupations you have engaged in? Why were those aspects influential?

The degree to which you connect with reflection points and activities will depend on how useful you find them at this point in your reading. I am not going to offer my own reflections regarding my influences here, as we will explore reflection, reflexivity and indeed career biographies later. But I do want to make a confession. My first degree (in sociology) was through the Open University in the UK and the course provided every student with excellent materials, full of exercises and activities. However, as I write these activities and reflection points and encourage you to undertake them in this book, I have a picture of me then thinking, 'Oh, let's move on!' That was 40 years ago and I am now better at slowing down, being reflexive and creating space to process my thinking and learning – I hope you will also develop that skill even if at the moment you too 'want to get on'. Knowledge of self is a prerequisite for working collaboratively and effectively with others.

The changing concept of career over time

In Collin and Young's edited book *The Future of Career*, published in 2000, the contributors discuss the fragmented nature of working life in postmodern times.

The book presents a 'kaleidoscopic' picture of career; charts the past meaning of the term and contemplates its future. The authors identify the challenges to fixed notions of career within the changing world of work. The entire book is an important contribution to the literature, but here I want to quote from the chapter by Collin (2000) 'Dancing to the music of time', which among other work draws on what Castells (1996) refers to as the network society in the information age.

Although Collin recognises that the concept of time and space is evident in many approaches that theorise career, she emphasises that in the network society 'social actions do not now require the sharing of the same time and place' (2000: 84). Collin employs the metaphor of navigation in terms of how people position themselves in time and space, by reading latitude and longitude 'from various *domains* of social practice' (2000: 87). After a detailed analysis, Collin states that the changes that are occurring now have worn away at the fixed notions of latitude and longitude, as the structures and norms in society and the world of work have fractured. In this reading the metaphors that have been used for career are outdated as they appear both fixed and linear. Within a working world where time and space (or place) have merged, future directions are difficult to anticipate; let alone predict. The notion of a career journey or pathway suggests continuity and a known destination, whereas serendipity will play a large part in the 'decisions' that are now taken. The terms we use for careers work will continue to evolve, as to depict the work as a bridge to employment and career development may seem at odds with the reality of the social and contemporary world of work. As Collin notes:

> Those views imply that, rather than being individualistic, and a personal trajectory, career has strong horizontal and networking characteristics. Thus despite what are predicted to be major perturbations in the experience of time and space, the future of career could still be a moving pattern of relationships between individuals, a dance to the music of time. (2000: 94)

The core competences and training required for effective careers work

Having looked at what we mean by 'career' and how this is contextually bound, but changes over time, it is useful to think about what skills, abilities and capabilities are required for the career practitioner to work effectively. There is a vast literature on work competences and, it seems, like everything else the word (and even the spelling of the word) is contested. There have been numerous attempts to define the core and supplementary competences that a career practitioner needs, the most recent in

Europe defined by NICE (Network for Innovation in Career Guidance and Counselling in Europe; Schiersmann et al., 2012). Any published list of competences needs to be more than a 'wish list'; such frameworks need to be underpinned by theory and practice, and cognisant of policy. But for the moment, work intuitively on the activity below.

Activity 2.3

From your experience and reading so far, make a list of what you think might be the skills, abilities and knowledge (i.e. competences) required by a career practitioner. There is no need to put these in hierarchical order, but you could put them in two columns, labelled:

1. Core or essential
2. Supplementary or desirable.

In the appendix, I have included the core competency framework developed by the NICE group of Higher Education Institutions across Europe. This is an overview, rather than detail as it took many people several years to: (a) agree on what we mean by competences and the limitations and expectations of using such a concept; (b) develop a framework; (c) support the framework with a curriculum; and (d) consider competences matched to roles (or levels). The work makes explicit reference to the literature within career guidance and counselling and to other frameworks that had been developed prior to the NICE project. That aside, I would expect that your list will resonate with the NICE framework – there will probably be things on their list that you have not thought about yet, but is there anything that surprises you?

Training for effective careers work

I mentioned discourse earlier. A discourse that I inhabit and that frames my thinking is, not surprisingly, related to the need for high quality education and training for the role and occupation of a career practitioner. The level at which a person is trained for this work will depend on the nature of their job and whether career guidance, career counselling, career education and/or career coaching is all, or part of their work role. The NICE competency framework is comprehensive and suggests that a professional 'career guidance counsellor' will meet, or be working towards, the competences listed. However, the profession is not regulated in the same way as teaching in the statutory sector in most countries; even taking into account policies to standardise careers work in a number of nations. My own view is that providing information, and offering advice on that information, does not need the same level of training as providing career guidance and counselling.

When suggesting the need for professionalism, I should make clear that this is not a wistful looking back to a time when a professional was viewed as the expert 'who always knew best'. My use of the term refers to a need for professionals to work empathically, reflexively and creatively with diverse clients/groups in multi-cultural as well as unpredictable contexts – often in circumstances where boundaries and requirements are somewhat fluid. So, to manage the complexities of education, training and career decision making in a fragile and changing employment market, a professional career practitioner needs a 'good enough' education. It seems odd that in 'hard times' when knowledgeable practice is required, applying minimum stand-ards of training, often on grounds of costs, may take place: this is reductive and does not serve the practitioner or their clients well. For the NICE group, education for the professional role requires undertaking courses in Higher Education at graduate or postgraduate level. However, others may be entering the profession via different routes, with or without degree level qualifications, where they are supported by training which aims to meet the recognised standard.

Activity 2.4

In your context where you work now, or where you are intending to work, what are the requirements for education and training for the professional career practitioner or career coach? If you do not know already, the web is a good place to research this.

The prevalence of 'Western' approaches in a changing world

Before ending this first chapter, I want to touch on another theme that will permeate this book. The dominance of Western values and beliefs leads to a particular view of how career decisions are made which will not 'fit' in many countries. Yet again this relates to the concept of discourse and the prevalence of Western assumptions in much of the literature (in the West). We need to remain mindful that any theoretical model should acknowledge cultural difference and must take account of social, cultural, historical, gendered, neo-colonialist and other world views in terms of sensitivities and insights. In other words, disregarding a colonial and imperial past and present (and the imperialists and colonists here came/come from across Europe and the USA) will fail to acknowledge the current influences that have a profound impact on our thinking about how the world is, or should be, organised (Said, 1994). In many societies, Western approaches will be viewed as overly individualistic, neglecting an understanding of the individual in relationship to a wider community. Our Western and largely rational approaches lack an awareness of the spiritual dimensions of career choice, which may be more present in 'Eastern' world views (Reid and West, 2014). Arulmani (2009) suggests a need to develop 'cultural preparedness', which resonates with ways of thinking and being within a particular cultural context. The aspirations of people from minority communities in the West are likely to reflect values and cultural beliefs that are different from the dominant culture. This point is worth remembering when working with both newly arrived and second and third generation people from a number of minority groups. Multicultural careers work will be examined later in the book, but to emphasise the importance of this concept a case study is provided, followed by a final reflection point in this first chapter.

Case study 2.5: Working with diversity

This case study derives from my own practice in the 1990s and is the first picture that came to my mind as I thought about what to write here. I was working in a school in an economically disadvantaged area. The school did not have a sixth form and students left at age 16 (or earlier for some). Approximately half of the students then went on to the local Further Education college to study on a range of courses, whilst the rest were looking for work, with or without training. As an area of town that also had what had been labelled as 'poor housing stock', it also became the destination for many families newly arrived from other countries who needed, or were placed in, inexpensive housing. A student with, apparently, very little English was 'sent' to see me, as at age 15 he needed to decide on his 'next step' beyond school at the end of the year.

Before he arrived I had no information about him other than his name, which was Hasan. Despite my efforts at building rapport and trying to get Hasan to talk to me, I failed to connect with him and he would not make eye contact with me and did not reply

(Continued)

(Continued)

to my open questions. I decided to end the session as he was clearly uncomfortable and I was frustrated, although doing my best to hide this; of course I gave an open invitation to return and see me if he wanted to later. He looked at me briefly for the first time, gave a half smile and left.

At the end of the morning I sought out the teacher in charge of the year and he told me that Hasan spoke very good English – this puzzled me. He then said he was newly arrived from Pakistan from a very devout Muslim family. It seemed likely, we thought, that Hasan had not been prepared to meet me – a white, Western woman and that he did not value the service I could offer him. Equally I had not been prepared to meet Hasan and was not culturally equipped for his world view either – we shared a different and conflicting cultural space.

Reflection point 2.4

What are your thoughts about this case study? Was anyone 'at fault' here? I did feel responsible, but what is your view?

I did have a colleague who felt that Hasan had to 'fit in with the social norms of the country he now lives in and he needs to see you, a woman, or go without'. Despite my feminist principles, this was not my view. Following a conversation with a contact I had in the local council authority, it seemed that the best way forward was to offer Hasan another session with a male colleague. The ideal solution would be for that colleague to be from the same ethnic background as Hasan, but, at that time and place this was not possible. Hasan did meet with a male colleague and they had a productive careers interview.

Chapter summary

This chapter has engaged with a number of definitions in order to clarify terms used throughout the book. It has also considered the part context plays in defining what is understood by the various activities and practices that fall within the scope of a book on career counselling and career coaching. In thinking about definitions, the concept of discourse was introduced alongside a discussion on the shifting nature of language and the meaning of words. Related to this, the chapter referred to the changing concept of career that takes place over time. At the start of the book it was also important to reflect on the competences and education that are required for professional careers work. Much of this discussion has not yet achieved real depth, but ideas have been introduced as 'ground work'. Finally the chapter introduced another important theme – that of multicultural competence – which, as with many of the concepts introduced in this first chapter, we will return to as we progress through the book.

Further reading

Kidd, J.M. (2006) *Understanding Career Counselling: Theory, Research and Practice*. London: Sage. I will make reference to this text frequently. Its scope is broad, combining theory, practice and research. It looks at careers work in a range of settings, covering tools and techniques useful for career counsellors and career coaches. There are examples and case studies to aid understanding, and the writing is clear and concise.

Savickas, M.L. (2011) *Career Counseling*. Washington, DC: American Psychological Association. This is a hugely significant text for the field. It is integrative (i.e. it draws together a number of theories and approaches in the development of the model) and tells the story of career with imagination and great skill. Firmly rooted in established theoretical understandings, it moves careers work into a generation of theory and practice that encompasses creative approaches for the current century. Beautifully written, with case studies, it provides clear explanations of concepts and introduces the reader to narrative thinking and the author's career construction model.

3

Career coaching and career mentoring

This chapter will:

- discuss the growing appeal and importance of career coaching and mentoring;
- make a distinction between career coaching and career mentoring;
- introduce a critical lens on coaching and mentoring.

Introduction

In the previous chapter the activity of career coaching was described as involving interventions to enhance self-development and performance, usually orientated toward setting and achieving goals. This chapter will begin by discussing the growing appeal and significance of coaching and mentoring within the context of careers work, before identifying the difference between the two: this will extend the description given in the previous chapter. Whilst upholding the benefits of coaching and mentoring, the chapter will introduce a critical viewpoint, with the aim of encouraging the reader to be reflective with regard to their practice. Later chapters in the book will examine the theory that can inform career coaching and the practical models that career coaches find useful.

Career coaching and mentoring: A growth area

In the previous chapter distinctions were made between different practices around careers work in an attempt to offer definitions and clarify our understanding – to work towards a shared language (at least within the confines of this book). However, it was also suggested that these traditional distinctions were beginning to break down as careers practitioners often find themselves operating in a range of contexts. In the UK, professional boundaries in the so-called 'helping services' have become less exact in many areas and the boundaries between public and private services are less distinct. This is due in large part to shifting government policies (from more than one political party), decentralisation of public services and economic recession. In relation to public career services the recession, from 2008 onwards, led to withdrawal of funding in some areas and significant cuts in others. This situation is not unique to the UK and is evident across Europe where widespread unemployment, and particularly youth unemployment, alongside financial failures in a number of Euro-based economies, resulted in significantly reduced spending on many public services. It seems unlikely that in any economic 'upturn', career services will be reintroduced in a format that existed before 2000 in the UK. As ever, we need to be mindful that services vary in their structure and operational contexts across Europe and internationally, but it seems likely that the appeal of careers coaching and mentoring will increase within this rapidly changing context. Part of that changing context for careers work generally, is related to the use of digital technologies and this will be explored in a later chapter; but for now the discussion will continue to focus on the rise of career coaching and mentoring.

Reflection point 3.1

Thus far, words like *appeal*, *growth* and *rise* have been used to describe the emergence of career coaching and mentoring as a significant practice. What do you think might underlie that appeal and growth?

Part of the appeal may be to do with language. As discussed previously the term 'career guidance', which is used in the UK, is not transparent to the people who may be considering use of the service. It appears to be about giving advice – crudely, an expert telling a client what to do. The meaning of 'career coaching' is perhaps clearer, as most would understand what a coach does. The term suggests an activity which is more personal, based on working with an individual's particular needs and specific goals. In practice there are of course many cross-overs (Yates, 2011); career guidance practitioners and career coaches would both be working with a range of 'clients' to focus on career choice and career management at various transition points. They may both be working within an interaction that is framed by a contractual structure with a clear beginning, middle and end. Both will be using a set of listening and questioning skills in order to understand the issues and develop strategies for development and action. The term 'career coaching' has an appeal and currency that the label 'career guidance' lacks: to use a present-day expression, it seems more 'fit for purpose' than the term career guidance. It may also reflect a prevailing discourse, which places responsibility for 'career progression' on the individual. That said, some practitioners in the UK, and many elsewhere, will prefer the term career counselling; but that may have negative connotations for clients who do not perceive the need for 'counselling', if this is viewed as an unnecessary therapeutic intervention. Even across countries which use the same language (in this case, English) the terms do not necessarily carry the same meanings.

In the next section, we will explore the differences between career coaching and career mentoring, but first what else can separate career guidance and career coaching? Yates (2011) identifies the main differences as:

- level and length of training;
- professional regulation;
- theoretical underpinning;
- use of tools and techniques.

Training and regulation will be discussed now and theoretical underpinning and the use of tools and techniques will be examined in later chapters.

Activity 3.1

From your own general experience and knowledge, (1) make a note of what you think the differences are in terms of length and level of training between career guidance and career coaching, and (2) identify the possible reasons for those differences.

An assumption is often made in the UK that career coaches are not as highly trained as career practitioners. It is difficult to be exact about this, but we can say that until recent changes in the provision of career guidance in schools, every professional career guidance practitioner working with young people in schools and local services received a level of training that was regulated by the requirement to reach a minimum standard. That standard was set at National Vocational Qualification level four, gained via training at work, or the qualification to practise was achieved through a relevant programme at a higher education institution at postgraduate and Master's level (Qualification in Career Guidance/Diploma in Career Guidance). Outside of career guidance work in the statutory sector it is less easy to be so definitive. Practitioners working in other settings such as universities, normally, will be graduates who may have undertaken training through courses run by their professional body. Career guidance practitioners working with adults, in public employment services or as independent practitioners, may or may not have qualifications at the same level as those working in the statutory sector.

Very little is known about the level and length of training of those working as career practitioners in areas that are not (or are no longer) public funded. There is a growing number of career coaching courses available, but not all of these are accredited and cannot therefore claim academic credibility, however useful they may be. Some are very short, perhaps a one-day course, whereas the 'traditional' career guidance training programmes take, on average, at least 18 months in work and one or two years if studied at university. There are exceptions and career coaching and career management training is now being developed at postgraduate level (Frigerio and McCash, 2013; Sheath, 2013; Yates, 2013).

A survey published in 2013 (Jackson, 2013) highlighted the many differences in terms of background and experience of people working with adults as career practitioners in the UK. Jackson notes how work with adults has had less policy attention than work with young people and that very little is known about the provision of careers work provided by those working in the independent sector. The National Careers Service, launched in England in 2012, is a publicly funded body working primarily with adults, but this coexists with a withdrawal of funding for services for young people in schools (Watts, 2010). The survey received 300 replies from career practitioners working with adults, through their national association, and from those working in the independent sector (and there will be cross-overs between these two groups).

In terms of training and qualifications, 90 per cent reported that they had professional training which was directly related to their work as a career coach or counsellor. Jackson's survey breaks this down further to examine the level, type and variations in qualification. It should also be noted of course that the survey does not claim to represent all those involved in the activity of career coaching and counselling. It might be expected that those who are members of a professional association, or who join other professional networks, will have or seek specialised training for their roles – there will be many others using the title 'career coach' who do not perceive this as a requirement for practice. And of course, people who respond to surveys often have a collective interest in promoting their area of occupational expertise. That said, the survey provides useful information on the changes taking place within career guidance, counselling and coaching for adults.

So, the differences in terms of length and level of training may reflect what is established for the 'traditional' occupation of career guidance, in comparison to the more 'novel' occupation of career coaching. Referring to the two groups represented in the survey (independent career professionals and association members), Jackson notes (2013: 11):

> It is striking that, although nearly all report having received specialist training, only a minority of both groups have a QCG/DipCG qualification. Many have other professional qualifications and it appears from the age profile that many in both groups have probably come to careers work after working in other related fields.

Many working as career coaches, then, may have or have had other work roles or occupations from where their qualifications derive; i.e. teaching, management or human resources. What this survey highlights is the diverse range of practitioners involved in careers work with adults and the broad nature of what careers work now incorporates. Regulating 'the profession' in such a setting and 'policing' professional standards for the work will be difficult. If used, standards need to be rigorous enough to ensure a 'good enough' level of quality, but eclectic enough to celebrate the diversity of the work – rigid boundaries will not be useful or desirable. And the question is always whose needs do such boundaries serve? A case study might add to this discussion.

Case study 3.1: A career coach's view about professional networks

'I work within the human resources department of my organisation and my professional qualification is in HR. I am also a member of the Chartered Institute of Personnel Development and have been for many years. In fact most of my CPD [continuous professional development] activities and qualifications have been gained via the institute. I work for a large organisation and it was felt sometime ago – about five years I think – that we needed a career coaching approach as part of the HR service and I got the post. People are referred to me by their line-manager and although that means they get the "time out" to spend with me, this has the potential for problems if we are not clear about why they are with me and what we hope to achieve. Before starting this career coaching service, we spent a lot of time designing it based on our HR experience and we were clear about contracting and confidentiality and so on, but I soon found that, occasionally, much deeper issues began to surface in what were supposed to be career coaching rather than career counselling sessions. I did not feel equipped to deal with this and there was no one else within the organisation I could refer to.

You cannot have rigid procedures about this, but I did find myself torn at times between having the goals of the organisation in mind and the more personal needs of the coachee. In these circumstances it is very difficult to be impartial. Anyway, I reached a point where I felt that I needed to learn more about career counselling. The activities are separate, but cannot be assigned to compartments when you are working respectfully with an individual who needs more than a terrific CV and impressive presentation skills! When I have worked with individuals who have been 'sent' for performance-related coaching, I have found that was often the situation when deeper issues emerged. My first step was to join a LinkedIn group and through that I found out about a short course at postgraduate level that I could study through blended learning. I didn't want or need a whole programme, but I wanted to develop my counselling skills in the context of my career coaching work; and I liked the sound of the mix of taught, distance and online learning.

So, now individuals may be coming for career development or career performance coaching, but if other issues emerge I am more able to contain these and listen effectively. I need to be clear, in my HR role I am not offering therapeutic counselling and do not have the same level or depth of training that I would expect a career counsellor to have, but my knowledge and understanding has increased through the course and access to the literature. If nothing else I am now clear about the boundaries of my own expertise and the importance of being open about that with the person I'm working with. I feel more secure about saying "I don't know" and I do have contacts now, through the network that I can suggest as referrals.'

Career mentoring

Thus far in this chapter we have explored the differences, similarities and crossovers between career guidance/counselling and career coaching. This section will consider the role of the career mentor. Yet again there will be overlaps. Earlier I argued that the roles are becoming integrated in many cases; however, knowledgeable practice requires an understanding of the potential differences so that we know what is appropriate action and activity in different circumstances. That said, the term career mentor is not applied widely – it is more likely that the term used would be one of the following: 'developmental mentor', 'learning mentor' (particularly with young people), 'peer mentor', or even 'buddy mentor'.

A good place to start would be to look for definitions for the word 'mentor'. The OED (1992) tells us 'mentor: experienced and trusted adviser'. The word derives from the Greek *Mentor*, the name of the adviser to the young Telemachus in Homer's *Odyssey*.

Colley (2003) suggests that mentoring is an activity that has grown rapidly as a result of the focus on social inclusion that is evident in many countries, but particularly in the UK and USA. In the UK, social inclusion was a major theme of policy initiatives brought about by the Labour government from 1997 onwards (Reid, 1999). Within schools 'learning mentors' were less likely to be professionally qualified and were employed with the specific intention of raising attainment in terms of examination results and/or preventing school 'drop out'. The inclusion policy initiatives resulted in the development of the Connexions service in England (disbanded by the coalition government formed in 2011) and brought about significant changes to the work of career practitioners. The focus was on helping disadvantaged young people who (to use the language of the time) were 'disaffected' or 'in danger of making an unsuccessful transition to education, training or work'. Much debate and criticism ensued about this targeted service that will not be discussed here (see Watts, 2001) and although it was later stated that the service was universal (i.e. directed at helping all young people with their decision making), it remained the case that the focus was on helping those who were, or might become, 'NEET' (Not in Education, Employment or Training).

Reflection point 3.2

For me, there is an interesting irony in the labels used. My preference would be to use the descriptor (when one is needed) 'disadvantaged', rather than the terms in inverted commas above. Why do you think disadvantaged might be thought more suitable?

Any word prefixed by 'dis' suggests a negative label – a deficit of some sort. However, at least 'disadvantaged' indicates that the individual or group is disadvantaged by their circumstances, i.e. their experience of, or place in, society, where they encounter barriers of one sort or another, which exclude them. 'Disaffected' suggests it is a personal choice, that an individual removes themselves from what is considered the 'mainstream'. It has a 'can't be bothered' ring to it. Williamson and Middlemiss (1999: 13) commented that the young people thus labelled included 'the temporarily side tracked, essentially confused or deeply alienated'. The longer term 'in danger of making unsuccessful transitions to education, training or work' was an attempt perhaps to ameliorate negative labelling, but did not offer the necessary shorthand term required when making bids for funding or for promoting policies that, genuinely, sought to help disadvantaged young people. NEET is possibly the most offensive. The upper case letters, the focus on 'not belonging' has an essentialising quality; in other words it suggests that this describes the whole person – 'they are NEET' – whereas their lives are much wider and more interesting than the label applied. The irony is that the language used is far from inclusive. Such issues around avoiding language and practice that is oppressive will be examined further in a later chapter. For now in the context of mentoring, the discussion is relevant if we are to avoid attitudes and actions that start from a position of viewing the individual as 'deficient' or 'lacking' in some way, or as 'needing our expert help'.

This discussion should alert us to the need to place mentoring in the broader social, economic and cultural milieu and to avoid falling into the trap of viewing this solely at the individual level. In other words the activity takes place within power relations shaped by class, gender, race, age, ability and disability, sexuality and other social variables. Colley's work (2003) pays particular attention to class and gender when considering youth mentoring: recognising the benefits of mentoring, but highlighting also the complexities within any mentoring relationship.

We will now return to the definition – 'mentor: an experienced and trusted adviser; an experienced person in an institution who trains and counsels new employees or students' – and extend this to the role of the career mentor, before describing an activity that can help to explore personal values before mentoring begins. Like previous attempts to offer definitions in the book so far, defining mentoring is not simple. Colley (2003) and Caldwell and Carter (1993a), chart the historical development of mentoring and emphasise the plethora of meanings applied to the activity. Both texts move away from a simplistic view (a myth in Colley's terms) of the modern-day mentor as a self-sacrificing and devoted adviser operating in a neutral environment that is not influenced and constrained by a wider agenda.

In using the term 'career mentor' we can perhaps illustrate this further by relating the role to a workplace setting; albeit we need to emphasise that career mentoring may take place within other relationships and contexts. Within a workplace this could be an informal role that does not have a set of intended outcomes outlined in a developed policy. Informal mentoring (particularly in the current economic climate) could be 'sitting beside Nelly' watching, learning and being helped by a more experienced colleague. Carruthers (1993: 11) states that:

> No matter the variations in the definitions of a mentor, most mentor interpretations fall into one of two categories:
>
> 1. those which emphasise the professional development of the protégé only;
> 2. those which emphasise professional and personal development of the protégé.

It is, however, difficult to separate the two and the basic premise of this book is that career and life cannot be thought of as existing in distinct compartments. An aspect of mentoring which, when occurring in the workplace, might help to work toward a definition would be to see the mentor as distinct from someone who line-manages or supervises a person who is new to a job role or post (although in some cases the roles may be interchangeable, particularly in small organisations). Where efficiencies and 'flatter' structures have removed the layers of management that were evident in former times, the mentor can take on aspects of the management role that the line-manger no longer has 'space' for.

Reflection point 3.3

So, pausing at this point, what do you think the differences are between a career coach and a career mentor?

Given that there are overlaps, according to the context which can vary, a **career mentor** is more likely to be someone other than a line-manager, who is more experienced in the job or organisation than the mentee, and can advise and guide them. The career mentor will usually be working in the same organisation and department, and will guide the mentee through a period of change or transition towards an agreed objective (possibly the ability to work independently). The role supports the occupational training, learning and development needs of the mentee, but is not about teaching specific tasks, and it should be independent of performance management. The **career coach** within an organisation is more likely to be part of the line management structure or have a role in a staff development or human resources department within a medium to large organisation. They may even be an external consultant brought in to coach an individual for a new role or for internal promotion if it is felt that the mentee's seniority in the organisation would necessitate coaching from outside, or that the required expertise is not available within the organisation. In some cases, the career coach may be expected to help the individual to reach a required standard of performance (for example in 'executive coaching'), although it should not be assumed this is the central role. The relationship with the career mentor may be perceived as more personal, developing over time – but again it is difficult to be precise as it will depend on the setting and the aims of the work and how they are agreed locally.

Kay and Hinds (2012), reflecting on the nature and scope of mentoring, indicate that an effective mentoring relationship will give rise to conversations that cover more than solving a particular problem, and may also include issues around career (the context we are exploring), personal and family matters. Of course, any 'helping' or guidance or coaching encounter can touch these areas if the relationship is 'good enough' and trust and rapport have been built. Along with knowledge and experience,

Kay and Hinds list the following personal skills that the effective mentor needs to apply in the role:

- Listening
- Motivating
- Influencing
- Fact-finding
- Liaising
- Counselling
- Time management
- Staff development. (Kay and Hinds, 2012: 27)

To be effective the time needed to engage in mentoring in the workplace needs to be recognised, allowed for and protected. Whether the role is in or outside of the management structure, the goals of the mentoring dyad need to be explicit and any reporting on the activities engaged in, clarified. Reporting may be simply a recording of when meetings take place and for how long; if more information is recorded it needs to be clear with whom this is shared, where it is stored and for what purpose it is produced and kept. Given that the argument here is that (a) mentoring does not take place in a neutral context and that a power imbalance is likely, and (b) the role is personal and not about judging the other, we need to address issues around the social variables mentioned earlier. Before engaging in any mentoring relationship – even one that purports to be about professional development only – a mentor needs to explore their own values. One way of doing this can be through devising a mentoring game.

Activity 3.2: Exploring personal values in mentoring

The game can be played in pairs or small groups of three or four players and is useful for any organisation that is considering introducing a mentoring scheme; the players can include other people, but ideally should involve potential mentors and mentees. For the game to work groupings need to be of different ages and from different backgrounds – in other words, the greater the 'mix' of social variables the more interesting the game becomes. It can be designed as a board game on A3 paper with a start and finish point, a die and coloured counters (clear wrapped boiled sweets work well and can be eaten

(Continued)

(Continued)

at the end). The game can be squares within a square or a snaking path and each player throws the die and counts to a square. On each square there is a question that begins a discussion between the players. The questions are designed to explore different views related to experiences when growing up. For example: (when you were growing up) did you have a telephone in your house? Could you watch the television whenever you wanted? Where did you go on holiday? Who decided what you would wear each day? When did you first go out in the evening on your own? Did you go to a mixed or single sex school? The questions reveal differences in experience and raise thoughts about cultural values between the players. Each player responds to the question and no player can land on an occupied square; e.g. if at the start, two players throw a four, the second player must jump over the first.

As an activity (rather than the game) find one or two people who are in a different age group or from a different background to you and use the questions to start a conversation. Explain why you are doing this, i.e. to explore different experiences of growing up. For the board game you would need many questions and not all of them will be 'landed on', but the discussion is the point of the exercise of course. At the end of the game it is useful to get the players to reflect on what they have learned via the game.

The game should be fun, but we always need to be mindful that for some 'growing up' may not have been a positive experience and the conversations could be upsetting. Becoming upset does not automatically assume that harm has been done, but it should be made clear before starting the game that 'joining in' is not obligatory and a person may choose to watch rather than take part. Appendix 2 provides a list of questions that could be included in the game.

Keeping a critical lens on coaching and mentoring

It is always difficult to decide on the placing of chapters in a book of this nature. The reflection points, activities and case studies are designed to illuminate the material and engage the reader in critical reflection. The concept of reflective and reflexive practice is explored in a later chapter, but it is important to clarify what is meant by the terms early on in the text.

A reflective practitioner is someone who is able to reach potential solutions through analysing experience and prior knowledge, in order to inform current and future practice. The internal process of reflection that is active and conscious could be described as reflectivity. Reflexivity is the process by which we are aware of our own responses to what is happening in a particular context (i.e. a counselling interaction) and our reactions to people, events and the dialogue taking place. A reflexive understanding will include an awareness of the personal, social and cultural context and its influence on both the speaker and the listener. Reflexive awareness in counselling practice, leads to a deeper understanding of how we co-construct knowledge about the world, and ways of operating within it, that are more meaningful for those involved. (Reid, 2013: 12)

Critical reflection then, as advocated in this book, is about an awareness of the social and political context within which career counselling, coaching and mentoring take place. It is not about taking a critical distance from clients, or being cynical, but is concerned with an acknowledgement of how any interaction or interview is influenced by a range of factors – not all of them conscious. We need to acknowledge that a relationship like mentoring (or counselling) which builds over time is not a sealed dyad, untrammelled by what is happening in the 'outside' world. Indeed in any interview it would be the case that there are more than two people 'in the room' as we all bring our life scripts and social, familial and cultural influences and defences with us. A case study may help to clarify what I mean here.

Case study 3.2: Sean reflects on his mentoring relationship with Jenny

'I was asked to be Jenny's career mentor because I have been in a team leader post for some time and Jenny was new to a management role. We work in the same organisation but not in the same office. The mentoring scheme is fairly well established and the policy makes clear what the aim is; in a nutshell, it is to guide and support a person experiencing change when moving to a new or higher professional position, so not about training, nor supervising and so on. So, we met, decided we would get on and agreed a contract – you know clarifying when and where we would meet and for how long and what we hoped to achieve, confidentiality, what was recorded and how.

(Continued)

(Continued)

Anyway, I thought it would be fine as I've been a mentor before, but Jenny is much older than me and well, she seemed a bit resistant to the process and I began to feel she was wasting my time. That sounds awful, but I'm being honest and I think my frustration must have been evident as she became more and more withdrawn. On one occasion I found I was on the verge of just telling her what to do – and I know that is not what mentoring is about.

I managed to rescue the situation as I did not want to fail as a mentor and I sensed that Jenny did not feel secure enough to ask for someone else – but I would not have wanted that either. It was tricky, but I spent some time thinking about what I was doing that might be affecting the relationship, but also wondering what else might be influencing our work together even before we started. There was something about Jenny that reminded me of my older sister, who always seemed rather 'needy'– was that affecting how I responded to her? And what about me, how did Jenny feel about working with a man so much younger than herself?

How did I rescue it? Well, by being honest and slowing down and making time to explore our thoughts about what was going on. There was no point pretending that everything was OK, we had to do this if we were going to get anything useful out of our meetings. I could not support her professional development without acknowledging that there were personal issues that needed to be considered – for both of us. It turned out that Jenny had had a bad experience of mentoring years ago and was very wary of the process. She was also not really enjoying her current role because of all the new responsibilities, but had felt unable to reveal this to me. She thought I'd think she was not up to the job, even though we both knew that mentoring is not about judging work performance. Age and gender may have had something to do with it of course – most of the team leaders are younger men and we talked about that too. The outcome was good – we have an effective mentoring relationship now – and Jenny said that! I've learnt a lot from this experience and want the organisation to think more about improving the training for mentors.'

This book will uphold the benefits of career counselling, career coaching and career mentoring, but as should be evident by now will continue to engage in critical reflection on the activities. As has already been stated, career coaching and career mentoring may be taking place within a range of settings and with clients of different ages, who are at different stages in their education and career histories. Aside from educational contexts, career coaching and mentoring in contemporary employment settings resonate with an approach that also views workplaces as learning organisations (Senge, 1990). They can be considered essential practices for organisations undergoing restructuring, but effectiveness can be undermined if the focus is solely on outcomes, competences, effectiveness and increased production (Caldwell and Carter, 1993b). It is in the relationship that a 'healthy' balance between the needs of the organisation and of the individual occurs. Career coaching should not be confused with practices that focus solely on educational or work performance – it is a developmental and supportive practice not a directive intervention.

Chapter summary

This chapter has discussed the growing appeal and the importance of both career coaching and career mentoring and offered a distinction between the two. In doing this it has stated that there are overlaps and that the meaning of all the practices described in these early chapters can vary, both across and within a particular country and culture. It has also introduced the concept of critical reflection which will be an approach taken throughout the work. In the chapters that follow, the theories that underpin career guidance and counselling and career coaching will be introduced – in order to give us further tools to think with.

Further reading

Colley, H. (2003) *Mentoring for Social Inclusion: A Critical Approach to Nurturing Mentor Relationships*. London: Routledge Falmer.
Although the book is focused on youth mentoring within a policy agenda of inclusion, it is exemplary in its analysis, critical stance and recommendations for effective mentoring practice. This is not a 'how to do it' book, but it does offer reflections on different models of mentoring and helps the reader to contextualise mentoring within wider political and power relations. The book uses case studies derived from an in-depth research study which serve to illuminate the discussion.

Connor, M. and Pohara, J.L. (2012) *Coaching and Mentoring at Work: Developing Effective Practice* (2nd edn). Maidenhead: Open University Press.
This is a very practical, highly regarded and accessible text which does exactly what the title suggests. This new edition offers illustrative case studies and examples explaining the coaching relationship, and includes new material on reflective practice and supervision. The writing is concise and has added 'frequently asked questions' in this revised edition.

Kay, D. and Hinds, R. (2012) *A Practical Guide to Mentoring: Using Coaching and Mentoring Skills to Help Others Achieve Their Goals* (5th edn). Oxford: How to Books Ltd.
As the title and the name of the publishing company indicate, this is a 'how to do it' book that offers a useful entry into understanding coaching and mentoring. The book contains

a number of scenarios which can help readers to comprehend the issues that can arise in practice.

Zeus, P. and Skiffington, S. (2000) *The Complete Guide to Coaching at Work*. North Ryde, Australia: McGraw-Hill.

This is more than a guide or self-help book and not only engages with the basic principles, but also with the key theoretical concepts for the implementation and effective use of coaching methods in workplace organisations. Case studies are used, alongside insights gained from academic disciplines and practical experience. The content is comprehensive and the format is accessible.

4

Established theories of career decision making

This chapter will:

- examine the place of theory for careers work;
- explore three theories established in the twentieth century;
- consider the integration of theoretical approaches.

Introduction

Theories of career decision making describe and explain how people make vocational decisions, but also suggest ways of assisting in that process. That is a nice, neat sentence that needs a bit of unpicking and critiquing before going any further. Theories and practice in the twentieth century focused on the scientific matching of personality traits to job factors, and the psychological development of the individual in terms of career; with a growing recognition that the social context of the individual was also influential. The term 'career decision making' suggests a freedom to make decisions unencumbered by wider factors; whereas choice may be limited by a range of social, historical, cultural and economic circumstances. In Chapter 2, a critical stance to the language used was introduced and the word 'vocational' was also examined. As the table offered by Savickas (2011) and reproduced in Figure 2.1 indicates, the theories, and the language used to describe their development, have changed over time and are not static. In what follows we will delve a little deeper into the meaning of 'career' before looking at specific theories. Theories aim to aid our understanding of *what* happens when people make career decisions and attempt to explain *why* this behaviour takes place. Most theories also offer models that practitioners can apply to help people in the process of identifying goals, making career choices, and decisions about what to do next. When considering the skills and knowledge required in 'helping' we also move into counselling theories, which will be the subject of Chapter 5: here, in this chapter, the focus will be on career theory (also referred to as vocational choice theory) established in the twentieth century and how it can be applied. The benefits and limitations of established theories will be assessed, alongside their longevity for career counselling and career coaching. It is worth repeating the point that the theories examined here are *established*, that is they have found acceptance and remain useful, but they are also subject to critique in a rapidly changing world of work. Newer theories and concepts are explored in a later chapter. The chapter will end by considering the merits of integrating theories.

In the latter part of the twentieth century theories were developed that recognised the importance of community influences and social learning. In brief, individuals acquire beliefs about their place in the world of work through interaction with others in their community which, in turn, shape their preferences and resonate with the values they learn within their social context. These will be discussed in Chapters 6 and 7. To progress in this chapter, the purpose of theory will be examined next.

Why bother with theory – what's it for?

When I informed a senior manager in the careers service in 1996 that I had accepted a post teaching in higher education on a career guidance programme, he said, 'Well, keep your feet on the ground Hazel, don't disappear inside all that theoretical stuff.' Having just completed a Master's degree in the Psychology of Career Guidance, I was well versed in the arguments for exploring, analysing and evaluating a range of theoretical approaches that can and do enhance practice; but I smiled and kept quiet. His point was, I think, that what we learn – the theories that underpin our practice – must be useful and their usefulness needs to be clear 'on the ground' of practice. However, an anti-intellectual mistrust of theory moves us away from being able to critique practice and to question what may be seen as practical 'common sense' (common to whom, we may ask). The discourse of 'just get on with the job' is one to be challenged, as it is a shallow, reductionist approach that blocks out critical thinking about what 'the job' is and/or should be. Critical theorising has at its heart the aim to improve services – to question the status quo and work towards finding better ways of supporting people who use the 'helping' services.

In writing about theory in this book I am mindful that theory, any theory, will not inspire practice if it is described in language that is dense and can only be understood by a handful of academics whose job it is to examine theory and explain it to other academics in peer-reviewed scholarly journals. My aim is to avoid an approach to writing that would patronise practitioners through oversimplification, but instead to provide access to theoretical writing in a comprehensible style. That said there is danger here in that the theories are detailed and summaries will render ('boil down' – if we go for a literal meaning of the word render) the original complexity. What is left cannot represent many years of elaborate and sophisticated theorising and can be criticised for 'emptying out' the detail (but see the further reading at the end of the chapter).

Reflection point 4.1

Before moving on, take a moment to note a few points on what you think are the purposes of theory for careers work.

Theories are tools to think with. A theory is based on a set of explanatory understandings that help us to grasp the behaviour that we are trying to make sense of. Usually a theory derives from research which aims to interpret, explain and anticipate human activity (the word 'predict' might also be used in the natural rather than social sciences). Theorising is something we all do to make sense of the world; in other words we draw upon our perception of the world and what matters to us, and we make decisions based on our knowledge, values and our assessment of the consequences of certain types of action. We do not always act with this level of reflexivity of course, but the point here is that theorising is not the preserve of 'theorists'. So beyond what we might call everyday theorising, theories in the natural or social sciences tend to be tested in more rigorous and elaborate ways and often involve a particular language and use of terminology. Theories develop, but may also outlive their usefulness and we then cease to pay attention to them; particularly when the ground of practice has shifted – sometimes in seismic ways. Similarly, theories may adapt and change to circumstances, albeit that too much adaptation may cause the theory to lose its internal coherence.

To answer the question posed in the reflection point above, theory can help to explain an aspect of the human condition that we cannot grasp; cannot explain because we are puzzled by what we observe, read or hear about. Reading theory can provide us with a language that supports the development of our understanding. It also provides a framework alongside a vocabulary to communicate that understanding to others, in order to share ideas. This does not mean that we 'swallow it whole'; a well-argued and well written exposition of a theory can be seductive, so we need to retain a critical questioning about what we read. This is not easy but, in simple terms, we can ask of our reading: what's good about this (the advantages)? What's not so good (the limitations)? How does it relate to my understanding of what happens in practice? What have others written on this issue?

Theory is important, then, for any practice that is thoughtful and informed; it helps to make practice knowledgeable and more than an activity based on a set of instructions on 'how to do' (in our case) career counselling and coaching. It avoids a narrow and instrumental approach to the work which, if taken, reduces complex human activity to check list, 'tick box' approaches which have limited value. Leaving aside arguments about what we mean by professional for the moment, a service that carries that stamp of quality (a profession) will be built upon a body of knowledge informed by research, theory and practice. As above, theory can also help us to think about how things may be changed for the better, can support us to think of new ways to improve the work: but theories need to be applied and tested in practice, thus the relationship is symbiotic and should not be separated. This symbiotic process is what is meant by the term 'praxis' – the intersection between reflection and action.

Activity 4.1

In the above I have, mostly, used the word theory, but I often find I use alternative words such as perspective, model and approach. It is part of the richness of the English language that we have many words that, on the surface, appear to mean the same thing and can be used interchangeably, but they do have different meanings in the context of discussing theory. In this activity, define the following words in the context of career counselling and coaching, in order to signify their different meanings:

Perspective
Theory
Model
Approach

My suggested definitions are offered at the end of the chapter – how do yours compare?

A wide range of theory

There is a wide range of theory that informs careers work drawing on a number of disciplines, including psychology, sociology, economics and management theory, learning theory, cultural studies and many others. Why so many? In part this question takes us back to thinking about what we mean by career and who is doing what with whom. Without repeating the points in Chapter 2, the following may help us to think further about the complexities involved.

As noted previously, career is a common term but has many meanings. There are other potential connotations that we can consider here which may not be recognised when working with clients. These aspects of meaning are connected, but their importance for the individual will vary. First, there is the social meaning of career related to roles and status, which might be referred to as social capital. Second, ideas about what is important to an individual in terms of career may change over time according to life experience, both planned and unexpected. Third, and related to the former, career links to an individual's sense of self, their place in the world and how their goals and values can be expressed within work. Fourth, career has strong links for many in terms of biography – our career story constructed with others in families, communities and organisations. This final suggestion moves us to what Savickas (2011) refers to as constructing a career where we move from describing an objective career (as outlined in a CV) to a subjective career, where the inner (private) and outer (public) worlds combine in an individual's understanding of what career means to them. The two worlds are not separated for the individual when thinking about past, present and future career decision making; or as C. Wright Mills expressed this for a broader context of understanding, 'Know that the human meaning of public issues must be revealed by relating them to personal troubles and to the problems of individual life' (1970: 247–8). Processes of employment and unemployment cannot, from this point of view, be understood if dealt with in the abstract as a social issue: to understand we also need to examine the effects as experienced in the context of the lives of individuals. This can be described as the *psychosocial* context for understanding the meaning of career.

When we begin to consider the complexities inherent in the word career, it is perhaps less surprising that the theoretical possibilities are multidisciplinary: this adds richness but also messiness. In terms of messiness, Schön wrote about the relationship between theory and practice where theory and research are described as occupying the 'high, hard ground', whilst practice resides in the 'swampy lowlands' (1983: 54). Alongside career theories, counselling theories are also used in the practice of careers work. A distinction was made earlier between career theories and career counselling theories: Kidd offers the following, which explains – clears up the messiness – further:

> the former [career theories] are concerned with how individuals experience their careers, how they make career decisions, and the environments in which careers are made. The latter [career counselling theories] focus on how best to intervene to assist individuals in their career development: they provide a basis for action. (Kidd, 2006: 7–8)

In the above I have demonstrated what was stated earlier, i.e. reading theory can provide us with a language that supports our understanding. Specifically, Savickas, Wright Mills and Schön are examples of 'theoretical friends' who help me to think about, and here write about, theory. When we are studying, writing or researching, our theoretical friends will be more or less important to us and our relationship with them will change over time as our own theorising develops. Some stand the test of time and we revisit them, others move away from us, but we also make space for new friendships to develop.

Reflection point 4.2

Why do I use the term 'theoretical friends'? When undertaking doctoral study, a colleague, from a height of 6 feet and 2 inches, posed the following question: 'What is your theoretical or conceptual framework for this research?' At the time, this question, as a relatively novice (and much shorter) researcher, was a scary question – I had read lots, but at that point no one theorist or overarching concept was distinct from others. I did not forget how stupid (and small) this question made me feel and when working with students at different academic levels, I never pose this question in this way. However, an exploration of potential theoretical or conceptual frameworks can be opened up if thought of as possible 'friends' to support thinking.

So, thinking back to any previous study you have undertaken – at whatever level and in whatever subject – did you have any theoretical friends, or influential writers, that gave you the tools to think with and the language to express your views? If so, who were they?

The reflection exercise above may help to demystify the term theoretical or conceptual framework – if not, don't worry, hopefully this book will introduce you to ideas, concepts and theories that will support your understanding of theory, and may even provide a friend or two. It is to theoretical and conceptual frameworks for understanding career that we now move.

Vocational choice theory in the twentieth century

It is worth mentioning at the start of this section that the theories examined here are informed by 'Western' approaches to thinking about career. Both formal and informal models were used in earlier times, and in various cultures, but the 'science' of career is thought to have begun in Boston, USA, in the early part of the twentieth century. However, early pioneers in the West included Dr Wolff in Germany, who instigated a department of vocational counselling that offered interviews to school pupils, and Maria Gordon in Scotland. Gordon published in 1908 *A Handbook of Employments Specially Prepared for the Use of Boys and Girls on Entering the Trades, Industries, and Professions.*

Already a distinguished academic specializing in geology, she made a significant contribution to the women's movement, and received recognition for her work on behalf of women in the League of Nations, becoming Dame Maria Gordon. When her father retired from Gordon's College in Aberdeen, she continued with his work helping students to choose and find employment. In the introduction to her book, she emphasised the need for an organised service for educational and employment information for all young people in Great Britain, in order that they would find work that suited them and rewarded them financially. The scheme was approved by the Secretary of State for Scotland and may have influenced the later Labour Exchange Act of 1909 in Great Britain (Peck, 2010).

Moving on, this chapter explores three theoretical frameworks that attempt to answer the question 'how do people make career decisions?' These are: person–environment fit theories; career development theories; and structural theories. The first two have their roots within psychology and the third is sited within sociology. Although these frameworks may be thought of as ways of explaining behaviour after the event, in other words when the decision is made, the exploration also helps us to think about how practitioners might intervene – help – in the process of decision making. Each one will be evaluated for their relevance for contemporary careers work.

Person–environment fit theories

The first significant theory of vocational behaviour arose at the start of the twentieth century, when Western societies were experiencing the effects of industrialisation, urbanisation and, in the USA in particular, immigration. The work of Frank Parsons, established in Boston, was developed to address the problem of how individuals could be matched, efficiently and effectively, to the changed nature of work. Sometimes referred to as the 'scientific matching approach', like all theories it was born in its time and was attempting to solve a social issue. Parsons' work, published in 1909, introduced a method for matching an individual's abilities and interests to the requirements and benefits of particular occupations. In essence, the central argument is that: (1) people are different from each other, they have different traits; (2) jobs are different from each other, they are composed of different factors; and (3) by studying both it should be possible to match a person to a job. Over at least five decades this trait/factor model evolved into person–environment fit theory, with John Holland being the main proponent.

Holland's (1985, 1997) congruence theory of vocational choice, as applied by practitioners, helps clients to increase their self-knowledge, find out more about jobs via occupational information and then pair self to job. Clearly for this to work people need to be able to explore their traits and have reliable information about potential occupations. The practical application of this theory requires the use of diagnostic tests, followed by an assessment and then a recommendation of the type of work that would be suitable. In the 1950s Rodger, in the UK, framed this within a Seven-Point Plan (1952) which provided a set of questions around seven areas to be addressed within a vocational guidance interview. It was used in the main by 'youth employment officers' working with young school leavers. The seven areas are:

1. Physical make-up
2. Attainments
3. General intelligence
4. Special aptitudes
5. Interests
6. Disposition
7. Circumstances

Activity 4.2

Bearing in mind the era in which this person-environment fit model was developed, and how use of words has changed since 1952, note down possible questions a careers adviser would ask under each of these headings. Rodger's list of questions (1952: 8–16) is outdated now in terms of language; you might want to rework the headings too.

Rodger conceived the seven points as 'pegs' to hang information on, not as a rigid framework for interviewing. The intention was to use the seven questions to record outcomes from a much more fluid interview. The one heading in the above list that might be puzzling is 'disposition', a word we are less likely to use currently. An alternative might be 'attitude' and questions could be about interaction with others, reliability, being a self-starter and so on. Although Rodger's Seven-Point Plan was used widely it was overtaken by approaches that were seen as less directive, but in its time provided a simple and useful tool for practitioners. And before we dismiss this approach as perhaps 'labelling' a client, we need to think about the informal assessments we make when we meet someone for the first time when they arrive for career counselling or coaching.

John Holland in the USA expanded person–environment fit theory over the 1960s, 1970s and continued to work on this into the 1990s. The elaboration of the theory of vocational personalities and work environments was published in a third edition in 1997. Holland was passionate about improving the opportunities for people to make informed decisions about working lives. Initially, and this is a sign of the times in which he was living, this was for young men living in relatively isolated rural environments, and he devised a number of self-assessment tests and tools that could be used. The theory focuses on individual differences, characteristics that make one person different from another: hence it is often referred to as 'differentialist'. Holland stated that individuals will seek occupations that match their interests and suit their preferences for particular work environments. In making choices, individuals choose from a 'hierarchy of preferences': in other words they will rank or prioritise what is most and least important to them.

Holland claimed that both people and occupational environments can be categorised into six types, which Kidd, drawing on Holland's theory (1985), describes as follows:

- **R**ealistic – likes realistic jobs such as mechanic, surveyor, farmer, electrician. Has mechanical abilities, but may lack social skills. Is described as: asocial, conforming, hard-headed, practical, frank, inflexible and genuine.
- **I**nvestigative – likes investigative jobs such as biologist, chemist, physicist, anthropologist. Has mathematical and scientific ability but often lacks leadership ability. Is described as: analytical, cautious, critical, curious, introspective, independent and rational.
- **A**rtistic – likes artistic jobs such as composer, musician, stage director, writer. Has writing, musical or artistic abilities but often lacks clerical skills. Is described as: emotional, expressive, intuitive, open, imaginative and disorderly.
- **S**ocial – likes social jobs such as teacher, counsellor, clinical psychologist. Has social skills and talents, but often lacks mechanical and scientific ability. Is described as: co-operative, empathic, sociable, warm and persuasive.
- **E**nterprising – likes enterprising jobs such as salesperson, manager, television producer, buyer. Has leadership and speaking abilities but often lacks scientific ability. Is described as: adventurous, ambitious, energetic, sociable, self-confident and domineering.
- **C**onventional – likes conventional jobs such as book-keeper, financial analyst, banker, tax expert. Has clerical and arithmetical ability, but often lacks artistic abilities. Is described as: careful, conscientious, inflexible, unimaginative and thrifty. (Kidd, 2006: 15)

Known as the RIASEC model, this is depicted as a hexagon to indicate closeness and distance between the different types. An important point to remember is that Holland was not suggesting that an individual is *one* type: instruments used to assess individual types will arrive at a code incorporating three in hierarchical order, which can then be matched to an occupational data bank, organised using the same categories.

For example, someone who is good at mathematics may find the test results indicate a strong match with teaching the subject and the code might be SIC; or (because we are all different) ISA if it is mathematics that is their strongest influence, but they are also social and have artistic talents: maybe teaching mathematics through creative demonstrations.

Reflection point 4.3

Take a moment now to consider your immediate reactions to person–environment fit theory. What is useful and less useful about this theory, in your view?

Advantages and limitations

When thinking about the advantages and limitations of person environment fit theory, it is important to acknowledge that it has proved useful for over a century and continues to be used. However, it is *one* approach and despite its continued influence it does have considerable limitations, alongside potential benefits.

The case study in Chapter 2 (2.1) illustrated the use of a computer matching programme that is based on this theory. This is an obvious example of one of the benefits, as many clients, particularly young clients, will have a limited conception of what jobs might suit them. To benefit from a matching programme, however, the individual has to have a clear idea of their likes and dislikes in order to answer the test questions. A set of answers mainly composed of 'don't know' will result in a very flat and unhelpful profile, of very little use to the individual. If completed at a time when they have not yet gained qualifications, the person must also have an idea of what educational level they may aspire to and include this. Failure to complete this part of the test (usually because this is less interesting and the person skips it), will again lead to a thin result in terms of possible occupations. So, such matching programmes, which must have regularly updated databases of educational, training and occupational information, are useful tools, but only when the individual is at the point of 'readiness' (Savickas, 2011), having already begun to think about their likes, dislikes and strengths (i.e. what do I like and what am I good at?).

Parsons', Rodger's and Holland's work was designed to provide an objective theory based on the proposition that people's job choices harmonise with their interests. However, the suggestion that this leads to job satisfaction has been questioned and Arnold (2004) suggests that occupational titles cannot encompass the complexities of work environments. The test result may have the feel of a 'prescription' about it and oversimplifies the match, not paying enough attention to the variables inherent in individual personalities and workplace cultures. Using a person–environment fit approach places the practitioner in the position of the expert who administers tests; this perception can diminish the role of career counselling. Indeed, such is the power of this idea of matching that in the UK, using an online matching programme can be viewed by many policy makers as 'good enough' in terms of public careers services for young people (and 'cost effective'). In addition, although such tests can provide useful information, they assume that clients know what to do with – how to make sense of – the information for their own circumstances. Furthermore, the notion that the person's career interests are fixed alongside a job market that is static clearly does not fit with our current experience of the world of work. Essentialist ideas about identity are also questioned: in other words a test could not possibly reveal a core 'self' that can be known, even to the individual. Ideas about 'who am I?' develop over time and are influenced by a range of experiences, both good and bad.

However, it is important that we do not 'throw the baby out with the bathwater'; contemporary person–environment fit models, if used thoughtfully, are more nuanced, negotiable and engage the client in discussion about the usefulness of the 'match' in the larger context of their lives. They can extend a person's ideas of potential occupations and the routes into these, helping them to process information and to think more strategically about current problems regarding choice and future possibilities (Rounds and Tracey, 1990). The theory and its applications remain useful, but it cannot be used as 'one size fits all': in working with clients, the job of the career counsellor or coach is to work alongside the person to assess what other types of interventions may be helpful.

Career development theories

Savickas states that in the middle of the twentieth century in the USA there was a rise in the number of middle class individuals living in suburban locations, employed by 'hierarchical bureaucracies located in horizontal skyscrapers' (2011: 4). Around the same time in the UK the then prime minster Harold Macmillan famously told us 'You've never had it so good' and that 'we are all middle class now'. In the United States a theory arose that demonstrated how aspirational individuals could climb the career ladders in hierarchical professions and bureaucratic organisations. Career development theory was informed by developmental psychology which charted the 'ages and stages' of man's psychological development – and yes, like trait/factor theory the concern was with man's employment, as woman's place in paid work in the first part of the twentieth century was not the focus. (This is not to dismiss the issue – it will be referred to later.)

What career development theory did do, in contrast to trait/factor theory, was take account of the wider processes in a life that contribute to ideas about, and preferences for, occupational choice. Although there are other writers who developed the idea that career decision making is a process that takes place over time (Ginzberg et al., 1951), we will focus here on the work of Donald Super. His original theory (Super, 1957) outlines the career thinking stages – how the individual conceptualises career at different 'ages', suggesting that that there are developmental tasks that the person can undertake. The theory posits that the individual can practice relevant attitudes and values, and can build competences in order to 'master' the appropriate career development tasks and reach their goals. The key concepts in career development theories are development stages, development tasks, career identity and career maturity (Kidd, 2006); all of which are open to career learning, hence this theory can be applied to career education. A programme of career education in a learning environment (schools or organisations) supplemented by a matching programme (as in person–environment fit) retains its usefulness, although there are limitations that are discussed below.

In Super's original theory (1957) he explained career development as progressing through five stages: growth, exploration, establishment, maintenance and decline. In this early version of his theory, Super attached ages to the stages:

1. Growth: from birth to 14, includes fantasy ideas about career, a range of possible interests and the development of particular capacities.
2. Exploration: from 15 to 24, tentative ideas are tried and tested.
3. Establishment: 24 to 44, although still trialling an occupation in the early part, the person's career role becomes stabilised.
4. Maintenance: 44 to 64, progression up the career ladder and maintenance of one's career position.
5. Decline: 65 and beyond, retirement and withdrawal.

Activity 4.3

We will move on to consider how Super developed his ideas, but note your criticisms of this 1957 version of the theory before we do.

Advantages and limitations

I imagine you did not find that activity too hard, but we have to remember what the world of work was like over 60 years ago – a far more stable place. Although the idea that individuals go through stages in thinking about career is helpful, the notion that this is fixed at certain ages is far less secure. In addition, hierarchical careers have disappeared in many occupations and the concept of a 'career ladder' appears outdated. Rather than conventional work patterns of starting at 9am and finishing at 5pm, from Monday to Friday, people work different hours, different days of the week in part-time, temporary jobs, more than one job, in a variety of locations, including from home and online. Added to this not only have working patterns changed, but linear progression is disrupted as many people have to retrain as the nature of the work itself changes and former skills and knowledge become redundant. Thus, the whole concept of what we mean by work has changed in a vastly different society to that which Super was examining in the 1950s. The notion of 'boundaryless careers' has been used (Arthur and Rousseau, 1996) to describe career mobility and the shift away from organisations and traditional patterns of working: although we would be wrong to assume this has happened in all occupations or work roles, despite global and local organisational change. In addition, the time it takes a person to progress through each developmental stage will vary and setbacks will occur. The process as described takes place over such a long timescale that the idea that an individual remains static in their career decision making also lacks credibility. You may also have thought that the stage 'decline' is rather morbid and would not be how we would wish to consider disengagement from paid work in current times.

Another major criticism is that the theory does not consider the career trajectories of women, who often enter, leave and re-enter the job market according to the demands of family and child care. Although in later models Super did include the career development of women and of 'minority' workers across the lifespan, the major thrust of his work was on the stages of exploration and establishment, as it is at these stages, according to Super, that the occupational self-concept is formed. Nevertheless, Super responded to the changing nature of work and society (1981), and to the criticisms aimed at his work. He extended his theory into a 'life-span, life-space' theory (1994) which aimed to incorporate the shifting ideas and expectations around life roles and work roles, and the moveable transition points when decisions are made. It can be said that career development theory 'developed' and was extended so far that its internal coherence was lost, but Super was willing to continually reconsider his ideas to include the changes he was living through. (For a comprehensive understanding of the man and the extent of his contribution, I can recommend the article 'Donald Edwin Super: the career of a planful explorer', written by Savickas in 1994.)

Super used diagrams to depict the reformulations of career development, illustrating this in the 'career rainbow' (Super, 1981) and then the 'career arch' (Super, 1994). The latter work was intended to demonstrate the various groups of determining features for an individual and their proximity to the personal and the situational. These are played out as roles in various theatres in a life, such as the home, the community, the school/education and the workplace. The roles can be: child, student, consumer of leisure, citizen, worker, spouse or partner, homemaker, parent and pensioner (Killeen, 1996a). Roles and their expectations change over the course of a life cycle and decision points are reached as roles develop, change or cease. So, in Super's thinking he moved significantly from the early model which charted the progress toward making *the* stable career decision to a more nuanced proposition that recognised that career interacted with, and was situated within, other life roles. He was aware that any career choice was likely to be a compromise and of the limitations of any theory – including his own. Finally, it needs to be reiterated that career development theory acknowledges that people change and jobs change and, thus, to learn about both and to make satisfying decisions about what to do, individuals can benefit from the help on offer from career counsellors and career coaches at a number of transition points. A case study follows to illustrate how a career coach might incorporate career development theory and 'matching' into their work.

Case study 4.1: Coaching for a return to work

Rosemary is a career coach who was asked to design a short course of four, two-hour sessions, by a community group that received funding to support parents back into work after a career break. She describes how she planned the sessions and the approach that informed the work.

'Well, in thinking about where these people were in terms of their lives, I knew that they would all be "adult" clients, rather than school leavers, and was told that to qualify for the course they had all been out of the paid workforce for at least four years. Parents include men of course and in the group of 12 there were two men. I decided I would use the DOTS[1] model to structure the sessions, as I would not be giving individual career coaching. And I know that Bill Law has developed this work further and thinks the DOTS model is old hat – but it is simple and provides a good starting point in my view; provided that you use it flexibly with lots of discussion and creative exercises.

So, anyway, each session was framed around the model but in SODT order: you know – **s**elf-awareness; **o**pportunity awareness; **d**ecision making skills; and **t**ransition management. We began with introductions and set ground rules, confidentiality and so on, and then did some exercises to get to know each other and explore people's general interests, likes and dislikes, what motivates them; and also to find out about any previous work experience and their current situation. We did this through talking in small groups, but also using imagery, drawing – whatever medium they chose from the examples I

---

1   Law and Watts (1977).

gave – including a bit of storyboarding[2] – Bill Law would approve of that! It was fun and brought the group together. In the following session we discussed the current employment market, constraints and opportunities and how to look for employment in general terms. I set them some 'homework' too, to see what they could find; different examples of occupations and vacancies, to follow up on the session. In the third session we looked at decision making skills, talking about how they make decisions normally and how this varies according to the situation, the factors involved – and then considered alternative ways of thinking about decision making. And we thought again about what motivates us to take action and what gets in the way, and ways of overcoming this.

So that linked with the final session. First, we looked at what they had found out after session two and how they had accessed labour market information, and then we thought about managing the transition from home to work – what's involved for them in their context. We thought about self-presentation skills, in a CV, on an application form and at an interview. I wish I had had more time with the group, as I would have liked to use a computer matching programme with them at that point. But I explained what these are and how to get the best from them, and as the sessions were in the community centre near the library, I suggested they accessed online resources there – for those that did not have access at home. And I also gave them a list of useful books that I know the library stocks, you know, the perfect CV, preparing for interviews and so on. There's so much more I could do, but at least the resources were available for these short sessions – to get them started.'

Reflection point 4.4

We have looked at two career theories that are derived from the discipline of psychology and we now move to theory informed by sociology – what do you anticipate this will mean in terms of a shift in focus?

Structural theories

Structural theories focus on socio-economic status and the organisation of work, viewed as stratified along class and gender divisions. In the theories above, derived from psychology, we can say (albeit this is a simplification) that they focus on the

---

2 See the Career-learning Café at: www.hihohiho.com

individual and assume the person has the ability to make a career choice. Structural theorists focus on the structures within a society that aid or constrain the possibility of choice. When choice is viewed as free, we can say that the person has *agency*; when their ability to choose is governed by their social context, this can be described as *socially determined*. Bourdieu (Bourdieu and Passeron, 1977) is most often connected with the phrase 'cultural capital': our cultural capital combines actual and social capital and is closely linked to social status and power.

In the UK, Ken Roberts, a sociologist, challenged the prevailing psychological and individualistic approach to career theorising (i.e. trait/factor and developmental), by arguing that for many young people choice is a chimera, since the first job gained is largely determined by social class. It is, in this theory, the family background and access to social capital that shapes the educational experience, career aspirations and career actualities for vast numbers of young people, constrained as they are by their socio-economic position. At the time, education in the UK was organised in a tripartite system where access to different types of schooling was determined at age 11, or in some cases 13. Trait/factor matching and career education programmes are therefore considered meaningless if entry into matched occupations is not possible, due to the limited opportunities available to those not in the 'higher' level of grammar school education. Most young people in these circumstances do not choose occupations, they simply take what is available. Roberts (1968) provided a stark and necessary reminder that no amount of career planning will obviate the very real issues that many face in industrial areas where employment is organised around the work that is available locally. Young people are less 'mobile' than adults and in difficult times are unlikely to move away from family and friends to find work elsewhere. In the 1970s there were youth riots and disturbances in many cities in the UK, where previous working communities, which offered young men apprenticeships and working status in traditional industries (broadly speaking in engineering and allied crafts, such as ship building, steel, coal) had broken down. The textile industry in the north of England, the potteries in the Midlands and other manufacturing industries, which also employed many young women of school-leaving age, had also declined. In this climate career education programmes were viewed by Roberts as pointless as they raised unrealistic expectations for many young people, and he viewed the outcomes of career guidance as limited within structural constraints (Roberts, 1977).

In later work, Roberts (1997) argued that the transitions for young people from education to working life have become more prolonged and their ultimate destinations more uncertain. With the decline in traditional employment routes for young people, they become warehoused in education and training schemes that do not necessarily offer the kinds of qualifications that are valued by employers or the society at large (in the UK it is academic rather than technical qualifications that remain the most desirable, and weak vocational qualifications with little real work experience are the least desirable of all in a competitive job market). The changes in the world of work, and increased youth unemployment and alienation, led to a shift in the discourse about unemployment and young people (Reid, 1999). The language changed from describing young unemployed people as being (socially) disadvantaged to being (psychologically) disaffected: the former suggesting it is the social context that is to blame, the latter that it is the young person who is responsible. Previously the closure of the factory, or the pit, or the steel works within a specific geographic area, resulted in a common experience of unemployment: a devastating, but at least shared experience. In more recent times work and occupations are diffuse and unemployment has become an individualised experience, where the individual feels personally responsible for their inability to find work.

The work of Roberts, and other structural theorists (Hodkinson et al., 1996), remains significant in areas today where unemployment or underemployment is endemic and the prospect of employment for young people is bleak. When we think of the employment situation for many young people across Europe and North America, life chances remain as dependent as ever on social class and access to educational attainment that is valued in the society within which the individual operates. The opportunity structures in a society (how work is organised), structure the opportunities that are available. We have to remember that Roberts was looking at the issue from a macro, structural perspective, explaining how the employment market functions, with its 'reserve pool of labour', to use a sociological term. Social class may be stratified in the UK along different lines in the twenty-first century, but there are more people than jobs and where jobs are available, they are often poorly paid, with conditions that are not considered acceptable to an indigenous population that is not itinerant. Structural theory is not claiming that this is *how life should be* for young people and others, but reminding us ('us' often being middle class, white folk with jobs) that this is *how life is* for many. Although Roberts' work focuses on young people, the above has relevance for adults, although adults do have more experience in terms of finding a job – any job. A case study may help to illustrate the point and the theory.

Case study 4.2: Beside the seaside

Dan is eighteen and has not worked in a full-time job since leaving school at 16. He lives in a coastal town that was once a centre for British seaside holidays, but is now blighted by widespread disadvantage and unemployment. It has a high street full of closed shops, charity or 'pound stores' and former hotels on the seafront are in disuse or occupied

(Continued)

(Continued)

by multi-occupancy tenants. As an 'independent-liver', Dan has a room in one of these buildings, paid for through housing benefits. He tells the career adviser at the job centre a little about his life and his prospects – as he views them currently.

'Well, I was doing all right at school, got OK grades but not really good enough to go to college and they did not want me in the sixth form – the courses were pretty rubbish in any case. My mum needed me to get a job, but with no experience I couldn't get one. I did a training course in retail, which I liked, and got some work placement in a supermarket, but they did not want me there after the course finished and there were no other vacancies. Well there were, but every time you go and ask they say you haven't got **enough** experience and they take adults who have more experience – whether it's in retail or not. I think employers around here aren't interested in young people. My girlfriend's sister has a job in a supermarket on the tills, but she's 21 and has been to university – it's ridiculous!

I couldn't stay at home after that and I'm living in an old B&B place on the seafront – it's horrible, I hate it. The area is full of people who have been sent there, ex-offenders, migrants; the young guy in the room next to me comes from a care home somewhere in London, doesn't know the town or anyone in it. What chance do I have to get a job – as soon as I give my address you can see them making all sorts of assumptions because locally they know the area. And it's no good telling me to go the next biggest town to look for work, as I do not have the money for the bus, not that there's many of those – huh!'

Advantages and limitations

The work of Roberts emphasised that contrary to the theorising of many career psychologists in the middle part of the previous century, the labour market was not structured on meritocratic lines. It may be that the individual has a high level of intelligence and has learnt about self and about career, but the entry points into employment were/are determined or severely constrained by socio-economic status. We might think that changes in employment legislation have ameliorated this situation in the UK, and of course considerable improvements have been made in terms of equality; but choice remains constrained by the amount of social/cultural capital an individual possesses and by the prevailing opportunities available within a competitive job market.

Roberts views the role of career practitioners working with young people as important, in order to ensure they can find work within what has become a more fluid and less fixed labour market. Practitioners, from this view, can help young people with the transition from education to work and, although they cannot change the status quo for large numbers of young people, they can make a difference to the lives of some young people. In other words, they can advocate on behalf of a young person and they can enable, but they are unlikely to empower large groups of young clients.

Unlike the previous two theories, opportunity structures theory does not give practitioners tools to work with (although the tools to think with resonate with practitioners' experience of practice 'on the ground' in many areas). The theory may leave the reader feeling pessimistic, but it should not lead us to think it is all too difficult and we may just as well give up and go home. It does warn us about raising aspirations that are beyond the current horizons for some young people, but it also suggests that we need to work alongside the individual to recognise what the difficulties might be and identify ways of dealing with likely constraints. There are other actions that can be taken in terms of the implications of the theory for practice. For example, practitioners can work with employers and training organisations in their area to promote opportunities for young people, including developing a fairer selection and recruitment process. Local labour market information can be gathered and kept up to date and made accessible for young people, to help them make the most of the opportunities that are available. Practitioners and their professional organisations can engage in lobbying activities with policy makers to support employers wanting to develop better 'modern' apprenticeships and work placement offers. Young people, who experience a number of barriers to employment, also need more time and practitioners need more relevant training to support them. Matching and career learning programmes will not be enough.

Problems with career decision making

The notion that career decision making is straightforward has already been 'problematised' and, as is evident in the above discussion, there are different ways of theorising this. Yates (2013) draws on the work of Gati et al. (1996) and Gati and Tal (2008) to examine the reasons clients may get stuck in the process. The research identified three broad themes and ten sub-themes that appear to be most telling. The first group of issues centres on a lack of readiness, which Yates states, 'can be split into people struggling with a lack of motivation, indecisiveness and dysfunctional myths' (2013: 79). The second group revolves around a lack of information about occupations and/or the process of making decisions related to self-knowledge linked to occupational awareness. The third group focuses on inconsistent information which may be the result of inconsistent or unreliable information – again about self and occupations. Yates offers coaching approaches that can be useful to work with these difficulties and I will refer to her suggestions later in the book.

Integrating theory

In this chapter, three theories, or theoretical approaches, were discussed separately. From the 1970s onwards it has become increasingly acceptable for practitioners to draw on different academic disciplines and to integrate aspects from various theories into their practice. On the face of it this seems sensible as, for instance, my client may not fit into my way of working if this is informed by a single theory. But there are limitations here too. Kidd (1996), drawing on the earlier work of Norcross and Grencavage (1989), warns that 'technical eclecticism' can lead to the integration of methods and techniques without examining or understanding the 'parent' theories, or the philosophical background that informs their development. This may be fine in situations where models have been developed from more than one theory to structure counselling work (e.g. Egan, 2007) or for single 'helping' interactions (e.g. Reid and Fielding, 2007). A problem arises, however, if the eclectic model is not proving useful and the practitioner does not have the knowledge to enable them to shift their approach by drawing on other theoretical knowledge. The alternative approach to integration would seek to synthesise theory through a process of 'theoretical integration'. This can avoid a reductionist approach that condenses career counselling to a series of techniques or list of competences to be ticked. But this is not easy and theoretical integration requires in-depth understanding of a range of theories and their application; which suggests that training for career practitioners must incorporate the development of a number of intellectual skills to enable them to critically evaluate their approach(es). We will return to this point later in the book.

On a more prosaic level, we can see the theories described above displayed in the space of a single *psychosocial* career encounter. Within a session the practitioner will be making an assessment of a client or group (although they may not be using Rodger's terms and this may not be via a test), they will be thinking about the developmental stage and career maturity of the person or group, and they will be considering what might be affecting their aspirations, goals and ability to act; in terms of the social context. And careers work is about using career information, it may incorporate giving advice and offering guidance – all of course at the point of readiness, and when relevant to the *current* interests, circumstances, needs and desires of the client or group that the career practitioner is working alongside.

Chapter summary

This book is an *introduction* to career counselling and career coaching, and a limited amount of theory has been discussed in this chapter. Even so, within the imposed constraints there was much to cover and it is one of the longest chapters. In the suggested reading that follows, I have indicated texts that embrace a richer discussion and deal with the arguments in greater depth. The chapter has included an examination of the purpose of theory for careers work and has explored three theories, or theoretical approaches, that became well established in the twentieth century. The discussion has indicated that the theories still have value, despite the major changes in the world of work and the meanings that can be given to the word career. At the beginning of the chapter, I 'signposted' that future chapters will examine the developments in theory at the end of the twentieth century and those that are emerging currently: we are by no means 'done' with career theory yet. Finally in this chapter a discussion took place that considered the desirability of integrating different theories, as relevant for the work that takes place with clients.

Further reading

Kidd, J.M. (2006) *Understanding Career Counselling: Theory, Research and Practice*. London, UK: Sage.
This is a well written and easy to access text, which deals in further depth with the theories introduced in the chapter. It also includes a chapter focused on adult career development.

Killeen, J. (1996a) 'Career theory', in A.G. Watts, B. Law, J. Killeen, J.M. Kidd, and R. Hawthorne (eds), *Rethinking Careers Education and Guidance: Theory, Policy and Practice*. London: Routledge. Written in a different style, the breadth and depth of this chapter by John Killeen is remarkable and explores the detail that it has not been possible to include here. Overall the book retains its currency, although due to wider social changes some parts may be dated; but this chapter in particular remains very useful for exploring career theory.

Lent, R.W. and Brown, S.D. (eds) (2013) *Career Development and Counselling: Putting Theory and Research to Work* (2nd edn). Hoboken, NJ: John Wiley & Sons.
Another sizeable text from American editors, which covers a wide range of established career theory, relevant for various careers work settings. Now in a second edition it includes new and emerging approaches.

Yates, J. (2013) *The Career Coaching Handbook*. Abingdon: Routledge.
Unlike many coaching texts this book pays attention to underpinning theory and includes several chapters on theories of career – relevant for both career counselling and career coaching. I particularly like the chapter on career decision making difficulties, with its use of recent research on the topic.

Activity 4.1: My definitions

Perspective: Words to associate with this would be looking, seeing, an overview: it suggests a standpoint (a place we look out from). Our perspective is informed by our worldview, how we think the world operates (our ontological viewpoint) and thoughts about what counts as knowledge (an epistemology of career). In terms of career theories, an academic discipline gives structure and an overarching perspective – this will shape our approach to theorising. An example of this would be a psychologist trained in cognitive-behavioural therapy.

Theory: The word theory is in the singular and suggests a particular set of explanations that attempt to explain human behaviour. It is informed by the theorist's perspective, but will develop as it is criticised by others and by the changes in society, but it should retain its core arguments.

Model: A model moves the theory into practice and suggests ways the theory can be applied in practice. A model may be working with one specific theory, but often it may integrate aspects from different theories.

Approach: An approach is what practitioners often talk about – down there in the 'messy swamps', particularly as they become experienced and develop their own approach, informed by their knowledge of both theory and practice. In careers work it is likely that they take an integrated approach, drawing on their learning and experience to negotiate what works best for a particular client or group. Schön referred to this as 'the artistry of practice' (1983). This of course does not negate the need to refresh our learning about theory or to engage in continuous professional development. From the above, you can see that these words are placed to indicate a progression from perspective to approach.

5

Counselling theories to inform career counselling and coaching practice

This chapter will:

- explore the principles of person-centred therapy for career counselling and coaching;
- consider the use of cognitive behavioural approaches, psychodynamic therapy and transactional analysis for career counselling and coaching;
- examine the boundaries between career counselling and coaching and therapeutic work;
- discuss the assessment of the needs of the client and link this to processes of referral.

Introduction

As explored in the previous chapter, theories of career decision making draw on research into how people make choices. Career counsellors and coaches also need theories that inform and underpin their interventions – to assist in the process of decision making – sometimes referred to as career guidance theories. Many of these are drawn from counselling and psychotherapy and, in terms of the estimated 400+ counselling models in use, this chapter will focus on the perspectives that are most usually adopted and adapted for career counselling and are useful for career coaching. The chapter will focus on person-centred theory and will also include cognitive behavioural approaches, psychodynamic therapy and transactional analysis. Specific techniques and skills will be considered later in the book. Within this current chapter the boundaries between career counselling and therapeutic counselling will also be mentioned; alongside considering the assessment of need and the process of referral.

Person-centred theory

Client-centred therapy was developed in the previous century by the psychologist Carl Rogers (Rogers, 1951). Client-centred therapy is described as non-directive, where the therapist's role is to come alongside the client, to listen and reflect on or restate the client's words, without judgement or offering interpretation. The goal of therapy in this approach is for the client to achieve personal growth via their increased awareness and understanding of their attitudes, feelings and behaviour.

The later, and more influential person-centred approach (Rogers, 1961), pays attention to the potential labelling implications of using the term 'client' and the power relationship between the 'client' who is 'helped' by the 'expert'. It was Rogers' view that if the person, who is the expert on their own situation, is given the space to think and is held at the centre of the work, they will find their own solutions. The theory posits that human beings have an innate tendency to work towards personal fulfilment (known as the 'actualising tendency'). To become 'fully functioning' and work towards 'self-actualisation' (Maslow, 1970), the physical and psychological environment needs to be such that the individual is able to be open to experience, trusting and trusted within relationships, curious about the world, creative and compassionate.

Within a psychotherapeutic context, the person-centred therapist works within a trusting relationship to maintain an environment that is free from psychological threat – by demonstrating deep understanding (empathy), genuineness (congruence) and acceptance (unconditional positive regard): the core conditions. A trusting relationship based on the core conditions helps to create the 'therapeutic alliance' – this is viewed as important in most counselling approaches. Although Rogers' ideas were developed for psychotherapy, the principles of a person-centred approach are valued and applied in counselling, and in professional helping situations that are non-therapeutic, including teaching, management, childcare, work within health and social care settings, mediation, and career counselling and coaching. That said I am mindful that the term client-centred rather than person-centred is used widely in career counselling and coaching, although, as above, this relates to earlier formulations of Rogers' work. Also, it is important to state that whilst the principles and skills derived from Rogers' work are used widely, person-centred therapy remains a distinct counselling approach (Mearns and Thorne, 2000).

Reflection point 5.1

Once again, language is important and perhaps earlier, in the introduction, you questioned the use of the word 'intervention'. It makes me feel rather uncomfortable, and it is unlikely that it would fit within Rogers' person-centred thinking – why?

The word intervention may have connotations of interference or intrusion by the practitioner into the life of the individual, and it unbalances the intention that the relationship is based on equality. Person-centred work assumes that the individual can take responsibility for their own behaviour (they have the *locus of control*), and that they have the free will and opportunity to make decisions independently (what was referred to previously as *agency*). The person-centred approach has its roots in humanistic and existential philosophy, which, if you are unfamiliar with that term, may need explaining. Humanistic-existential philosophy suggests that human beings can use reason as a capacity for making freely willed choices, unencumbered by the influence of religion or society. It is an individualistic approach rooted in a search for values, suggesting that the individual has an essential self or identity, created through living a life. Critics would accuse this philosophical approach as elevating *reason* above *being*. As a therapy the focus is on thinking persons being able to develop self-awareness and thus work towards personal growth in order to realise individual potential. I want to pause here. In offering definitions as we progress through the book, I should clarify that these are my attempts to provide access to terms and concepts that are complex or expressed in a specialised language that can feel exclusionary. But, there is always the danger that I will propose my preferred understandings and others may disagree. Further reading, in order to develop a deeper understanding and question any superficiality found here, is suggested at the end of each chapter.

Activity 5.1

Before moving on, using the critical approach outlined in the previous chapter, evaluate the benefits and limitations of the person-centred approach – as you see them at this point (and make some notes).

Rogers believed that personal development and learning occurred in both individual and group therapy, and his willingness to record and share his work has enabled others to understand the approach and the attitudes required, and to observe what are generally known as counselling skills. The major criticism of his work is that as a Western, white and individualistic approach, it pays inadequate attention to wider social, political and cultural factors. However, Rogers saw his work and personhood as always 'becoming', as in the title of his best known work *On Becoming a Person* (1961) and in his final book *A Way of Being* (1980), he regretted the lack of attention to the social context. The approach relies on the personal qualities of the therapist and their 'way of being' in therapeutic relationships; in other words, the ability to build a non-judgemental and trusting relationship. Nevertheless this is not a quality that can be switched on and off; hence the work is not suited to all. The relationship is the bedrock of the approach, which we will explore next through discussing the core conditions, before relating these more explicitly to careers work.

To work effectively alongside a client, the practitioner will focus on the relationship. Within counselling this is known as the therapeutic alliance. The principles of a person-centred approach which inform this are summarised by Westergaard as:

- we are all unique;
- human nature is fundamentally 'good' and positive;
- we each possess the drive to self-actualise (to become who we want to become);
- we all need to be loved and valued by others;
- we are best placed to make decisions about our own lives. (Westergaard, 2011a: 42)

Rogers' person-centred approach does not offer interview techniques and his work is not goal-focused. The emphasis remains on the attitudes of the practitioner; attitudes that are said to help clients develop self-awareness and locate their inner resources and strengths. The attitudes (the core conditions) are usually expressed as:

- **empathy:** understanding the client from their frame of reference (not from the practitioner's experience) – in other words to see the world as the client views it;
- **congruence:** being genuine and real within the relationship;
- **unconditional positive regard:** having a respect for the client which is accepting and non-judgemental.

Westergaard (2011a) explains these attitudes in detail, but a case study follows to illustrate where these attitudes are lacking.

Case study 5.1: The core conditions – getting down to business

Carly has an appointment with a young jobseeker called Ali, who she has worked with for a number of weeks. Ali is often late and sometimes forgets the appointment. Carly has a busy day ahead of her and feels irritation mounting as Ali is again late this morning; but he does eventually arrive. He explains that his benefits have been stopped and he had to borrow some money as his meter had run out and he had no electricity. Carly notes he looks cold and more dishevelled than normal and that his clothes do not smell good, but she decides that she needs to 'get down to business' in order to support Ali in this current crisis, which requires immediate action.

'Hmm, well that's difficult, but we need to decide what you will do to look for work, so that your benefits can be started again don't we Ali. I'm sorry, but we haven't got much time. So, what do you think you should be doing now?'

Comment: It is reasonable for Carly to feel irritated that Ali is late again and she is under much pressure to work with a number of people. She has 'placement targets' that are important for the funding of the work. Carly does want to help Ali and she knows that he needs his benefits, and she will work with him to see that he can reapply. She does need to take action today. However, she does not listen and respond with empathy to Ali's explanation; she avoids the trap of sympathy, for example 'Oh, you poor thing, let me sort this out for you', but she does not demonstrate empathy. Her getting down to business approach is perhaps more to do with her busyness than an accepting and non-judgemental attitude towards Ali. She acknowledges that his situation is difficult, it is a crisis, but she is not prepared to give him the time which would demonstrate genuine caring for Ali and his personal circumstances. Being congruent does not mean that she would say, 'Look I'm really busy today and you are late, you need the money, so we'd just better get on with it'. But it feels like she is playing the role rather than being person-centred, she does not sound sorry, and the open question at the end of her response is not really helpful either. His life **is** his responsibility, but his situation is stressful and it is unlikely that he can think on his own. And although she has not commented on his appearance, was she checking out her feelings and responses to Ali and being mindful of her approach? It is unlikely that he feels valued and trusted – she is not exemplifying unconditional positive regard as a way of being with the client. Without 'living' the core conditions, what do you think the likelihood is of this approach facilitating change with, for and by the young person?

Activity 5.2

Keeping within the boundaries of a professional approach (taking Ali home or giving him money from one's own pocket would not be professional), how might Carly have worked as a person-centred practitioner? Try to rewrite the case study, to demonstrate the core conditions.

It is naive to suggest that our own experiences as practitioners, and our lives outside work, do not affect our reactions to our clients; the core conditions are not always easy to maintain. The person-centred counsellor will, however, strive to understand self, through reflexive processes, and work constantly to build a therapeutic alliance through exemplifying the core conditions – in order to work for the best outcomes for their client. Carly is not working with Ali as a therapist, but she could demonstrate the core conditions in an alternative approach, despite the pressures that she is working within.

The principles of person-centred work in career counselling and coaching

For many practitioners working in career counselling roles with young people in schools – or with young people and adults who are seeking work and may or may not have a range of barriers to finding employment – time is likely to be a key issue. There are other concerns relating to restricted resources, workloads, legislation and the need to evaluate and quantify action – the meeting of imposed targets and the like. So how might Carly have responded, bearing in mind her need to care for herself alongside caring for her client?

Case study 5.2: 'Living' the core conditions in restricted circumstances

Carly has an appointment with a young jobseeker called Ali, who she has worked with for a number of weeks. Ali is often late and sometimes forgets the appointment. Carly has a busy day ahead of her and feels irritation mounting as Ali is again late this morning; but he does eventually arrive. He explains that his benefits have been stopped and he had to borrow some money as his meter had run out and he had no electric. Carly notes he looks cold and more dishevelled than normal and that his clothes do not smell good, and she recognises that this is a crisis situation which needs immediate action.

Carly: 'I can see that you are cold Ali and that you have had a lot to deal with this morning, would you like a hot drink?'

Ali: 'No thanks, I got some money from a friend and bought a tea on the way here.'

Carly: 'Well thank you for coming, I do have other appointments this morning, but we'll use the time we have to ensure that you can reapply for your benefits – am I right in thinking that is your priority for this morning?'

> Ali: 'Yeah, 'cause I need to pay my friend back the money and then buy some food and stuff.'
>
> Carly: 'OK, well before we do that, just tell me what else is going on for you at the moment, how are you coping living in the flat, for example?'
>
> **Comment**: Carly recognises her irritation caused by Ali's lateness and she knows that the time she can spend with him is limited, as she has other young people booked in. She also knows that this is a crisis situation and that Ali is anxious and will need to know that she is going to help. Her opening response is empathic and, as the kitchen is next door to the interview room, it would not be hard for her to make a hot drink if he would like one. Although he refuses, it is more likely that Ali senses that Carly is concerned for him. She is also open with him as she does have limited time, but she checks out that her interpretation of his immediate needs is correct. Above all she stays alongside Ali and does not rush to action, as the relationship will not end today and she will want to work on his wider needs, including career ideas, beyond the immediate issue. She knows his life is likely to be chaotic – he is living on his own, on benefits, which have been stopped; he has no electricity and has probably been unable to wash his clothes. She wants him to have the opportunity to talk about his situation before they deal with the benefits reapplication.

As I think about Carly, in both scenarios, I wonder about the organisational support she receives and whether supervision is available – we will explore support and supervision for career counselling in a later chapter.

Although Rogers was not interested in career counselling, others have applied his approach to the field. Patterson (1964) was one of the first to do this, recognising that one of the most important factors for making progress in an interview is the relationship between the careers practitioner and the client. Bozarth and Fisher (1990) prefer the use of the term person-centred approach in careers counselling, as it emphasises both the egalitarian nature of the relationship and the person-to-person interaction, rather than expert to client intervention. They outline four 'axioms' of person-centred careers work:

1. The person-centered career counsellor has attitudes and behaviours that focus on promoting the inherent processes of client self-actualization
2. There is an initial emphasis on a certain area of client concern, that of work

3. There are opportunities for the client to test his or her emerging concept of personal identity and vocational choice with real or simulated work activities
4. The person-centered career counsellor has certain information and skills available to the client through which a career goal can be implemented. (Bozarth and Fisher, 1990: 53)

Working through each axiom, Kidd (1996) notes that: the first emphasises that the locus of control remains with the client; the second acknowledges that this is careers work, but that other issues may arise; the third suggests the need for broader career learning and development; and the fourth recognises that information should not be introduced until the appropriate time.

Thus far the focus has been on considering the person-centred approach in therapy and career counselling, but what about career coaching? Rogers' work remains so influential across a number of sectors, as noted earlier, that much of the same discussion applies to career coaching. In essence it is about humanistic attitudes and beliefs rather than goals and techniques, hence its applicability and significant place in this chapter, albeit that there are contextual limitations. Although coaching draws on psychological theory and practices it is not viewed as therapy and yet Zeus and Skiffington, writing about workplace coaching, make the links with 'existential issues' and humanistic work clear:

> Coaching is imbued with notions from humanistic psychology – a science created by Abraham Maslow which is concerned with higher human values, self-development and self-understanding. Coaching involves examining and clarifying an individual's needs and values and working with these to develop goals that will lead to personal and professional development. (Zeus and Skiffington, 2000: 10)

They also cite the work of Carl Rogers when they state that a successful coach offers 'unconditional acceptance and warmth' (ibid). Whitmore (2009), in discussing the principles and practice of coaching and leadership, also draws on humanistic psychology, particularly the work of Maslow and Rogers. The development of goals in both career counselling and career coaching is perhaps the departure point from person-centred therapy.

Moving on, within the word limits of this chapter, three other theoretical psychotherapeutic and counselling approaches will now be introduced. This is however, only a brief introduction; where appropriate for career counselling and coaching, techniques that derive from them will be discussed later in the book.

Using cognitive-behavioural approaches

Many career coaches will draw explicitly on cognitive-behavioural therapy (CBT), such as solution-focused approaches. Before looking at solution-focused work in more detail in the next chapter, a summary of CBT will be offered here. The key idea underpinning CBT is that it is our beliefs that influence our thoughts, values and actions, rather than events. Thus if our beliefs are in some way self-limiting, or even self-sabotaging, they will present barriers to fulfilment, or in our case, career success. Put another way, 'faulty' thinking (cognitions) or Negative Automatic Thoughts (NATs), can lead to unhelpful or limiting behaviour.

The development of CBT draws on cognitive-behaviourist psychology. Behaviourist psychologists (e.g. Pavlov, 1927; Skinner, 1953; Watson, 1919) posit that behaviour is a learned response to a particular stimulus. In other words, rather than we are who we are because of how we are made (*nature*), we are who we are due to our experiences (*nurture*). In terms of therapy, if this is learned behaviour it can be unlearned and more effective behaviours can be developed. Cognitive approaches, however, suggest that *thinking* plays a more important part in determining behaviour. The work of Kelly (1955), Beck (1976) and Bandura (1977) would be referred to as cognitive psychology.

Reflection point 5.2

Pavlov is mentioned above. His stimulus/response experiment is well known – can you remember what it was? If not, a quick web search will give you the answer. But, can you think of an example of an experience – learned behaviour – from your childhood that influences your action as an adult?

Westergaard offers a useful example that compares the two approaches (behaviourist and cognitive):

If we have been burned by touching an electric fire, behaviourists would suggest that we learn, by stimulus and response, not to touch it again. However, our thinking (cognition) tells us that if the fire is turned off, then it poses no threat. Furthermore, our cognitive processes enable us to make a judgement about whether or not to touch the fire, based on an analysis of how recently it has been turned off and what risk it might still pose. (Westergaard, 2011b: 95)

Childhood experiences can lead to irrational beliefs which will influence behaviour in later life. For instance, as a child, like many others, I had a fear of spiders. No amount of parental explanation, telling me that they were harmless and they were probably more afraid of me, given that I was several hundred times larger and more powerful, could alter my behaviour. It was having my own children and not wanting to reproduce this irrational behaviour that led to a change in my cognitions – thinking about the 'danger' that spiders posed. I am now able to pick them up – carefully – and remove them to a safer a place when necessary. At this point, a case study may help to relate the principles from CBT to careers work.

Case study 5.3: Identifying self limiting beliefs

Zainab is a career coach working in a large public service organisation. She has been asked to work with Gill who, according to Gill's line-manager, is no longer 'performing well' since she was given a more senior post. Zainab asks the line-manager what Gill's performance at work was like previously. 'No problems at all, quite the opposite, which is why she was promoted, but she is not managing staff well and I get nowhere trying to discuss this with her.' Zainab is then told that if the work does not improve, it is likely that Gill will be removed from the post.

Zainab arranges a first meeting with Gill, away from Gill's office space. Gill appears reluctant to engage with the coaching, stating that she has no problem with her new role aside from the amount of work she is being asked to do. Little progress is made in this first session, but another meeting is arranged, when again, although attending the session Gill still appears defensive and her body language suggests she does not want to be there. Zainab senses that she has started to build trust with Gill in the relationship but, whilst remaining person-centred, wants to explore this resistance.

Zainab: 'Gill, I'm wondering what is getting in the way of us being able to work together?'

Gill: 'What do you mean?'

Zainab: 'I sense you are reluctant to be here and you look very uncomfortable.'

Gill: 'Well, I've been sent here because I'm not good enough!'

Zainab: 'Tell me more about that, Gill – is that what your line manager said?'

Gill: 'Not directly, she said that I need coaching to help me develop my skills managing staff.'

Zainab: 'OK, that was my understanding too, but I'm wondering now why you interpret that as "not good enough", when you were promoted because you were judged to be the right person for the post. Can we spend some time thinking about that?'

Gill agrees and it emerges that her reluctance to engage with the coaching is based on a fear of failure and insecurities she feels regarding her new role. Gill felt to discuss this with the line-manager would be embarrassing, a sign of weakness and might mean she would be demoted. The main issue seems to be that Gill finds it difficult to assert her authority in difficult situations in her new role. Zainab recognises that Gill has self-limiting beliefs (NATs) which are producing a barrier to successful work in the new job. They agree to meet again when they will explore these beliefs. Zainab wants to question the reasons for these negative assumptions – are they rational? Could Gill be mistaken in holding these beliefs? Would she reach the same conclusion about another person in a similar situation? And why would she continue to think and act this way if there were no good reason to hold these beliefs? In the next session they work with Gill's faulty thinking and then continue to work on the development of Gill's management skills, in order to enhance the many strengths she has – the strengths that were recognised by the organisation when she was promoted.

Insights from psychodynamic therapy

The career coach in the case study above might have spent time exploring with Gill from where those self-liming beliefs originated. Much of our thinking about self (both positive and faulty) is conditioned by past experience as we were growing up, in the family, community, at school and with friends. But, a psychodynamic approach will not be appropriate without the time to develop and deal with the issues that may emerge. That said there are many insights that can be gained from psychoanalytic theory for career counselling and coaching. In the United States more attention is given to these insights than is found in the UK and many practitioners, in both careers counselling and coaching, are trained in psychodynamic therapy.

Psychodynamic theory, derived from and widely influenced by the work of Freud, uses interpretation to explore unconscious motivation and the deeply held reasons for the problems that are presented in therapeutic work. As the name suggests, the underlying dynamics that inform psychological behaviour (usually present from the person's early life) are assessed and worked with.

Activity 5.3

Before investigating this further, what might underlie the following behaviours in terms of fears, apprehensions or relationships problems?

1. A line-manager who micro-manages staff.
2. The colleague who seems aloof and never shares personal stories.
3. The client who arranges job interviews, but is always late in arriving.
4. A student who asks obvious questions all the time.

There may be numerous causes for the above behaviours and without a full exploration within the safe space of a counselling or therapeutic relationship, we would not be transferring 'answers' from this activity to practice. The point of the activity is to make us think beyond being perplexed or irritated by the behaviour of others.

We can create all manner of early life experiences that may have motivated the behaviours listed above. But in terms of fears, apprehensions or relationships problems, the first might be a fear of losing control, the second problems with intimacy, the third fear of the unknown and of success even, and the fourth a lack of self-confidence and ability to believe in one's own ideas. In psychodynamic therapy the experiences would be explored, but in careers work it is more likely that the effects of these beliefs would be worked with – as in the cognitive behaviour work discussed above.

So, ideas from psychoanalytic theory and psychodynamic therapy can help us to think about aspects such as anxiety, defensiveness and the unconscious communication that may occur during career counselling and coaching. Traits such as anxiety and defensiveness may, initially, seem like behaviour to be avoided – but within counselling exploring them can be beneficial, in order to gain a richer understanding of what is influencing the behaviour and the working relationship. Bearing in mind the cautionary note above, psychoanalytic ideas are worth introducing to highlight their explanatory power. In what follows the concepts of *anxiety* and *defensiveness* are discussed, and then *transference* and *counter-transference* are explained.

Anxiety and defensiveness

Anxiety is part of the human condition and our defences are there to protect us when we are uncertain or feel threatened, as in the case study above. Often these are unconscious responses that affect the way we behave and react to others. They function to help us to minimise the threat and retain a sense of control over our circumstances.

Defences can lead to behaviour such as denial (refusing to accept that something bothers us), projection (attributing our feelings or characteristics onto someone else) and repression (burying the anxiety as deeply as possible).

Within careers work a client might be challenged by issues that are not perceived as threatening by others. These issues may be difficult to explore as the practitioner may not be working in situations where they are able to develop a therapeutic alliance. In short-term work there is unlikely to be the opportunity for the client to explore deeply held feelings and beliefs. A client may hide behind their defences if the relationship does not provide a safe space to contain and explore these feelings. In-depth work, from this perspective, recognises that anxiety and defensiveness can be experienced on both sides of the relationship. So the practitioner may also be challenged by the difficulty of expressing feelings or of 'stuckness', incompetence even, when it comes to work with clients. Such feelings can evoke in clients and practitioners '"adolescent" feelings, including a desire to hold on to what may be under threat, and a resistance to change, for fear of the alternative' (Reynolds, 2006: 31).

Transference and counter-transference

In the explanation above, you will have noticed that insights from psychodynamic therapy are valuable for thinking about the career counselling and career coaching relationship – in that a relationship has two sides (or more than two of course if we are discussing group work). The purpose of exploring the relationship is to deepen the perception of the practitioner's understanding of the client's needs. A reflexive career counsellor or coach will examine their thoughts, feelings and actions towards the client and the 'helping' relationship. Transference can take place when something in an interaction triggers a resonance with a past event or relationship. The client can then react to the present situation in the same way that they responded to the past event. In many cases what is evoked is a relationship to an authority figure, but it might also be transference from someone who was very caring or over-caring. The feelings that can be recalled and exhibited (albeit unconsciously) might include anger, hostility, resentment, warmth, love, helplessness or resentment.

Reflection point 5.3

To think about this further, imagine what might have been happening for Gill in the case study above, in her relationship with Zainab in the early sessions – what transference might have triggered her defensive behaviour?

Counter-transference refers to the unconscious feelings experienced by the practitioner towards the client. If the practitioner is puzzled as to why they are behaving differently to a particular client than they do toward other clients, counter-transference may be taking place. The career counsellor or coach can reflect on their own feelings in relation to this person: for example, why do they feel irritated, bored, sleepy or overwhelmed by this person? These are complex matters that can emerge in relationships with clients and in therapeutic work would be addressed within a supervisory relationship (Reid and Westergaard, 2013). Supervision is a place where the unconscious communication taking place in the 'helping' relationship can be worked with, understood and explored. To look at other ways in which people communicate, Berne's Transactional Analysis (1964) is the final theory to be introduced in this chapter.

Transactional analysis

Like many others who went on to develop their own ideas (e.g. Carl Rogers, Fritz Perls), Berne's original practice was rooted in psychoanalysis and the work of Freud (Freud of course is often referred to as the 'father' of psychotherapeutic work). The focus on Berne's work in this chapter is on how people communicate – transact – with others. Berne moved on from the superego-id-ego states in Freudian analysis and devised a model for understanding transactions made up from three distinct ego states: Parent, Adult and Child (Figure 5.1). In so doing McLeod (2003) notes that Berne demystified psychodynamic ideas by using everyday language and concepts.

The key principles underpinning ego state theory are summarised below, but it should be noted that there are many other concepts within transactional analysis (TA) that are worth exploring. In particular the concepts of *life scripts* and *game playing* are illustrated in the case study offered. The core beliefs of TA are:

- People are OK.
- Everyone has the capacity to think.
- Everything we experience – actions and feelings – is stored within us.
- Feelings associated with past experiences can be reactivated in the present.

Westergaard (2011c) explores transactional analysis in the counselling of young people in some depth and analyses the concept of crossed transactions in detail, but it is important to say something more here about the structure of the ego states. The first point to make is that the ego states of Parent, Adult and Child are always expressed in the upper case inside adjoining, but not overlapping, circles (as in the figures below) – to distinguish them from an actual parent, adult or child. In TA, ego states relate to behaviour, thoughts and feelings that are 'acted out' in the different roles that make up part of who we are at different times.

The Parent ego state is divided into: Critical Parent, seen as controlling, setting rules and judging others against those rules, and can become disapproving; and Nurturing Parent, seen as caring, supportive and protective, but can become over-protective and rescuing. The Child ego state is usually divided into: Adaptive Child, where behaviour is adapted to please others and real feelings are suppressed; and the Free Child where feelings are paramount, seen as spontaneous and uncensored. A third state can be the Intuitive Child who adapts behaviour to please others, but gets their own way. Adult ego state behaviour can be described as thinking, reasoning and analysing. A response from the Adult ego state to a Critical Parent or an Adaptive Child transaction can 'save face' and avoids the 'hooking' of the corresponding ego state.

Case study 5.4: Critical Parent hooks Adaptive Child

For example, a meeting is set for 11am and a senior manager has to travel 50 miles to get there. He arrives worried he is late having driven probably faster than he should. He is told on arrival that the meeting has been changed to 12 noon, but no one remembered to inform him. He gets cross and shouts about his rush to get here, the difficulty of the journey and why wasn't he told. The meeting coordinator physically shrinks under the onslaught, mutters apologies, twice, but the senior manager is still angry. His Critical Parent has hooked her Adaptive Child. Her Free Child may have said something rude which would not be helpful either. An Adult response might go something like this, 'I can see that you are angry and that you have had a difficult time to get here. I do not usually make mistakes, but this has happened and I apologise. Now let me offer you a cup of tea or coffee – which would you prefer?' This response comes from the Adult ego state. It is important that his anger and frustration are heard and recognised – this is often the crucial aspect, as having being heard the anger is likely to dissipate. In this situation an apology was required, but not repeated from a stooped Adaptive Child ego state, it needed to be clear and then transactions can move on.

Berne observed that the people he worked with were often stuck in particular communication patterns, which can become dysfunctional. Patterns of communication are developed in childhood in order that needs are met. We make 'decisions' about life and the world around us in our early years, but these can be changed as we become responsible for our choices and actions. The theory suggests that communication takes place consciously on the social level, when we select our words to convey thoughts and feelings; albeit that those words can contain Parental messages, for example 'I should', 'I ought' and so on. But communication also occurs on the psychological level, through tone of voice and non-verbal behaviour (such as facial expression, body posture and the like). The latter is often an unconscious communication – transaction – and can conflict with the words we are using. In other words there is a tension between what is being said and how the message is being conveyed – for Berne the psychological message was of greater importance in terms of analysing the deeper meaning of the communication.

Time is important in terms of roles – when we exhibit different communication ego states – but it is important to remember that age is not. How we respond is learned behaviour and most of us balance this correctly and behave appropriately to the situation, but when stressed or psychologically unwell, we can revert to communication patterns that have been learned in the past – from a parental figure. For instance, if a parent sulks on a regular basis the child will appease the parent to get back the love that appears to be withdrawn, and, in turn, learns that sulking gets attention. In adult life sulking might become the default behaviour – behaviour from the past that is ultimately not satisfying.

When unexpected responses cause poor communication, we can refer to these as crossed transactions. An understanding of Transactional Analysis can be used by career coaches for solving problems caused by crossed transactions, or miscommunication, and can be an approach used for resolving conflicts in the workplace. Crossed transactions in careers work are depicted in the Figures 5.1–5.3 below:

As a career practitioner, as in counselling, it is important that we are aware of our own ego states when working with clients (and in life generally). And to repeat, as this is learned behaviour, it can be unlearned. Practitioners can work with clients to help them understand the way they communicate and that they can choose to

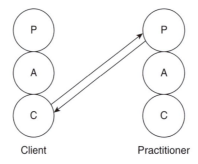

Figure 5.1   Client = Adaptive Child/Career Practitioner = Nurturing Parent

Client: 'It doesn't matter what I do it feels as though everyone is against me.' (AC)
Practitioner: 'That must be awful. Don't worry, I can sort this out for you.' (NP)

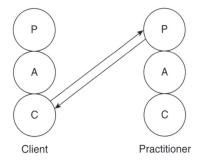

Figure 5.2   Client = Free Child/Career Practitioner = Critical Parent

Client: 'I don't care whether I get a job or not, I'm having a great time with my mates.' (FC)
Practitioner: 'OK, but you'll need to work at some point won't you?' (CP)

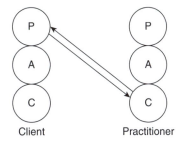

Figure 5.3   Client = Critical Parent/Career Practitioner = Adaptive Child

Client: 'I've come to see you now twice for career coaching, but nothing has changed. It's a waste of time!' (CP)
Practitioner: 'Oh dear. I'm sorry you feel like that. What else can I do to help?' (AC)

communicate – transact – in more satisfying ways. It is also important to say that someone who is in Adult all the time is likely to be boring company; we all need to be the Child that plays and will experience times when we want and need to be nurtured. The irritation that Carly felt with Ali earlier led to her transacting in Critical Parent. A self-aware Carly would have noticed these feelings and shown empathy and then worked from Adult.

The case study below comes from my own practice. Alongside the TA concepts of *life scripts* and *game playing,* it also includes the *drama triangle*. A life script is an unconscious life-plan developed in childhood, reinforced by parental figures and apparently justified by subsequent experiences. Life scripts culminate in a chosen perspective on life, a life position that enables us to make judgements about the world and our place within it – positive or negative. I'll explain the drama triangle after the activity.

Case study 5.5: Ah yes, but...

You have an adult interview booked and have information that your client is between the ages of 40 and 50 and has been in the same part-time occupation for several years, whilst looking after her children. She is now looking for a 'career'. During the interview your client tells you that her job (part time housekeeper to a National Trust property) is not satisfying her and she wants to do something 'more worthwhile and interesting'. Having agreed a contract and (you think) built rapport, you ask a number of open questions about what she thinks she may like from a new job. She gives vague 'don't know yet' answers. You try to find out what she does not like about her current job and she appears to dislike every aspect. She says she would not mind taking a short course in something. You ask her if she has seen any courses she finds interesting in the college prospectus she tells you she has looked at. She says it is too difficult as she does not know what it is she wants to do – that's why she has come to see you! You think maybe a Computer Aided Guidance program may help and suggest using one together. She tells you she has already used the program and got a list of suggestions. You ask if she researched any of these and she says she printed information but none of the suggestions were any good really. You realise you are doing most of the talking, beginning to run out of ideas and you wonder how you can help this person who is paying for your expertise.

Activity 5.4

- What is happening here?
- What are you trying to do?
- What are the client's expectations of you?

So, in TA terms, what's the problem? How would you analyse the transactions that are taking place? What might be this client's life script/life position? What could you do to change direction with this client? A Critical Parent response would be 'I can't help you if you won't help me'. Can you think of an Adult transaction that does move the interview (and the client) forward?

This case study is based on an interview I had with someone a little while after studying Transactional Analysis. About 20 minutes into the interview I realised I had interviewed her before, although two years previously. As the interview progressed, or rather did not make any progress, I realised that I had placed myself in a drama triangle, where roles switch between Victim, Persecutor and Rescuer. She behaved, initially, as a Victim but my every attempt to Rescue her made the roles switch, until I felt like the one being Persecuted. I paused, recognised my feelings of both frustration and growing incompetence, and wondered about her life script and the position she inhabits in the world.

I identified this as an 'Ah, yes, but' game (Berne, 1964). My client wanted help – that's why she booked and paid for the interview – but her life script seemed to be 'No one can help me and you're no different'. This could be an Adaptive Child ego state. To every suggestion – rescue attempt – she replies, 'Ah yes but, I tried that', or 'Ah yes but, the suggestions were no good', and so on. This felt to me like a Critical Parent ego state (I was no good – as she expected). So when I fail to rescue her, her life script is strengthened. In other words, 'There you are you see, I told you, you would not be able to help me and you didn't, no one can help me as it's all too difficult – life is as I say it is.'

My approach was then to test out what I perceived to be the barrier to us working together. In part two of the book the challenging skill of immediacy is discussed, but this is how it worked in this situation. I stopped digging myself deeper into the hole I was stuck in and from Adult, said, tentatively, 'I'm not sure what is happening here. Perhaps I did not explain clearly at the start about how we could work together. It is clear that you are looking for answers, but I do not seem able to help you. With every suggestion I make which would involve a change to your situation, you appear to find reasons or barriers that stop you from considering it further. And I wonder why that it is?' This Adult position, which was also congruent, ended the crossed transactions.

What happened next surprised me, as my client stopped frowning at me and started crying. Although this was not my preferred outcome, she then explained that she thought she was afraid of change, change had brought bad things into her life and even though she was not happy in her current job, it was a job she knew – it was safe. A new job, or training and education for something different, was unknown and scary. She was a single parent, she said, and there was much to consider. We talked about her fears and concerns for the rest of the interview, and she decided that she needed to think about this some more, before making a decision about what to do next. She had regained her composure by then, was communicating in Adult, thanked me for listening and left. (If you want to learn more about TA, see the suggested reading list at the end of chapter.)

Navigating the boundaries

In this chapter, three perspectives from psychotherapy and counselling have been introduced. From these overarching perspectives many theories have developed. I am aware that during this chapter the terms psychotherapy and counselling have been used at times interchangeably; and attempts to differentiate between the two are never completely satisfactory. It may be better to talk of counselling approaches and therapies derived from psychological principles. However, the fourth major perspective is multicultural counselling, which draws on other disciplines and will be considered in Chapter 8. When applying theory from psychotherapy and counselling to careers work, a further issue arises. In Chapter 2 the differences between various roles in careers work were explored and the conclusion was that there are many overlaps, but I want to end this chapter by highlighting that there are also boundaries. Knowing what those boundaries are is an ethical task for the career practitioner and in essence it is about knowing the limits of your own expertise. When faced with a situation that is outside of this expertise, it is important to assess the needs of the client and suggest a referral (and therefore know to where you can refer your client, and who you can offer as a contact).

Assessment of need and knowing when to refer

Assessment for careers work is described by Reid and Fielding (drawing on the UDACE model, 1986) as helping people:

> … to obtain a better understanding of their abilities and aptitudes, as they may relate to either personal, social, educational or career development, or the management of change in their lives. This is in order to enable them to make sound judgements about the appropriateness of particular courses of action. Such assessment may involve a range of methods, informal or formal. (Reid and Fielding, 2007: 26)

For many the word assessment may sound like a test will be involved, and there are many formal methods of assessment that can be used in careers work for matching individual personality traits, likes and dislikes to job profiles. These are known as career inventories. Psychometric tests are also used to assess other attributes alongside occupational preferences, for example personality type and decision making styles. Overall the role of assessment is to assist the individual with their decision making. Kidd (2006) provides a useful chapter on assessment tools and techniques, which covers both formal and less formal methods. McMahon and Watson (2015) have edited a book on qualitative assessment that explores theory and tools for careers work, drawing on 'new' and creative methods.

Assessment of the client's needs is slightly different. This may be through a formal process that uses an assessment tool, particularly where helping agencies may be working together, to assess which is the right service for the person concerned. In careers work it is likely to be an informal method, where through an interactive process of contract setting and sharing purpose and information, the practitioner makes a judgement about the suitability of what they have to offer. This might be an assessment of a particular approach to use, but it may be that the individual requires a different kind of counselling or coaching than the practitioner is able to provide. If the latter, then referral to different or specialist help may be necessary. However, within the principles of a person-centred approach, the client needs to be involved in this assessment and agree to the referral; it is undertaken with them, not done to them.

Chapter summary

This chapter considered the three major theoretical fields in psychotherapy and counselling and reflected on their relevance for careers work. A large part of the chapter explored the principles of person-centred therapy because of their use across most counselling approaches where a therapeutic alliance is central. The chapter also introduced cognitive behavioural approaches, psychodynamic therapy and transactional analysis – an understanding of each is useful for career counselling and coaching. In drawing on therapeutic approaches the nature of boundaries was also emphasised. The effective, ethical and reflexive practitioner will know the limits of their expertise. Finally, the chapter discussed the assessment of the needs of the client and linked this to processes of referral.

The case studies, reflection points and activities in this chapter have been used to illuminate an understanding of the theory – application of models that derive from these theories will be discussed in later chapters, including counselling skills. The previous chapter introduced the concept of integration. Integrative practice is where we draw on a broad knowledge of a number of approaches. It is important that we know how they are different and can consider the particular strengths and potential weaknesses of each, in relation to the work we are doing and the client or clients we are working with. This can lead to more effective work as we have more options to draw on than if we operated from a singular approach. The next chapter takes integration further by considering social constructionism and interdisciplinary approaches to career construction.

Further reading

Berne, E. (1964) *The Games People Play*. Harmondsworth: Penguin Books.
The seminal text on transactional analysis: short, well written and revealing.

Kidd, J.M. (1996) 'The career counselling interview', in A.G. Watts, B. Law, J. Killeen, J.M. Kidd, and R. Hawthorne (eds), *Rethinking Careers Education and Guidance: Theory, Policy and Practice*. London: Routledge.

This chapter deals with a number of theoretical orientations that can underpin career counselling and career coaching; including approaches that are not mentioned here. It also discusses theoretical integration.

McLeod, J. (2009) *An Introduction to Counselling* (4th edn). Maidenhead: McGraw Hill/Open University Press.
This is a key text for anyone practising in or interested in counselling. It is comprehensive, thorough and extensive – this 4th edition has further updates. It is enlivened throughout with short examples and case studies.

Nathan, R. and Hill, L. (2006) *Career Counselling* (2nd edn). London: Sage.
This book covers many of the concepts included in the above chapter, drawing particularly on the work of Carl Rogers. It includes a chapter on the role of career counselling in work organisations, which career coaches will find useful. Throughout, case studies are used based on the authors' experience.

Reid, H.L. and Westergaard, J. (2011) *Effective Counselling With Young People*. Exeter: Learning Matters.
Jane Westergaard's chapters (three, five and six) examine person-centred, transactional analysis and cognitive behavioural approaches in counselling. These chapters provide some of the detail that could not be covered here. Case studies are used to illustrate the theories in action.

6

New and emerging approaches

This chapter will:

- outline the shift to constructivist approaches for career counselling and coaching;
- explore solution focused career counselling;
- consider motivational interviewing;
- introduce the concept of 'green guidance'.

Introduction

This chapter will define constructivism, constructivist and social constructionism, the latter described as a new paradigm in career counselling. The terms will be explained and an overview will be given of the relevance of these approaches for career counselling and coaching. Two specific approaches will then be explored: solution focused counselling and motivational interviewing. Narrative career counselling is looked at in depth in the next chapter and a multicultural, or transcultural, approach is examined in Chapter 8. There are other 'new' approaches which will be referred to, but space limits further discussion here. In discussing new and emerging approaches it is important to note that decisions about future education, training and employment take place in a global context where sustainability issues are also under consideration. Many clients want to make what they regard as ethical or moral choices; this could be described as a commitment to 'green careers'. The chapter will conclude by discussing what career counsellors and coaches may consider in order to frame their guidance appropriately.

Social constructionism and constructivist approaches

As ever when defining terms we run the risk of being too shallow or going too deep. However, it is important that language and terms that are thought to be shared are examined from the start of the discussion. In thinking about the terms introduced in this chapter we bump up against other terms such as poststructuralism and postmodernism. In brief, poststructuralism recognised the instability of the earlier twentieth century 'grand narratives' approach to theories in the human sciences. Structuralism argued that human culture could be understood by the examination of various social structures, but poststructuralists argued that such thinking fails to acknowledge the inherent complexity of being human: in other words we cannot stand outside the structures we inhabit and arrive at objective conclusions. Post-structuralists pay specific attention to detailed historical analyses of how social systems have evolved to operate in the way they do. Social systems include health and education, social welfare, policing and so on – within such social systems we are all socialised and 'disciplined'. As individuals – subjects – we operate within language that is shaped by certain discourses that establish boundaries around what counts as 'truth', knowledge, cultural values and socially defined norms of behaviour.

Postmodern refers to a 'post-industrial' age (at least in Western economies) where explanations of the world, and how we act and behave within it, cannot be accounted for via scientific reasoning alone. The term postmodernism is also questioned and some social theorists will use the concept of 'late modernity' to indicate that contemporary society has not broken away from modernity (as the word postmodernity suggests), but continues; albeit in a world that feels insecure, fragmented, where identity is difficult to define within contrasting lifestyles and cultures. This ambiguity has led to the term 'liquid modernity' (Bauman, 2006) being used, to indicate the more fluid relations that exist where an individual can move through various roles, experiencing continuous change: a provisional, some-times rootless and often insecure life. Perhaps what we can take from each concept is what they have in common, rather than what separates them. All are concerned with the nature and degree of change and the impact this has on the way we construct the realities of our lives, within the social contexts we inhabit.

To clarify the difference between constructivism and constructivist, we can say that the former is focused on the individual and is cognitive, and the latter pays more attention to interpersonal processes and relationships. Definitions for social con-structionism vary, but Monk, Winslade and Sinclair, drawing on the contribution of Gergen (1994), state:

> Social constructionism (some argue that the word social is redundant) points to the way our experiences are constructed rather than determined in advance as part of the natural working out of biological processes. (Monk et al., 2008: 5)

As indicated in earlier chapters, we should remain mindful that counselling perspec-tives for individual decision making can ignore the structural constraints that define access to opportunities for many. Retaining the word *social* reminds us that interactions in career counselling and coaching are always culturally situated.

Constructivist methodology indicates a link to approaches that work alongside an individual as they construct meaning in their life and, within the subject of this text, their career. For most people, managing a career biography has become more unpredictable and uncertain as well as a more individualistic exercise. This is especially the case in marginalised communities where traditional structures of work that provided continuities across generations may have been lost under the impact of globalisation and neo-liberal economics. Constructivist approaches in careers work move from a hitherto dominant Western, 'scientific' orientation of measuring traits, using 'objective' psychological testing and matching these to occupations to a greater focus on *meaning*, in which subjective understanding is taken seriously. In the previous sentence social context is important, which returns us to the need for the word social, i.e., meaning is derived from the self in relationship to others or social constructionism.

Reflection point 6.1

The concepts above are likely to make you frown if this is your first encounter with them, but a passing familiarity with the terms is needed before we move on to explore a paradigm shift within careers work. The discussion above is all about paradigm shift(s) – what meaning does this term have for you?

Does careers work need a paradigm shift?

There appears to be widespread recognition of the need for a new paradigm for careers work. Bimrose (2009) concludes that the matching model (outlined in Chapter 4), which was devised in the early twentieth century, retains its dominance, despite its flaws when considering careers work in a 'liquid world' where jobs for life and clear career pathways, have dissipated. The case for a paradigm shift has also been argued in the USA and across Europe. (A paradigm shift being a change in the basic assumptions, or paradigm, within the ruling theory of science, but now also used in non-scientific settings. Within the context of career theory, this would mean a profound change in the belief in the absolute use of established models.) In a detailed examination of career theory, culture and constructivism, Watson (2006) argues that career counselling needs to be deconstructed and reconstructed for current times and that practitioners should examine their own constructions of how the world operates in order to 'understand and accommodate the cultural contexts in which their clients live and work' (2006: 55).

It seems clear that new frameworks, approaches and models are needed to respond to the changing nature of work and career in a globalised world. This was the premise of the European/American research group that formed to develop the 'Life Design' approach, based in social constructionism, as outlined by Savickas and colleagues in 2009.

In developing the Life Design approach, the research group recognised that there is a danger in discounting previous theoretical approaches. By so doing they acknowledge that there remains a place for a range of services, but emphasise that these approaches cannot be used exclusively in the contemporary world. This need to integrate modern and postmodern career theory, research and practice is also argued for by Sampson (2009). He outlines the problems in assuming the two are incompatible, or that postmodern approaches are superior, and concludes that individual needs and cost-effectiveness should be the deciding factors with regard to the approach taken. Thus in an increasingly vulnerable and globalised context, there is a call for a new way of thinking about career, and what is required to manage this; one more fluid and attuned to the twenty-first century. It is important to stress at this point that what is not being suggested here is one new, alternative 'model' for working with clients; this would be counterintuitive to the philosophy behind the development of a constructivist approach. What is being suggested is a framework for rethinking the epistemology (or theory of knowledge) for careers work. This fits with the move to transdisciplinary and integrative approaches in many of the helping services.

In the preface to an influential text that elaborates career counselling and constructivism, McMahon and Watson state:

> Constructivism has become an increasing influence on career counselling. Indeed it has been claimed by some authors that the adoption of constructivist approaches will ensure that career counselling remains a relevant and helpful discipline in the 21st century. (McMahon and Watson, 2011, preface)

Activity 6.1

It will be useful at this point to return briefly to Chapter 4 and review your evaluation of the three established approaches discussed there. What did you note as the benefits of each approach, and in terms of the contemporary world, what are the limitations?

Examples of constructivist approaches in practice, deriving from the work of the Life Design group and including other new and emerging approaches, are available in a comprehensive text edited by Nota and Rossier (2015). For a widespread paradigm shift to occur, analysis (drawn from research undertaken with my colleague Linden West) suggests that the lack of space for creativity and reflexivity in UK careers practice is, for some, a barrier to innovation (Reid and West, 2014). We argue that the shift needs to encompass *psychosocial* ideas that contrast with still dominant, highly cognitive approaches to learning and professional development. By psychosocial we mean, in simple terms, the combination of ideas from both psychology and sociology. It would seem a shift is needed, but innovation is easier said than done and any framework, new or old, has to be evaluated in context. Often a failure to innovate can be rooted in the desire to defend current practices, however outdated these may appear. On the Master's programme at my institution, we teach 'new and emerging approaches', but students on work placement can often be faced with such responses as 'there's no time to try new methods', or 'we have a check list that we must follow', and 'forget what you have been taught – welcome to the real world'. This can be dispiriting for the student and the teacher, but it would be my view that it is the university's role to introduce the student to new constructs and approaches. If inspired, students will (and do) work to find ways to engage in practice that is likely to be more meaningful for their clients in the twenty-first century. This text will now discuss two approaches that contrast with the established theories explored in Chapter 4. There is a wide range of approaches that could be included, but the two examined below are particularly useful for both career counselling and career coaching. Further reading will be suggested at the end of the chapter for a broader understanding of alternatives.

Solution focused approaches for career counselling and coaching

The first thing to say about solution focused approaches is that they are not new. The approaches are well established in counselling, but have been less evident in careers work until recent years. Solution focused models are often adopted by coaches as they are seen as probably the closest 'therapy model' in terms of the aims of coaching (Zeus and Skiffington, 2000). In other words, the approach focuses on reframing the problem and presenting alternative possibilities, works towards developing achievable goals (in small, incremental steps) and then develops a workable action plan to meet the goals. 'As with coaching, this type of therapy is based on the belief that answers reside in the individual's own repertoire of skills and is always framed within a context of human competency and our ability to change and adapt' (Zeus and Skiffington, 2000: 11). Yates (2014: 119) sees the benefit of a solution focused approach for career coaching in the way it 'turns the traditional approach on its head, by focussing exclusively on possibilities': this, she states, can be 'enormously empowering and uplifting'. Other coaching texts, for example Starr (2012), will use the concepts without necessarily referring to solution focused therapy, as the purpose is not to explore or build theory, but to offer strategies. But what is the theory that underpins such work?

In therapeutic practice, counsellors using the solution focused approach do not assume that it is necessary to explore an issue or 'problem' in depth or to analyse its causes in order to work with clients. The approach pays attention to solution building and identifying what is working currently for the client, in terms of moving towards and achieving desired outcomes. It is a constructivist approach as it departs from earlier 'positivist' or scientific methodologies, by recognising that perspectives on 'reality' are constructed by individuals in relationships with others. The main aim is to keep a focus on the intended outcomes of the work, using these as a means to structure the counselling intervention. Through working alongside the client, the focus should be specific and both the counsellor and the client should be clear about the direction of the work and the steps to be taken, albeit that these may change as they progress.

When clients are 'stuck' it can be difficult for them to believe in their ability to make decisions and to move forward. Solution focused career counselling assumes that change is inevitable – it is already happening as the individual is seeking help. Interventions, from this standpoint, will build upon the individual's strengths. This is seen as furthering the client's motivation, to enhance a belief that change is possible. The outlook is positive and problem-saturated stories are avoided; although the issue that brings the person to career counselling or career coaching must be clarified. The purpose of career counselling or career coaching is to work together to find solutions: it is future orientated. The process should not be rushed, however; the relationship needs to support the potential for change. Within the confines of this chapter, concepts from solution focused counselling that can be used in careers work include the following:

- Searching for the detail in the story told – asking 'tell me more about' questions to get beyond a superficial understanding.
- Considering what works now and building on this – looking for solutions that fit the client and their context.
- Finding exceptions to the problem – searching for what works for the client in terms of other decisions in life.
- Outlining the desired future – identifying where they would like to be and working backwards, rather than identifying the barriers from where they are now.
- Identifying strengths – clarifying the client's competences, which they may not believe they possess.

Techniques include:

- Scaling questions – to review progress.
- Miracle questions – to build a sense of possibility.

- Setting small goals – to foster success.
- Enlisting the support of others – to clarify boundaries and use resources.

Miller applies the above in detail to what she terms 'solution-building career counselling' (2006: 126). Within this approach career counsellors aim to help their clients to:

- clarify their reason for coming to counselling in terms of the preferred future that they want (goal setting questions);
- identify and amplify aspects of their lives that are working well (exceptions questions);
- re-discover important aspects of their context including resources, successes and strengths (self-helpfulness questions);
- clarify and envisage how life would be different if the problem were suddenly solved (miracle questions); and
- assess progress towards their goals (scaling questions). (ibid.)

She goes on to give examples of the above and other concepts that are applicable to careers work, but stresses that the client's interest in working in this way needs to be engaged from the start: the approach is both constructivist and collaborative. She also clarifies that the search for meaningful goals and ways of working towards these does not mean that the practitioner withholds information (which is part of their career 'expertise' maybe), but that they delay sharing information until 'needs, aspirations, strengths and skills' (2006: 134) have been explored.

Reflection point 6.2

The point about not rushing to solutions is important. The work derives from Solution-Focused Brief Therapy (de Shazer et al., 1986) and has an appeal for policy makers and fund managers. What is the appeal, do you think?

My guess is that you identified the appeal with ease – the clue is in the title and that is where the risk lies. It can be thought of as a 'quick fix' that moves people to outcomes in a short period of time; but this is contrary to the ethics of the approach. 'Brief', in therapy, means from one up to twenty sessions, rather than ongoing over a longer period. As in other approaches we look at in this book, time is needed to build trust and rapport, and the working relationship that supports effective change for and with the client. Focused listening – listening for the positives and for the client's success stories and working towards their own goals and solutions – cannot be hurried. And it is worth emphasising here that the approach does not suggest that it is the practitioner who finds the solutions: the role is to facilitate the client to find their own solutions, which will work for them.

Amundson (2006) recognises that many career counsellors do not have the luxury of regular hourly meetings with their clients and that many interventions may need to take place in much shorter periods of time. But this should not lead to the conclusion that the work becomes hurried or reductive; it suggests that career counsellors need to 'know more' (about a range of approaches), and be able to choose the most appropriate method for the work in hand within the time available. Amundson writes about an approach called 'active engagement', where there are a number of resonances with solution-focused work which build optimism for the future. In emphasising the need to provide space for the active engagement of the client, even when this may be in short segments of time, he uses the interesting metaphor of the 'backswing'. Using a hammer, an axe or a golf club, a backswing, Amundson explains, generates power to move forward:

> … there is a need to move backwards before going forwards. Applying this to counselling, many people come for help because they are discouraged and also confused about what steps they should take. They need to explore and clarify issues and also remember some of their past accomplishments in order to rebuild their confidence and develop goals for the future. (Amundson, 2006: 89)

If you are not familiar with this approach and its usefulness for careers work, you will want to find out more through accessing the texts referenced above. Within solution focused counselling, the work of Bill O'Connell (2005) is significant and can help to explore the approach further; other material is suggested at the end of the chapter. To end this brief introduction to solution focused careers work, a case study follows.

Case study 6.1: Finding strength to imagine future possibilities

Sally is an independent career coach booked for two, one-hour sessions to work with a member of a design team, Josh, in a specialised service industry. She understood the 'problem' to be that since moving to a new department and management structure, Josh appears to have disengaged from the company's career/staff development process. Staff development is a key activity for this organisation and is always discussed in staff appraisal. The department head says Josh is 'gifted, highly creative and well qualified' and they want him to progress but, despite asking, she cannot understand what's wrong. Before an initial discussion, prior to agreeing to the work, Sally was concerned that she might be asked to mediate between the two; but that does not seem to be the case. She decides that she needs to identify the problem and work with Josh to find a solution. She describes her approach and the work so far.

'Well, what I didn't do was make assumptions or be too directive at the start, I wanted him to trust me, so there was quite a bit of ground work to do before we could start the process. I invited Josh to talk about his job and about the move – he was vague and did not say much, other than things were not going well and he understood that his manager was trying to help. Once we had built some rapport, I asked him a number of open questions to try to get at the core of the problem, which was not obvious: so, you know, "tell me more about that, what was that like for you, what happened next" and so on. Although we did not dwell on it, it seems that he has always found change disturbing and he offered personal reasons for this, which I do not need to discuss here. But we thought about how he had managed in a past situation, what worked for him then and how he could use that strategy in the current situation. I gave him some positive feedback as clearly he demonstrated some real inner strength in that previous situation, and he said he had never really thought about it in those terms before.

We then discussed the future – how he would like his career to develop. He went a bit silent at this point, I waited but he seemed to have lost some energy. I asked if we could try something different and asked him to imagine he woke up tomorrow and he was feeling very positive, settled for now and working in his dream job – I said, don't worry about what it might be called or where it may be taking place, just what you would be doing, with whom or with what, how would you feel. He engaged with this well and talked about his ideal design job. As he had livened up a bit I asked him to try another exercise. Normally when a career goal is identified, the work is then to identify every next step on the way – which can make the goal seem too far away and the energy can diminish. So, I asked him if he would go and sit at the other end of the room, to get a different perspective as it were – it was big enough to do this, otherwise you can use a corridor if appropriate. I find this helps the client to get a different perspective and to think about what it might be like to have already arrived at the new goal. It can also inject some energy – just the moving from sitting in the same place.

Where was I, oh yes – so, I asked him from his new position to imagine he was already in that job: "Tell me again, what does it feel like, how did you get there, what interesting things happened on the way?" This does not always work and with any technique if it works keep doing it, if not do something else! But, he became quite animated at this point and was clearly enjoying the exercise, which made the goal feel more like it could be a reality. Anyway that was all the time we had in that first session, so I took my chair over to where he was sitting and we summarised what had been achieved, and we agreed he would think about the dream job some more; so that next time he could describe it in more detail. In our next session we will think about the small goals that he could work on to build success for his plan and about how his manager could help – as clearly she is interested in Josh's future in the organisation.'

Activity 6.2

Re-read the case study and see if you can identify some of the solution focused concepts and techniques listed above.

Motivational interviewing

Another approach that is about the potential to change behaviour for positive out-comes is motivational interviewing. At the core of motivational interviewing is an exploration of the desire for change and people's resistance to change. As human beings we can all engage in behaviour that is 'not good' for us (over-eating, smoking, drinking too much alcohol, not doing enough exercise) and we know intellectu-ally that the effects are likely to be negative, and yet we continue. Similarly people engage in relationships or communicative and/or emotional behaviour that can be destructive, but find it difficult and sometimes impossible to change this behaviour. Even with supportive help from a professional, change can be resisted – why is this?

Reflection point 6.3

What are your first thoughts on this? There are of course psychiatric issues that are beyond the expertise of careers work, but in 'everyday' life, can you think of an example in your own life, or in the life of someone you know well perhaps, where despite the obvious negative consequences, behaviour that is limiting or even damaging, continues? What might be the reasons for this?

In all counselling interactions, avoiding simplistic advice-giving would be fun-damental to good practice – and being told something is damaging is unlikely to change our actions. But if I were to examine my own behaviour, I know I experience some ambivalence when it comes to, for example, that second glass of wine. I am in 'two minds' – on the one hand I will tell myself it is not a huge glass and I'll not have a third, and on the other I will argue that wine drinking should be kept to the weekend only. How do I balance the enjoyment of the wine with my understanding of the adverse effects of alcohol, even in relatively small amounts, on my health? What is more important to me? What am I motivated to do?

In motivational interviewing it is the values and motivations of the client that are important, and exploring and understanding the client's *ambivalence* and *readiness for change* is essential. Assumptions about what is good for the client and what strategies will be helpful need to be set aside until commitment to change is examined.

The work of Miller and Rollnick (2002) is well established in the area of substance abuse within counselling, healthcare, social work and youth justice. It is becoming evident too in areas such as educational welfare, career and youth counselling (Reid, 2011). Rather than viewing it as a 'therapy', the authors see their work as a method of communication and define motivational interviewing as both directive and client-centred. The aim, however, is to 'direct' the work towards generating behavioural change, via helping clients to explore and work with areas in their thinking about the future where there is ambivalence and indecision. The goal is for the client, not the counsellor, to present the arguments for change. It is also important, from this standpoint, to move away from language that polarises the concept of motivation – i.e., that a client is either motivated or not motivated – as motivation is always situated in a context, in particular time periods and in relationships with others. So, in that sense, we could say that motivation is socially constructed.

There are a number of core behaviours for the practitioner in motivational interviewing that would be evident in other approaches in counselling and relevant for careers work. These can be summarised as:

- understanding the client's frame of reference and world view;
- expressing acceptance, affirmation and demonstrating unconditional positive regard;
- finding and supporting the client's own self-motivating statements and recognition of issues and problems, their desires, intentions and abilities to initiate change;
- being mindful of the client's readiness for change and avoiding resistance to change (which can be caused by the practitioner moving forward too quickly);
- affirming the client's rights to make their own decisions, including not changing.

Alongside the above behaviours in the practitioner, Miller and Rollnick (2002) also describe four general principles for motivational interviewing:

- expressing empathy (which also accepts ambivalence as normal behaviour);
- developing discrepancy (working alongside the client so that the client sees for themselves where any discrepancy lies between their values and their behaviour);

- roll with resistance (not imposing new perspectives, but recognising that resistance is a defensive position and supporting the client to lead on 'change talk');
- supporting self-efficacy (encouraging a realistic belief that change is possible; enhancing confidence for the client to act for themselves).

There are other techniques within the approach that recognise that when working towards change, resistance is a natural reaction. One more that can be included here is the diagnostic use of the 'wheel of change'. This is also referred to as the 'transtheoretical model of intentional human behavioural change' (TTM) and can be explored further through the work of DiClemente and Velasquez (2002). Yates (2014) also devotes a chapter to motivational interviewing in her book on career coaching. The wheel of change is reproduced in Figure 6.1 and, drawing on Rollnick and Miller (1995), the stages are explained in what follows.

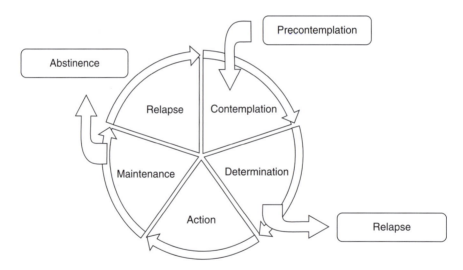

Figure 6.1   The wheel of change

www.sobermusings.com/stages-of-change

- **Precontemplation**: the person has no intention of changing their behaviour and does not see a problem. The stage is demonstrated as, 'I'm OK – problem – what problem?'
- **Contemplation**: the person is aware that a problem exists but they are not yet committed to change – they experience ambivalence. The stage is demonstrated as, 'I'm not sure, I don't know'.

- **Determination**: the person has made a decision to change and is motivated to move forwards, but needs a clear goal and action to support change. The stage is demonstrated as, 'I've decided, I know what I want to do, but need to know how to make it happen'.
- **Action**: the person is moving from decision to action, supported by the counsellor. Collaboration is needed to work together on the action required, time is needed and support is ongoing. At this stage Relapse can occur. The stage is demonstrated as, 'I know *what* and I think I know *how*, and now I'm taking my next step'.
- **Maintenance**: the person has taken action to consolidate the change, but still requires some support to maintain the new behaviour while their confidence builds. The stage is demonstrated as, 'I can do this and I am getting there'.
- **Relapse**: this can happen at any stage and the old behaviour can reassert itself – but this is recognised as normal when going through a process of change. The model is not always linear; hence the support of the practitioner is required. Their role is to ensure that the client knows that Relapse is viewed as normal and expected behaviour, but that the practitioner is there to support them towards the change they desire.

Using the wheel of change can help the practitioner to diagnose where in the process a client may be and their readiness for change. It can aid the development of appropriate strategies for support and action, and can also identify possible causes of 'stuckness' – in terms of the recognition and desire for change and action taken (or not). It is a useful tool for the practitioner to question whether it is their actions that are causing the stuckness: for example, are they jumping ahead of the client's readiness for change, are their own actions congruent with the client's values? Using the wheel of change can, then, avoid inappropriate and ineffective interventions.

Activity 6.3

Using the wheel of change, can you identify where the client is in the process of change in the vignettes below? My answers are included at the end of the chapter.

1. **John** is a careers counsellor working with a young person, Amy, who is now clear that she wants to leave school and study at college. Amy seems keen on a course in travel and tourism, but when they talk about going to an open day, Amy says she could 'try and go', but her tone and body language are not convincing.

(Continued)

(Continued)

2. **Claire** is a college counsellor working with Stacey who is not attending her course and is likely to lose her place at college and perhaps her benefits. The situation needs urgent action, but Stacey appears unconcerned.

3. **Meena** is a career coach working with Alex who has decided that he is going to change career direction and apply for a teaching course in science. They have worked together for some time and he now has a clear goal and plan of action – he is ready to discuss the next step.

4. **Franco** is working with a number of young people in a youth training agency and is meeting with Carla to discuss her progress. Carla is not really engaging with the training, but is willing to meet up with Franco, although she is not very clear about what she does want to do at this first meeting.

5. **Joseph** is a tutor working with young people on a plumbing 'day release' college course. He is really pleased with the work of Kate who was a reluctant student at first, but has progressed well. He has spent less time with her lately, but notices that her enthusiasm has waned and her portfolio has not been handed in yet. He decides that she may need some additional support to continue.

6. **Sam** works as an independent careers practitioner and receives an email from Charlie, a sixth form student she was helping with her university choices. Charlie thanks her for the help and says that she has now made her choices, completed her application form and booked university 'open day' visits. It will all depend on her grades, she says, and asks if she can keep in touch for now. Sam replies, encouraging her to let her know how the visits go and what offers she receives and yes, do contact me again, she says, if I can help some more.

Green guidance

Discussion about global warming takes on a particular urgency with each new 'natural disaster' that causes widespread disruption, particularly when lives are lost. Alongside this in recent times are criticisms of individualistic and global capitalism in the pursuit of profit. When careers work considers only the needs of the individual and views their career interests as separate from their contexts, the guidance given may be seen as part of this wider problem.

Peter Plant is the academic who is most closely associated with literature on the development of 'green guidance' and the final section of this chapter draws explicitly on his work. Plant explains (2014) that many young people realise that individual energy consumption, as one important example of a global ecological issue, has an impact on the lives of the world's population and on the sustainability of Earth itself. This realisation is not unique to a younger generation of course, but those who advise young people need to consider how their career decision making theories and interventions measure up to this disdain for capitalist growth and global competitiveness; where it ignores the ecological impact of such individualistic behaviour. Economic growth cannot be achieved without environmental sustainability if the future of humankind is to be secured. These are deeply complex issues and it is easy for us all to pay 'lip service' to the philosophy. Many of us in the so-called 'developed nations', and I include myself here, are used to a disposable world, used to being able to travel where we like, have endless supplies of water, expect the power to our homes to be available 24 hours a day and so on. In other places in the world, clean water is a miracle. And the West has had its industrial revolution, so it can be viewed as rather patronising when we criticise newly industrialised countries for their 'polluting' behaviour. And yet, as Plant suggests, it is from 'non-Western' countries that inspiration for an alternative way of thinking about the world can be drawn. Plant cites the work of Arulmani and Nag-Arulmani (2004), drawing on the ancient Indian tradition of *ashramas,* that views life as stages of learning, placing career in family and community as being aspects that are intertwined and integral with nature, the environment and the cycle, or spiral – *Jiva* – of life.

All of this does not mean that personal fulfilment is to be abandoned, but it does mean that the cost needs to be counted – in terms of the implications beyond the individual or indeed the community and of course the global organisation. More than just a political issue, this is, as Plant and many others point out, a moral issue of devastating significance. There are signs that many organisations are engaging in corporate responsibility and that factors that assess company performance now also include aspects such as carbon emission, dealing with waste, and other environmental measures such as use of power and water. Careers work cannot change the world, but our clients may be more interested in ecology rather than the economy.

Reflection point 6.4

It is difficult to write about climate change and environmental catastrophe without it sounding like a polemic or as something so potentially earth shattering (literally), that you and I as individuals can feel overwhelmed and powerless to make a difference. But think about careers or jobs that you would find unacceptable from a 'green perspective'– what would be on your list?

There is a danger in list making. My list would include work that involves exploitation of disadvantaged people, but do I always know where my clothes have been made – do I check the sources? I would advocate career choices that foster social inclusion, and I have engaged in voluntary work for a number of years, but I could do much more. I would not work for an organisation that is involved in the manufacture of armaments, but I have worked on an education project with the British Army. I do always want to work in an organisation that cares more about people and their education/lives/careers than the profits that can be made; but 'surplus' is vital for my institution to survive, we are told. So, these are not clear-cut issues and like any approach in careers work, we need to think about our own position before we can, ethically, work alongside others. Saying it is complex, however, does not mean it is too difficult to engage with – but how?

Activity 6.4

When we have looked at a number of theories for careers work thus far in the book, core principles have been summarised. What would you say are the important core or guiding principles for a career practitioner who wants to promote 'green guidance'?

It can also be useful to have an inspirational list of ecologically sound careers and activities. We have to remember that we cannot all be employed by charitable organisations or work as volunteers. People need to have livelihoods and in some contexts, and where poverty is widespread, this may strip out any choice. Plant offers the following and his last point emphasises that within 'ordinary' jobs, green choices can be made:

- Green activist working with neighbourhood ecological gardening;
- Green greenkeeper working with a no-pesticide approach to maintenance of sports grounds;
- Green lawyer working with environmental cases;
- Green transport engineer working with non-pollutant means of traffic and transport;
- Green farmer working with ecological practices in fields and stables;
- Green painters using non-toxic and degradable paints;
- Green builders using natural insulation materials;
- Green fishers, working with sustainable fishing;
- Green hairdressers … etc. In short most careers can be seen as potentially green. (Plant, 2014: 314)

And what about those guiding principles for working with clients? In the same work, Plant suggests the following, and you could add others that you identified above:

- Guidance should take account and create awareness of the environmental impact of vocational choices;
- Guidance should play an active role in establishing training and education opportunities with a positive contribution in environmental terms;
- Information materials on career options should include environmental aspects;
- Guidance should be measured, not only by an economic yardstick, but also by green accounting, (i.e. by relating environmental goals to guidance activities);
- Guidance theories and practices should address common career development issues in addition to individualistic approaches – with a focus on environmental impacts of career choices;
- On a much smaller scale, guidance workers themselves should inspect their own practices: how green are my routines re recycling waste, cutting down on power consumption, etc? How is ICT used to cut down on my travelling, for example? (Plant, 2014: 314)

Finally, Plant stresses that environmental issues do not have boundaries in a globalised world and a commitment to working towards green careers is needed from both practitioners and their clients. 'With this kind of approach, the individual career fades into the background, and common goals come into focus, including social justice issues' (Plant, 2014: 315).

There are other approaches to career counselling that are gaining significance and which need a specific mention before this chapter concludes. One is the systems theory approach to understanding career influences by McMahon et al. (2013), and another is Pryor and Bright's (2011) chaos theory of careers. Aside from these specific references, these and other new and emerging approaches can be explored in McMahon and Watson (2015) *Career Assessment: Qualitative Approaches.*

Chapter summary

In this chapter the shift from established approaches to those based in social constructionism for career counselling and coaching has been argued for and explored. But the intention was not to 'throw out the baby with the bathwater'. A place for established approaches remains, but as part of knowledgeable practice; in other words negotiated decisions about integrating what works best for the client. Although there are various theories that fall under the banner of constructivist, two particular approaches were discussed, as both are viewed as useful for career counselling and career coaching: these were solution focused career counselling and motivational interviewing. Others will be discussed in the next chapter. Finally, the concept of 'green guidance' was introduced in this chapter on new and emerging approaches for career counselling and career coaching.

Further reading

When thinking of what to read around new concepts and theories, academic journals are a useful source. In particular the three listed below can be recommended:

- *The British Journal of Guidance & Counselling*
- *The International Journal of Educational and Vocational Guidance*
- *The Journal of Vocational Behaviour*

McMahon, M. and Watson, M. (eds) (2011) *Career Counselling and Constructivism*. New York: Nova Science.
This text will help the reader to access the concept and thinking around career constructivism. Each author explains their approach and illustrates this with practical examples.

Nota, L. and Rossier, J. (eds) (2015) *Handbook of Life Design: From Practice to Theory and From Theory to Practice*. Göttingen, Germany: Hogrefe Publishing.
This impressive book builds substantially on the work of the International Life Design group. It begins by explaining the theory and concepts that underpin the paradigm shift taking place in career counselling, and then grounds this in practice. The contributors are leading researchers in the field, and they provide rich and varied examples of life designing in careers work across different age groups, sectors, and cultural and social contexts.

Plant, P. (2014) 'Green guidance', in G. Arulmani, A.J. Bakshi, F.T.L. Leong and A.G. Watts (eds), *International Handbook of Career Guidance*. Dordrecht, The Netherlands: Springer.
As stated in the text, Plant is the leading writer on the development of green guidance and this chapter provides a comprehensive discussion of this important and emerging approach.

Reid, H.L. and Westergaard, J. (2011) *Effective Counselling With Young People*. Exeter: Learning Matters.
Reid's chapters, seven and eight, examine motivational interviewing and solution focused approaches in counselling. These chapters provide some of the detail that could not be covered here. Case studies are used to illustrate the theories in action and further reading is identified.

Activity 6.3: My answers

This is not always as precise as the wheel may indicate, but my diagnosis was as follows:

1. John/Amy – Determination;
2. Claire/Stacey – Precontemplation;
3. Meena/Alex – Action;
4. Franco/Carla – Contemplation;
5. Joseph/Kate – Relapse;
6. Sam/Charlie – Maintenance.

7

Using narrative approaches in career counselling and career coaching

This chapter will:

- examine the foundations of narrative career counselling;
- consider the benefits of approaches that focus on career biography;
- outline ways of working alongside clients in narrative ways for career counselling and coaching.

Introduction

Following on from the previous chapter, this chapter will examine narrative career counselling in more depth. The foundations in narrative therapy will be looked at, before focusing on how a narrative approach can be applied to careers work. A particular model is outlined in some detail, but the chapter will also make reference to others that have a focus on narrativity or biographic approaches for careers work. Constructing a career narrative suggests a purposeful activity that places career into a life, giving life meaning and purpose. How an individual develops a narrative identity, or is prevented from doing so, in a context with others, needs to be evaluated and the chapter will discuss the issues involved. Ways of working alongside and supporting individuals as they construct their career biography will be outlined.

In the previous chapter it was suggested that, for most people, managing a career biography has become more unpredictable and uncertain, and has evolved into an individualistic exercise, where the person takes responsibility for their own career/ work patterns. It was noted that this is more evident in marginalised communities where traditional structures of work across generations may have been lost under the impact of globalisation and neo-liberal economics. Structural changes in the world of work have led to calls for changes in the way we theorise career. The movement is away from what was a dominant Western, 'scientific' orientation of measuring traits, using 'objective' psychological testing and matching these to occupations, to a greater focus on constructing *meaning*, in which 'subjective' understanding is taken seriously. I have also cautioned against the slide into psychological approaches that place all the focus on the individual, which may assume we are always in control of our own destiny. As argued previously, people can have various degrees of *agency* within the social, economic, historical and cultural structures that affect their particular life chances. So starting with those themes, the chapter will now move on and explore narrative approaches for career counselling that can also be developed for career coaching.

Biographicity and career identity

Careers work is learning work, whether we are working one-to-one with a client or with a group of individuals. We all learn about the self in a process of construction, sometimes as active agent, as mentioned above, at other times placed in the position of experiencing an event passively, within structural forces outside of our locus of control. But at turning points in our lives, sometimes seismic in their impact, there are stories to be told which may question and trouble our perceptions of what constitutes our sense of who we are. Our biographies get disrupted. At career transition points we can also experience disturbance, particularly when we have to make decisions which affect 'our future', with all the weight of consequences that term carries. There are likely to be numerous factors to consider and other people in our lives will influence, and be affected by, the choices that we make. We may be more or less able to make that choice on our own, due to a whole range of social and economic circumstances and cultural expectations. Lives transact with other lives and our views, as practitioners, on how individuals make those decisions cannot be based solely on a psychology of the individual from the 'inside out', as it were; we must also pay attention to the 'outside in'– to what has been referred to elsewhere in the book as the *psychosocial*.

Reflection point 7.1

Thinking about your own career biography, reflect on a major transition point. How did you weigh up the internal factors (in other words, your thoughts and feelings about the decision to be made) and the external factors (who or what influenced the decision made)? What did you pay most attention to?

In hard economic times, where work becomes fractured and progression is no longer linear, there is a greater expectation that people will take responsibility for their own career trajectories. In such contexts, the concept of *biographicity* (Alheit, 1995) has been used in thinking about how individuals construct a career identity (Savickas, 2011). Biographicity is taken to mean the processes by which individuals reflect on new and often troubling experiences, rethinking and absorbing them into their life story. The identity work involved may entail constructing an altered view of self in order to cope with the changes encountered, some of which may be traumatic. A conscious engagement in such a process can help individuals to identify what is important for them in the context of their own lives, enabling them to evaluate choices, where choices exist, that are integral to their values. For example, redundancy as a result of the closure of an industry, an acquired disability, or a disappointing examination outcome may result in the need to rethink a career identity and to reshape a view of self and what is possible, but without moving away from core values. Central to a narrative approach for careers work is the ethos of working alongside a client to explore their life themes in order to build biographicity and a career identity. All too often in career guidance and counselling the space for exploration is limited; indecision is seen as a bad thing, rather than a desirable space for reflection and consideration. The narrative career counselling approach encourages biographic agency by reframing disruptions as transitions and turning points (Savickas, 2011). This is not a denial of the impact that a change may have caused, and it is not an assumption that all career decisions derive from trauma either, but the aim is to provide a connection to the future which links with continuities from the past. New ideas, experiences and information can be built on existing knowledge in a way that has meaning for the individual.

One way of achieving this is through linking stories from the past to the career issue of the present, finding the core interests in the stories and relating these to the possible choices for the future (more on how to do this later). In turbulent times, where fixed and linear careers are no longer the norm and the next job needs to be found, reflecting on core interests retains its importance. Even acknowledging that for many a job – any job – has to be taken for basic livelihood, where there is choice (however restricted) engaging in autobiographical reasoning – biographicity – can help individuals to manage change and transition.

What's the appeal of narrative?

Narratives are central to our ways of making sense of our lives and our interactions with the external world. They function between history and biography, between cultures and particular lives, and between the storyteller (the client) and the audience (the practitioner). It is difficult to think about a world without narrative; from story books shared with children to the stories we gather about past lives in our families and communities. Storytelling can liberate the emotions when we describe a difficult day or a wonderful experience. And we have all had the experience of another offering advice, even defending us, when all we want is to be heard and understood. An experience we should always remember as practitioners. Although it is not our role to solve problems for the client, we wonder how useful we have been sometimes if the client does not leave with a clear outcome; but if we have heard the client's story we should never underestimate the power of being listened to. We also tell stories to ourselves, internally, when reflecting on our day and our lives, helping us to evaluate our intentions and action; although these interior narratives can be limiting as well as positive in terms of their outcomes. Stories, whether spoken or written down, are at the core of what it is to be human. It would be difficult to think of any therapeutic or counselling work that did not involve narrative to some extent.

Alongside all the benefits of globalisation brought about by ease of travel, digital and virtual technologies where we can be connected to others instantly, there can be a loss of private spaces. Instant access means that we can become colonised by email and other communication technology, never out of reach, never truly 'on leave', as in 'left alone'. How do we present ourselves to others when we check our email and respond at night, at the weekend? Building an identity, shaping a biography, holding on to our values, knowing what and who to believe, can be challenging in an uncertain world. We may search for facts and visible certainties; for career information and advice that can tell us what to do and how to do it. We may yearn for simplicity in what is a complex world. Narrative approaches seek to slow this process down, by spending time exploring what people think and feel about themselves, what matters to them subjectively: this can be enabling and potentially empowering.

However, individual narratives are situated in a context, we are not encapsulated beings and the stories clients tell (and what we hear) reflect and constitute power relations and competing discourses within the wider society of particular cultures. When the client tells their story, there will be more than two people 'in the room'; in other words there are other voices (friends, parents, authority figures, the media and so on) that can be detected, either positive or negative in terms of their influence. By virtue of being social as well as psychological beings, meaning cannot be separated but 'is rendered both public and shared' (Bruner, 1990: 13). Narratives, the telling of one's story, can also serve as a means of resistance, a way to challenge dominant regimes of truth – or, as Foucault (1979) claimed, where there is power, there is resistance. Telling stories to an attentive listener can help us to manage who we are and might be; in the 'saying it out loud' to another we can rehearse a different story and, with further work, make it more real (Savickas, 2011).

Activity 7.1

What was your favourite story as a child? For many this will be a book, but it might also be a TV programme – what was the narrative content? Why do you think it holds a place in your memory – what's its significance for you? Can you make some notes on this – a rough analysis?

We will revisit this activity later in the chapter.

Narrative therapy

Within narrative therapy and counselling there is recognition that 'telling the story' is not a mere reporting on the facts in order to find solutions. In the telling of the story the teller and the listener are constructing a narrative to help them understand something that happened in the past, through the lens of the present conversation. In order to gain a new perspective on the issue, time is taken to listen to a *re-presentation* that can be heard, explored, challenged, deconstructed and reconstructed. Part of the deconstruction in narrative therapy is searching for the other voices that may be present in the stories told. Using narrative methods can access thoughts and feelings that are repressed and preventing the therapeutic work with the client from moving forward. This is not a wallowing in past problems, however, but a search to identify the themes that are affecting current and potentially future behaviour and action.

As indicated above issues related to power are at the heart of narrative counselling, thus the therapeutic space seeks to be collaborative and agentic. Michael White and David Epston (1990), working in the context of family therapy, are usually cited as the developers of narrative counselling. A core principle of the work is captured in the 'externalising' statement of Michael White, 'The person is not the problem; the problem is the problem' (1989: 7). This highlights that often individuals ascribe the results of injustices that cause them distress to something lacking in themselves, rather than the social factors that may cause the problems they experience. In addition, those in power, and this can include the various helping agencies they encounter, often, albeit implicitly, exacerbate that feeling of hopelessness and powerlessness (Payne, 2006). Separating the person from the problem is the first step in such narrative ways of thinking about an individual, as the focus is not solely on the client and moves away from the language of deficit. Winslade and Monk (2007) provide very good examples of working with young people in school counselling contexts, where they use a narrative approach combined with solution focused work. As do other authors working in this approach (e.g. Besley, 2002), they draw on the work of Foucault and of White and Epston (1990) in the avoidance of problem-saturated stories. In other words, they question the label that often brings a person to the attention of helping agencies and counselling, and search for the alternative story. They recognise that the person in context has other stories to tell, other competences which get buried under the weight of 'the problem'. The counsellor, the therapist, the teacher, the career practitioner may be tempted to work with this partial story, rather than the whole person and the client can 'perform' accordingly, or, to put it another way, live up to the label they are given:

> We live our lives according to the stories we tell ourselves and the stories that others tell about us. (Winslade and Monk, 2007: 2)

Much more could be said here about narrative counselling but perhaps to summarise, however reductive this may be, we could say that the aim is for the client to discover their own competence and resourcefulness and work towards finding a solution that is meaningful to them (Reid, 2011). (It is to be noted that in narrative counselling, words like 'client' and 'helping' are problematic, as they retain connotations of unequal power relations.) There is a rich literature on the use of narrative counselling and examples are listed at the end of the chapter. The remainder of this chapter, however, will focus on narrative careers work. First it will make reference to ways of working 'narratively' with clients in career counselling and coaching, and then it will outline a particular model.

Reflection point 7.2

Have you ever experienced being given or presented to others with a 'label' that you felt was reductive and not coherent with your view of self? Often this happens when you are presented as a 'problem' of some sort. The one for me that comes to mind is 'class comic', and yes I deserved it to some degree, but what went with this on the school report was 'and will never achieve much academically'. Perhaps I agreed with this assessment as I left school at age 15.

Narrative careers work

When, in narrative careers work, we ask a client to recall an early story from their life, many will worry about how 'true' the story may be. We are all aware that time changes our memory and we can only ever view past events through the lens of the present and the narrative repertoires that are available to us. Within narrative careers work the aim is not to recall a factual report of a childhood memory, but to *re-call* stories that have meaning in the present, related to the issue a client brings to the practitioner. In that sense the story told, as a *re-interpretation,* is telling – it counts for something. Stories live on in the present, they are not fixed in aspic in the past, and thus the teller is constructing a present reality shaped out of past events. Used within a career counselling context the telling recalls and develops a sense of self – biographicity – while the stories can be a means for building reflexivity. At career transition points, this can be important where a decision taken can rest on deciding what to take forward from the past (continuity) and what to leave behind (change) within a life theme. As noted above some people often come to career counselling not expecting their stories to be valued. The aim then of telling stories is to engage the person in a kind of reflexive play, to encourage creativity within what Winnicott (1971) referred to as a safe transitional space, in a search for more meaningful career narratives.

Activity 7.2

This activity asks you to recall a past event, as an example of reflexive play. Think back to your first day at school, what do you remember? Whether or not others would agree with your memory is not the important issue – what meaning did that day have for you? What pictures come to your mind? For some this may be an emotional exercise, for most it is likely to involve mixed feelings. Note down your thoughts on this.

Within career guidance and counselling there is a growing body of work that employs narrative and biographic methods (McMahon and Watson, 2015; Nota and Rossier, 2015). And the plural is important here as this book and others mentioned welcome the range of approaches and would not advocate **one** approach in the use of narrative in careers work. The point of any model is to engage the client in a reflexive process of finding a career/life future that is meaningful for them within their context. That is not the same as saying 'anything goes' and the point has already been made in this book that practitioners need to understand the foundations of any approach that they use, rather than 'surface mining' across a range of approaches with very different philosophical and epistemological underpinnings.

The work of Mark Savickas has already been mentioned and within the career counselling field he is the acknowledged expert, drawing on previous theoretical foundations that have been explored in this text (i.e. Parsons, 1909; Super, 1994) and the work of Adler (1956) and others. Adler, Savickas tells us, 'portrayed an individual's "line of movement" or *life line* as proceeding from a felt negative to a perceived plus' (Savickas, 2011: 31). The concept of plotting a life line is evident in career coaching approaches where visualisation techniques may be used (Yates, 2014).

The notion of life lines and life themes figures in many theories of personality development. Savickas makes reference to Csikszentmihalyi and Beattie's (1979) explanation, 'A life theme consists of a problem or set of problems which a person wishes to solve above everything else and the means the person finds to achieve a solution' (1979: 48). Narrative careers work, or what Savickas calls 'career construction theory' (ibid.) draws on this by working with an individual to identify patterns in their life related to their *pre-occupations*. The term is used to identify the issues (or problems) that shape the important themes in a life and the career choices that resonate with these, and in the language of career construction theory, career becomes the means of solving the problem. Extending Adler's phrase above, Savickas states:

> In moving from victim to victor, the individual turns tension to intention, preoccupation to occupation, obsession to profession, negative to positive, weakness to strength and lemons to lemonade. People convert symptom into strength through *actively mastering what they passively suffered*. (Savickas, 2011: 33 – my emphasis in italics)

Reflection point 7.3

I struggled with the point above (emphasised in italics) for some time. I think it was the word 'suffered', as I could not see what I had suffered and how I had 'mastered' this in the career choices I had made. But having engaged with the approach and taught it to others, I needed to understand this in the context of my own life. I now do. If I return, for example, to the label applied to me at school, the facts of competition for girls' places at an exclusive grammar school in the area I lived in, being the youngest in the family with two older brothers who did go to grammar school, hearing my mother say 'Well she can leave school at 15 as she'll probably be married by the time she is 18' (I was not) – then what does becoming an academic say about me?

Does the phrase mean anything to you in terms of the career decisions you have made? An immediate response may not be possible, but it is worth coming back to this reflection point later as you develop your own career and work with others developing theirs. Biographicity is concerned with reflecting on patterns in the stories told in order to identify life themes.

Again when engaging in an individualistic exercise such as the one above, we must acknowledge that for many 'career' may not be central to their lives; work may be simply the means to survive and opportunities for career development may be severely restricted. I find the approach fascinating and with my colleague Linden West and a number of career practitioners, we have 'tested' the model in practice in the UK (Reid and West, 2014). However, in advocating any approach for career counselling and coaching it would be foolish to suggest that what works in one context and culture will automatically work in others; and indeed it will not work all the time for all the people in the same context. That is not the intention here or in the work of Savickas et al. (2009). What is offered is a framework, not a prescription, and the possibilities and constraints within a particular context need to be acknowledged. Career decision making is a dynamic, non-linear process, influenced by multiple perspectives and informed by personal belief patterns. The philosophy behind narrative and other constructivist approaches views an individual's identity as psychosocially constructed through the process of social discourse with others.

So aside from the important work of Savickas (2009) and Savickas et al. (2009), who else is working within this broad 'interpretive' paradigm? As noted above, there is now an increasing body of international literature which can provide journal articles and substantial texts for both trainee and experienced practitioners (to avoid overwhelming the reader I have added these as a footnote and they are included in the reference list[1]). There is less explicit evidence to be found of the use of interpretive, narrative or biographical theory in the coaching literature, but as noted previously most coaching texts pay more attention to practice without discussing any underpinning literature. There are exceptions and Yates (2014) does draw to some extent on the literature mentioned above as appropriate to the techniques she describes for career coaching, as do Nathan and Hill (2006) in a career counselling text which can be applied in organisational settings. It is an area for development in career coaching and has a place within the collaborative conversations that professional career coaching occupies. If career coaching is grounded in evidence-based practice (Yates, 2014), then the evidence is there to be drawn upon from the literature mentioned above. Coaching borrows from a range of therapies and could incorporate aspects of narrative and biographical approaches; albeit the knowledgeable professional will want to have a working understanding of the underpinning theory. The model described below has a playfulness about it that is likely to appeal to career coaches.

Aside from the examples referred to above, other narrative methods can be used drawing on creative practices; which may include poetry, song or drama. Such

---

1   Cochran (1997); Peavey (1998); Young et al. (2002); Law (2003); McMahon and Patton (2006); Grant and Johnston (2006); Maree and Molepo (2006); McIlveen and Patton (2007); Guichard (2009); McMahon and Watson (2010); McMahon and Watson (2011); Savickas (2011); McMahon et al. (2012); Lent and Brown (2013).

approaches can enhance reflexivity in the work but, like any 'unusual' intervention, they need to be agreed to and introduced once rapport has been established. Asking someone new to career counselling or coaching to express their feelings via a song or drama for example, may induce a panic of self-consciousness. Creative approaches used in career counselling and career coaching are explored later in Chapter 13, with examples of their use in practice. In the last part of this chapter on narrative career counselling, the model that follows offers a helpful framework for practical application. The chapter will conclude with reflections on the usefulness of the approach.

An interview structure for narrative career counselling and coaching

In a later chapter in the book a generic framework for structuring careers work is offered (Reid and Fielding, 2007). In essence this has three stages: a beginning, a middle and an end. These stages, like the model by Egan (2007, 2013) from which it derives, may or may not take place in the space of a single career intervention. In the research project mentioned above (Reid and West, 2011a, 2011b, 2014), we adapted the Savickas narrative career counselling model that can be found in a range of publications, and specifically in Savickas (2011) and on DVDs (Savickas, 2006, 2009). Our adapted use of the Savickas model is detailed in what follows.

Stage 1 Beginnings – negotiating a contract

The first stage begins with a clarification of the expectations from the client and the establishment of a contract – or ways of working together. Interviews are rarely as linear as a bullet point list suggests, but the work may begin like so:

- Questioning: How can I be useful?
- Asking: Tell me why is this important now?
- Explaining: Format, number of meetings, note taking and so on.
- Identifying: Topics and related issues.
- Agreeing: Aspects of confidentiality, how to proceed – an agenda.

Stage 2 Middles – exploring the story

At this stage it is important to create a space where the person can 'play' with ideas. This is likely to move beyond their expectations of what 'an interview' is like and the practitioner will need to be persistent and not 'give up' too quickly. But, explaining why you are doing what you are doing is always helpful, e.g. 'The reason I asked that question is ...', or 'What we could try here is... it may help us to think about... how would you feel about trying that?' If the client is involved in the decision to try something different, there can be a real sense of experimenting together in using the approach, with the option of using an alternative approach if found not to be fruitful. It is at this second 'stage' that Savickas' six favourite questions can be used:

- Role models (3) when young (these can be a 'real' person or a character from a book, TV show, cartoon).
- Magazines/TV shows (favourites, ones that are looked at regularly).
- Hobbies/interests (e.g. 'What do you like to do in your free time?').
- Books – all-time favourites (could be films or other entertainment media).
- Favourite saying/motto (best describes an approach to life), could be a t-shirt message or a 'tag'.
- Favourite school subjects, and those disliked.

For many clients the questions alone can be revealing in helping them find the solution to their career 'problem'. The answers they give can help them to identify patterns and the important life themes that the method is aiming to foreground in the work. In this way the questions can be incorporated into other models of career counselling and career coaching. We will continue to look in detail at stage 2 after the next activity.

Activity 7.3

You can probably guess what this activity is going to ask you to do. You can write down your responses to each of the questions and remember no one is looking so be honest (and you have already thought about this in a previous activity). In other words a favourite book does not have to be *War and Peace* or something worthy, this is not about censoring our choices in case we do not impress others. But, an even better approach would be to record this without the filter of committing words to paper. Most laptops, mobile devices have a recording facility – this will make your responses more spontaneous and less 'considered' (which is what happens when we make marks on paper – they seem more permanent somehow). Engaging with this exercise can also help to reinforce the point about the importance of rapport, in order that the responses are meaningful for the client and not their audience. In giving your answers, extend this; say why the role model is important, why that story is the favourite and so on – what are the qualities of the characters involved or why is that activity so important to you? Again capture your first responses and note what you say/think with emphasis. I have offered a case study below, but work on your story first.

Case study 7.1: Finding the patterns and life themes

Moira found it difficult to find three role models. It took time, but in the end she identified *Lassie* which she watched on TV as a child, Miss Lloyd her junior school teacher, and a family friend who always listened, and who introduced her to a love of Shakespeare. When asked what it is about Lassie that makes her a role model, Moira said Lassie was always 'coming to the rescue, saving the day, but without any big fuss'. Miss Lloyd was described as 'young, independent, smart, efficient, wore neat clothes, the classroom was always interesting but tidy, she drove a "bubble car" (and this in the 1950s)'. The family friend owned a farm which she visited regularly as a child and young adult, and long conversations about life and literature took place late into the night.

Magazines did not figure much in Moira's life, but currently she never missed the TV series *ER* (a hospital drama). Hobbies involved reading, travel, walking in interesting places; she liked exploring woods, because they reminded her of happy times when she was young, but she also loved the moors, fells and glens – 'wide open spaces'. Books were important, 'as a child, reading for hours, lost in the story' – favourites as a young child were *Milly Molly Mandy* and *Heidi*. 'Milly Molly Mandy lived in an old timber-framed house in an extended family in a village, she had a friend, a boy who seemed to get into trouble a lot, and she spent time helping the family. Heidi lived in the hills, with Grandpa in a loft room where she could look at the stars and the snow, she had a friend called Peter who did silly things and she had to rescue him occasionally'. Later reading, 'if I had to pick one book, which would be very difficult, what would it be? – *Jane Eyre* – strong, despite all the difficulties of her life, where she lived, when she lived, she won, was the strongest in the end'. Motto or favourite saying was 'There's always a way'. School subjects – favourites were English Literature and history; she disliked maths and science, but that may have been more to do with the teachers, she said.

You would need to be working with Moira to identify the patterns, but what comes to mind as you read the case study? What qualities are evident here? There seems to be a pattern about wanting to solve problems, rescuing people, there may be something about independence – being strong and efficient, and also neat and tidy. An interest in reading is emphasised and the outdoors maybe. Something about winning, not being defeated, coming through, despite difficulties, and the motto suggests that there is always an answer to a problem. Clients will often pick a family member as a role model; it can be important to clarify that role models should be outside the family as we do not choose our family, but care needs to be taken with this of course. And other terms may be more useful, such as 'someone you looked up to or admired when you were young, maybe a "cool character"'. Also, the term motto does not always work – t-shirt message or tag can work better with young people. An important point to note here is that a question about school subjects is last on the list. Many career interviews with young people focus on this question first and it often has the effect of a wet blanket thrown over any spark of interest they may have had in the process.

Moira may have found enough insight from the discussion around the responses to the six questions, but where a deeper approach is thought useful, the exploration can continue by visiting stories from childhood. Savickas (2005, 2006) suggests the stories selected reflect the current dilemma that brings a person to career counselling at this 'turning point', past in present and present in the past. These are the *telling* stories, meaningful at the present time, which is why they come to the fore in the session. It is important to stress that this is not a conscious process of 'selecting' a story, but the stories that emerge *rehearse* the problem and can lead to insight and potential solutions. Continuing with stage 2, the approach progresses along these lines:

- The client is asked to recall a significant story from early childhood – the first thing that comes to mind. The practitioner searches for the detail by asking what happened next, and so on? The practitioner notes down the key words that the client uses.
- The client is asked for two more stories, using the same approach. If the person is really stuck it **may** be helpful to prompt, e.g. 'How about when you were in primary school … when you moved up into senior school?' It is important that the client knows the story is not being judged; they do not *recount* a story to impress the listener. This is usually, although not exclusively, an enjoyable activity (although more on this later) and needs to be spontaneous.
- The client is asked to summarise the essence of each story by turning them into headlines for a newspaper (important to note that it is the client who does this, although the practitioner can reflect back the words the client used in the stories if it helps).
- The practitioner listens for the first verb the client uses each time and notes it down.
- Taking the answers to the questions and the headlines from the stories, the practitioner summarises the stories, feeding back actual words and working with the person to identify patterns and potential themes.
- Working **collaboratively** these are related to the presenting issue at the start of the conversation. This is not the practitioner interpreting and analysing the client's stories, but about working at joint identification of the life interests, in order to relate these to future education, training and/or career goals. The practitioner will be doing this through using reflective feedback, 'You said earlier that … and I wonder …', and summary skills, 'What I heard you say was … and the words you used were …' (these skills are explored in a later chapter of the book).

Activity 7.4

In an earlier activity you were asked to think back to your first day at school and note down what you remembered. In that activity the topic was given to you. Now think about the first story that comes to your mind when you think about yourself as a small child. This needs to be your memory, not a story told about you. What's the story, what's the detail – write it down? If you were to turn that story into an article for a local newspaper, what would be the headline? These are usually short and should contain a verb.

The point of the exercise above is to have a go at this. In teaching the model it is not possible to do this through role play, as the responses need to be authentic and personal, or they are unlikely to be coherent and meaningful to the individual for their understanding of how the model can work. Participants in a training workshop, however, may not be trying to solve a personal career problem when they engage in this activity. But often the stories are revealing as even when in work, most of us are future focused, wondering what might be the next career path ahead. You could try for two more stories from later childhood and early adulthood and see if there are any patterns emerging. And are the patterns related in any way to your responses to the six questions above?

Stage 3 Endings

Having identified the goals, there is agreement on what action is required. This might progress as follows:

- Identifying potential action.
- Evaluating potential action.
- Clarifying the action steps.
- Checking/asking – 'So, what has been achieved today?' related to the initial question, 'How can I be useful?'

Savickas states that there needs to be a period of reflection after the meeting where the client has an opportunity to test the ideas. It is in the follow-up meeting (which does not have to be face-to-face) that 'reality checking' takes place – shaped by the client's subsequent reflection and the experience and evaluation of the action taken. Follow-up questions for that meeting might include:

- What did we get wrong?
- What are your reflections on the discussion and the initial action?

- What are the goals now – are these the same or different?
- What further action is required?
- How will that be reviewed?
- What else needs to happen?

Case study 7.2: Wild child

In the research project, one of our practitioners worked with a young woman who was having difficulty making her university choices. She talked about business studies and management courses, but with a complete lack of energy or enthusiasm. Her t-shirt message (how she would best describe herself) was 'wild child', which she said with some emphasis. Her subject interests suggested maybe media or psychology as future courses at university, but her stories were all about the outdoors, exploring nature and having adventures. At the point this was fed back to her, she said that business studies was a sensible choice to ensure an income for the future. When the patterns and emerging themes from the interview were examined further, she could see the mismatch and became energised about ideas related to an outward bound course she had attended (which was in one of her stories). The practitioner and client then talked about courses related to physical geography and the kind of campus university she would like which offered the outdoor activities that inspired her. She became enthused and they created a new story headline, 'Wild Child Chases Twisters'. Her action was to find out more about courses and places that resonated with her life themes. She left the interview, pointing to her heart and saying, 'That was great and it all came from me' (Reid and Scott, 2010).

Reflection point 7.4

Having read through the model and engaged in the activities, what are your initial thoughts about this approach? Do you have any concerns? If so, what are they? The next section will share the reflections of those on the research project.

The usefulness of a narrative approach in career counselling

In discussing what proved useful with practitioners, they liked the systematic structure that the Savickas career construction model gives for interviewing. At the beginning of interviews they sought permission to 'try something different', which helped with the engagement of the client. Explaining what they were doing and why enhanced the collaborative process and the effectiveness of what took place. Resisting a 'check list' approach was important to avoid a shallow exploration: that said, a prompt sheet can be helpful when trying a new method and can be offered as a document to give to clients at the end of the interaction (see Savickas, 2011: 49–50). Language may need to be adapted for the particular context – for instance, magazines and television could be replaced by other media and books, and movies by community stories and tales. In the storytelling phase there is a need to stay with the story and not to rush on to the next phase, asking follow-up questions, such as 'tell me more about that' or 'what did that feel like?' resulted in richer material. Indeed, such an approach provided a reflective space for clients to think at a deeper level, increasing their confidence to tell a story and enhancing rapport between practitioner and client. In some contexts this may enable the client to be more honest with their answers, reflecting their personal interests rather than the interests that may be culturally expected. Of course, using any 'model', however creative, can result in a mechanistic approach if adherence to the model and any prescribed stages takes over from the relationship in the interaction. So whilst structure is helpful, flexibility is important.

In the reflection point above you were asked to consider any concerns that you had. In our project a particular concern for our practitioners was how to identify the themes. Training in the UK leads practitioners to avoid taking on what they perceive as a 'directive' role. It is clear in the literature that the identification of the life themes results from reflecting back particular words that the client used. The practitioner notes down the client's words, particularly those used with emphasis, and uses them when they search together for patterns and themes.

Some practitioners liked the very positive feel to the interview that they observed on the Savickas DVD (2006), and this should also appeal to career coaching with its emphasis on positive psychology (Yates, 2014). Others were concerned about the degree to which they might be expected to analyse the client's story. However, Savickas is clear that it is the client's words and phrases that are fed back and that an analysis is not the primary aim. But, these perceptions were meaningful to the practitioners involved and point to the importance of understanding the context within which career counselling and coaching take place. Even where British and American (Savickas) practitioners may share a language, 'meanings' (which are at the core of constructivist work) can vary and models, and the terms used to explore the life themes, need to be adapted for particular cultural settings.

At the point when the client is asked to summarise the stories in the second stage, by providing headlines for a newspaper, the interview moves from story-telling to life theme identification. This can be the turning point when the client can gain insight, see the patterns and begin to identify their life themes. Another concern relates to 'getting' the client to work in a different way to that which they might be expecting from a more conventional career guidance interview – what if they 'just don't get it'? For example, identifying role models (up to three) can involve using silence (which is a skill) and giving the person space to think: in other words, trusting that they can think while knowing they are not being judged. A caution is required here – it can be easy to impose the practitioner's knowledge of the role model if they are a known person or character. So, the task is to wait and concentrate on what it is about the role model – *their qualities* – that the client finds admirable.

A further concern is worth a mention. In facilitating storytelling it was important to assure the client that this was not 'tell me all about your childhood', but 'tell me about the first story that you think of'. With the focus on the latter, this also avoids the temptation, however unconscious, to search for a 'good' story to please the listener. Alongside this worry, practitioners wondered what they would do if the story or stories told were traumatic, would they be opening 'a can of worms' that the client did not want to reveal. This may happen, and did for two of our practitioners, but both felt that it was the story that the client wanted to tell at that time, it was important that it was heard and they were able to contain the story in a supportive way. From a sad story they could identify a time when the client was scared but found resources to be brave, times when they may have felt helpless but might have found strength in their favourite character in a book or a role model that becomes a 'blueprint' for later life. In one other case, having heard a worrying story that might have safeguarding implications for an under-aged young woman (in terms of the relevant child protection policy), the practitioner switched to another approach as she felt that further therapeutic work might be required (and she also offered a referral). That said, we need to remember that being upset, expressing emotion, is not the same as being harmed – it can be cathartic. Overall these experiences were the exception; the norm was an enjoyable and insightful interaction for both client and practitioner.

Returning to the concern about 'interpretation', how did the practitioners in the research project work with clients to recognise patterns and identify themes from the questions and the stories? Their solution was to ask the client: one said, 'I didn't know what to do next, so asked the young person what they thought!' Others used an explanatory introduction before asking this: 'The theory goes that the stories that come to your mind are connected to the decisions that you are trying to make – so what do you think now, having worked on this together?' To recap, the stories told in the narrative career counselling interview are not thought through before the interview, they are not prepared in advance, but are what come to mind when the questions are asked. They are stories that relate *at this point in time* to the career problem that the client is trying to solve. So, following a summary, other examples used effectively by practitioners were: 'So, where has that discussion got us to?', 'What is your thinking now?', 'What clues have emerged, do you think?'

Building trust and rapport is essential in any intervention or the approach used, however collaborative, will not work. Many of our practitioners in the project worked with young people whose answers to questions are likely to be 'dunno', to use a British colloquialism; they probably do know, but often do not trust the practitioner enough to tell them. Used with careful and respectful curiosity, the narrative career counselling interview demonstrates genuine interest in the person, alongside investing time in respectful listening. The approach is applicable to all ages, again depending on what the client needs from a career counselling or coaching session. Any approach that is built on a concept of biographicity and identity work requires a sensitive attitude, not because it is inherently difficult, but because of the complexity of people's lives. There will be situations where an individual does not have the resources to enter the career of their dreams, but engaging in narrative and biographical work that helps them to identify their core interests can help them to manage change and transition. For example, discovering that they cannot become a veterinary surgeon may be disappointing, but confirming their interest in working with animals can lead to job satisfaction when they are the favoured assistant in the pet shop or pet rescue home that everyone comes to for advice. In this way Savickas suggests that the narrative career counselling approach has the potential to build resilience and help clients to 'articulate their intentions', and it 'clarifies the current choices to be made and enhances the ability to decide' (Savickas, 2011: 131).

Chapter summary

The chapter examined the foundations of narrative career counselling by exploring the concept of biographicity and identity work in the context of career decision making. It outlined the contribution that narrative plays in counselling work before moving on to consider the benefits that can be derived from applying interpretive, narrative and biographical approaches. Finally it described in some detail an approach that is located specifically in the career construction counselling work of Mark Savickas. By making reference to a research project in the UK, it evaluated the usefulness of the approach for career counselling. The chapter also suggested that with an understanding of what underpins the approach there is scope for its development within the career coaching sector. Narrative approaches have at their core a desire to work collaboratively with clients in reflexive and inclusive ways. Social justice and inclusion are key ethical principles that are central for many career practitioners working in various contexts with diverse individuals and groups: both are explored in the next chapter.

Further reading

McMahon, M. and Watson, M. (eds) (2015) *Career Assessment: Qualitative Approaches.* Rotterdam, Netherlands: Sense Publications.
I mentioned this book earlier in relation to assessment methods; I include it here as its focus is on qualitative assessment in order to work with the client to help them construct their career. The content outlines relevant theory and also includes examples of 'how to do' qualitative and narrative work in practice.

McLeod, J. (1997) *Narrative and Psychotherapy.* London: Sage.
This text provides a very clearly written introduction to narrative counselling. If the reader is interested, then the works of Michael White and David Epston are also highly recommended.

Reid, H.L. and West, L. (2014) 'Telling tales: do narrative approaches for career counselling count?' in G. Arulmani, A.J. Bakshi, F.T.L. Leong and A.G. Watts (eds), *International Handbook of Career Guidance.* Dordrecht, The Netherlands: Springer.
This is the most comprehensive account of the research project we undertook with practitioners who were trialling the approach. It includes both phases of the project and the details of the model used.

Savickas, M.L. (2006) *Career Counseling – DVD, Series II – Specific Treatments for Specific Populations.* Washington, DC: American Psychological Association.
This is an excellent resource for seeing the narrative career counselling approach in action. The introductory discussion and the detailed analysis of the interview that follows the example are also illuminating.

Savickas, M.L. (2011) *Career Counseling.* Washington, DC: American Psychological Association.
This is the essential text for those who want to understand both the philosophy and the practice of constructivist career counselling using a narrative approach.

8

Working with diversity

This chapter will:

- discuss the relevant concepts and offer definitions for the terms used;
- outline the multicultural principles in counselling that underpin the chapter;
- suggest guidelines and practical tasks to support career counsellors and career coaches for effective multicultural and transcultural work.

Introduction

What is meant by 'working with diversity'? In the context of careers work, it is taken to mean recognising diversity as an all-encompassing term that acknowledges and respects 'difference', such as gender, ethnicity, sexuality, socio-economic background, disability, religion/faith, age and other variables. In a multicultural society, ethical career practitioners will acknowledge diversity in their work and avoid practice which may lead to oppression. Multicultural awareness should permeate all the work that career counsellors and coaches undertake, but this can often be reduced to knowledge of policies of 'equal opportunity' or concerns over 'political correctness'. The latter refers to language, ideas, or policies that address perceived or actual discrimination, but, when used negatively, implies that these considerations are excessive or applied because they are required rather than desired.

When working with diversity, a multicultural approach requires a practitioner to be aware of any barrier (to clarify, not 'race' alone) that can have an impact on an individual or group's access to services and opportunities. Beyond equal opportunities, this involves a way of 'being' that welcomes diversity, strives for social justice and is anti-oppressive (Thompson, 2011). This chapter will discuss the concepts, draw on the multicultural approach in counselling (Ivey et al., 1997; Sue et al., 1996) and make suggestions to enable those involved in careers work to develop an appropriate awareness, and to practise multiculturally across different cultural groups, i.e. transculturally. But first we need to be clear about the terms used.

The language of diversity

It may be boring to repeat the point already made in this book, but language – the words we use – is important and of particular relevance within the context of multicultural work. Where to place this chapter in the book has been a problem, as it is at the core of career guidance and counselling work from its foundations in the work of Frank Parsons, his contemporaries and successors. My expectation is that anyone involved in this work is interested in the wellbeing of others and would in all probability see themselves as non-judgemental and open to the benefits of diversity. However, the issue is multilayered and complex, requiring examination. In recent years there has been concern that being 'politically correct' can, on the one hand, be reduced to paying 'lip service' to equality, and on the other, stifle critical debate of contentious issues.

Reflection point 8.1

It is important to pause at this early point in the chapter and think about your perspective on this topic. What do the terms equal opportunity, political correctness and multiculturalism mean to you? Note down your thoughts.

This is not straightforward. Views differ about the terms 'equality of opportunity' and 'equal opportunity', and the meaning is contested in various disciplinary fields, including philosophy and the political and social sciences. For the context of this book we could focus solely on employment issues, but it is the premise of this work that career is more than just a job and that life and career are closely connected. Aside from employment, the concepts relate to access to a range of services, as noted above, such as financial services, education, housing, the justice system and the right to vote in a democratic state. One way of thinking about the difference is that 'equality of opportunity' connects in abstract ways to the theories which underpin the concept. 'Equal opportunity' is, generally, more grounded in the context of employment practices as a legal right to prevent discrimination.

The literature is extensive and this section of the chapter cannot do full justice to it, but will give a brief overview. *Formal equality of opportunity* is based on the principle of *non-discrimination,* where there is no evidence of *direct discrimination*; i.e., where people may experience disadvantage from discrimination on grounds of supposed race, ethnicity, religion, gender, sexual orientation and so on. Direct discrimination occurs when a condition applied equally to everyone can, in reality, only be achieved by a smaller number of people within that population. Under the UK Equality Act (2010), the former technical requirement to prove that certain treatment was less favourable than would have been received without a particular attribute, or with a different attribute in the same or similar circumstances, has been removed. The new test, known as the 'comparitor test', focuses on whether or not certain treatment was unfavourable to the person claiming discrimination.

Substantive equality of opportunity or *fair equality of opportunity* is broader in its approach and concerned with *indirect discrimination,* i.e., where people may experience unfairness from certain conditions imposed on an individual that have an unfavourable impact.

The definition of indirect discrimination within the 2010 Act has also been simplified by removing existing technicalities and has provided further clarity around the factors to consider in determining whether a requirement, condition or practice is reasonable in the circumstances. Indirect discrimination takes place when an individual imposes, or seeks to impose, a condition or practice that will have the effect of disadvantaging people with a protected attribute. This is rather complicated and an activity might help by providing examples to work with (adapted from www.victorianhumanrightscommission, 12/03/14).

Activity 8.1

Which of the following is direct discrimination and which indirect discrimination?

1. A garage owner will not train a young female apprentice to use a new piece of machinery as she may find the lifting involved difficult.
2. An advert for a cleaning job asks for fluency in speaking and reading English.
3. A department store requires a photographic driving licence for identification purposes before a customer can collect an order.
4. A letting agent refuses an application from an African Caribbean man for a tenancy on a flat, on the basis that the owner prefers indigenous tenants.
5. A restaurant requires all waiters to be clean shaven.

My answers are at the end of the chapter.

Equality of opportunity

'Fair equality of opportunity' is associated with the work of philosopher John Rawls (1971), who suggested that equality of opportunity occurs when individuals with the same innate talent and ambition have identical prospects of success in any opportunity for which they compete. However, in terms of access to that competition in the first place, most (all?) societies in which equality of opportunity is sought, are unequal, as there will be significant disparity in terms of wealth, power and influence. Rawls prefers the word 'equity' which he views as superior to 'equality', as treating everyone the same, regardless of the advantages they inherit, reinforces and reproduces social inequality. In other words, if we make reference to the metaphor of providing a 'level playing field' for equality of opportunity, it is evident that individuals and groups in a given society do not compete as equals. Some are advantaged, by birth, income and the like and start 'the race' half way up the course, and others are disadvantaged and 'handicapped' by the same criteria, starting the race behind the blocks and in some cases at the rear of the crowd. And, the notion of the playing field also assumes everyone wants to join the game and has the same goals.

No amount of meritocracy (in broad terms, the notion that we can all make it if we try hard enough) will counter this disadvantage for the majority of 'competitors'. Thus the moral and just idea of equal opportunity for all is problematic, as some people are simply more able to benefit from the opportunities available. That does not mean that it is all too difficult and as practitioners we cannot make a difference – we can, and suggestions at the level of practice will be made later in the chapter. As Sultana notes (2014: 7), 'Working within the system, however, does not preclude working against aspects of it'. And working collaboratively with our clients to enable them to progress despite the system, where required, can make the job personally and professionally fulfilling.

Equal opportunity

Having skimmed the surface of the broad philosophical debate around equality of opportunity, this section focuses on the term equal opportunity, described above as grounded in employment practices. Equal opportunity demands that all people should be treated similarly and not be subject to any social barriers that prevent access to a range of services and experiences that are open to others, unless there are very particular requirements that can be justified as exceptions. In terms of employment, the value that underpins this is that any opportunity is awarded to the most suitable person in terms of qualifications, experience, capabilities and competences.

Those who recruit others should select on the basis of stated criteria and not on the basis of random or irrelevant choices. Where someone lives, their socio-economic background, their gender or peer group relationships, sexuality, disability, religion, race, or age should be immaterial. There are very few exceptions to this in terms of the legislation in the UK (Equality Act, 2010) and any intended discrimination (positive or negative) would need to be verified. It should not be assumed either that the legislation that operates in the UK is identical in Europe or across the so-called developed world. Before the legislation of 2010 was enacted in the UK, there were several pieces of legislation to cover discrimination, including: the Sex Discrimination Act 1975; the Race Relations Act 1976; and the Disability Discrimination Act 1995 (see the website reference at the end of this chapter).

In essence, at the point of selection for an opportunity and for advancement and employment rights within education, employment and training, an individual should succeed or fail based on their abilities and not on any other unrelated factors. In contemporary society it would be difficult to argue against this and indeed political parties of various persuasions would lay claims to upholding equal opportunities. There are close associations in the UK with the UK Human Rights Act (1998) which states that the government, the police and local councils, for example, must treat everyone equally, with fairness, dignity and respect. This applies to every person resident in England or Wales, regardless of whether or not they are a British citizen or a foreign national, a child or an adult, a prisoner or a member of the public. The human rights within the Act are based on the articles of the European Convention on Human Rights (see HRA, 1998). What is evident in the ethos behind such conventions is a desire for social justice, beyond 'equal' opportunities, which can hide deeper social divisions; but the terms are sometimes used interchangeably – what's the difference?

Social justice in the context of careers work

If we accept that life chances (our opportunities to be what, as individuals, we consider to be successful) are not distributed equally, then a belief in social justice implies that we should ensure that all have equal chances to succeed in life. There is a sense of mutual obligation here to support others and, by extension, a need for a redistribution of opportunities, although how such redistribution could or should occur is contested (Gale, 2000). Again, the philosophical work of John Rawls (1971) is influential in this debate. Acknowledging the responsibilities of all, Rawls argues for a balance between social equity and individual freedom, but there is a tension here that is not easy to resolve.

> ## Reflection point 8.2
>
> Most (all?) people working in the helping services would claim a commitment to social justice and inclusion, but can you see the paradox here in terms of upholding the values of diversity alongside social inclusion? Note down your thoughts about the possible tensions.

On the one hand, inclusion is a liberal desire for all to be included within a society, but on the other, valuing diversity suggests that plurality in social life (different ways of living and participating in society) is acceptable, even where this deviates significantly from the norm. To suggest that full inclusion can be achieved through policies and political activity is a liberal utopia and some would argue that difference – plurality – cannot and should not be overcome by politics (see Biesta, 2006 for an extended argument). Liberal theorists such as Rawls, however, would not be suggesting that people of difference should be assimilated into the 'mainstream' culture. In order for people of difference to be included, their difference has to be de-politicised when included in the mainstream; in other words, that which makes people different gets pushed out of the political sphere and into the private domain (Mouffe, 1993). And as part of this discussion, we could also question the terms diversity and difference. 'Diversity' can be viewed as 'variations on a theme', making the differences we see in 'others' reducible to mere cultural aspects. In effect this can lead to an unquestioning acceptance of the norms, values and particular interests of the majority group. 'Difference' recognises that difference **cannot** be included into a society, via some kind of 'tossed salad' approach. Those 'doing' the including do so from a particular (powerful) position and cannot know and understand what it is like to be 'the other' (Biesta, 2006). However, this argument should not be taken to mean we should not engage with difference because we can never fully 'know' what it is like to be someone else. Instead our responsibility as practitioners is to take an ethical stance, recognise that our understanding and knowledge will always be limited, and identify how this is shaped by the historical, social, economic and political frameworks that structure the communities within which we live.

These academic concerns are all very well, and, I would argue, an awareness of such political issues is vital, but what happens on the 'ground' of practice? In the context of careers work, an important edited collection of papers published in 2005 by Irving and Malik challenged career practitioners to acknowledge the wider political contexts within which they operate. Career education, guidance and counselling, and career coaching, are not neutral activities; they can be viewed as part of a narrowly defined agenda that serves the needs of the labour market and government employability goals. The work can, in effect, reinforce inequality (Irving, 2005). For instance, this might include: guiding individuals into 'suitable' academic and non-academic pathways early within secondary schooling; fitting them into the 'realistic' choices for training and jobs at age 16; working within a discourse of pragmatism that does not challenge the status quo with regard to options for higher education; and moving the unemployed into unsustainable short term and available 'opportunities' to meet the demands of a target culture and provide evidence of progression. All of this is political and we need to question whose needs are being served. As Irving states:

> The uncritical acceptance of such goals acts to move discussion away from a wider exploration of the concept of work in advanced capitalist countries, consideration of inequality and justice, and ways in which human value and worth are socially derived. (Irving, 2005: 4)

As argued in an earlier chapter, much career theory has focused on the individual and the choices they make. A call to think more profoundly about the causes of social exclusion (see Levitas, 2005), how to advance social inclusion and to promote social justice, requires the career practitioner to think more deeply about how we operate in a social and political context for careers. As stated before, we must work across disciplines and have a political awareness alongside an understanding of *psychosocial* approaches. If our interventions derive from narrow worldviews and the use of singular approaches within confined disciplines, we deny the social (Sultana, 2014). So, in the development of careers work, we need to engage with the individual and social/political context. To repeat Wright Mills' words, public troubles (the political) cannot be separated from private experiences (the personal): 'Know that the human meaning of public issues must be revealed by relating them to personal troubles and to the problems of individual life' (1970: 247–8).

Thus, in our education and training for career counselling and coaching, we need to adopt a more complex view of social justice and multiculturalism in order to be able to work effectively with diversity. Since the Irving and Malik book was published, there have been ongoing changes in the state provision of career guidance in the UK to 'include' and support both young people and adults with their career choices; none of which could be described as an unqualified success (Watts, 2013).

Reflection point 8.3

Not everyone practising in the careers field will be working with individuals on the margins of society and it may be the case that some readers are, or hope to be, working in a context where social justice is not perceived as an issue. What about you, what are your thoughts on the issues raised in the discussion so far?

There is a danger here that the reader can be overwhelmed by a perceived require-ment to act 'politically' in order to promote social justice. As practitioners we can feel weighed down by the imperative to address the needs of every, diverse individual we may encounter. In so doing, at the macro level, we may run the risk of ignoring the needs of the 'main' and majority group. Perhaps the apparent growth of the UK Inde-pendence Party, or other far right and/or fundamentalist groups, is an indication of the dissatisfaction with multicultural polices. The xenophobia is evident in the feel-ings of injustice belonging to those who consider their 'Britishness' at risk (and this includes settled communities of individuals who immigrated to the UK in previous years). We cannot ignore these political issues and as practitioners we need to hold onto our own selfhood. There may be times when we do not agree with the client's political views or cultural expectations. For example, when interviewing a young woman whose father also attended the session, I could not collude with what were, in my view, the father's sexist views about his daughter's future, nor could I ignore this difference. My response was, 'I have a very different view and I doubt we will agree on this point, but I am more than willing to continue working with you both, keeping our different cultural perspectives in mind.' The resource to offer another adviser from the same cultural group would have been useful, but was not available.

Within the constraints of practice, the efficacy of careers work in terms of its impact on the status quo can be overstated – grand claims cannot be made. There are resonances here, however, with the previous debate in an earlier chapter with regard to 'green careers'. Despite the social and economic restraints that affect the services we can offer or operate in, we do aim to make a difference at the micro level of practice, and we can all enhance this further if we have a thirst for social justice in our work. Drawing on the work of Gramsci (1971), Bauman (2006) and Sen (2008), Sultana emphasises that this is not an all or nothing approach and sug-gests that 'social justice is a "stance" rather than a state' (2014: 10). He also warns against a retreat into blaming the economic context for an inability to act in support of social justice. How we might develop a social justice 'stance' is outlined in a later part of this chapter. Whole books could be written on social justice, but I would like to end this section with a quote from Sultana. It reinforces the points made here, and arguments made in earlier chapters with regard to the dangers of individualistic and neoliberal approaches.

> Career guidance approaches that eschew the social may very well end up reinforcing these broader trends, which is why the bigger picture cannot be forgotten, even as we struggle to live up to the demand of social justice in the face-to-face encounter with the 'other'. (Sultana, 2014: 15)

A recently published and truly international text on career development that offers us insights into 'the bigger picture' has, at its core, the desire for human flourishing in multiple communities (Arulmani et al., 2014). This international handbook provides an extensive edited collection in response to the call to broaden the concept of career. It recognises that the field needs to move on from criticising the dominance of Western (individualistic) approaches and explore and disseminate models that are relevant for different cultures in current times. It is an extraordinary achievement to bring together authors from developed and so-called developing economies, in order to provide an in-depth analysis that is both multidisciplinary and transcultural. The authors offer a wealth of strategies through practical examples of the application of theories and concepts for diverse groups, in multicultural settings. As such it covers areas that cannot be included in this text, for instance, the career needs of indigenous people, older women, immigrants, international students, those practising in workforce development, mental health services and workers engaged in traditional communities of rural or craft occupations, and many more.

The challenges for careers work

The discussion so far indicates that the challenges for career practitioners are many, but that we should not be overwhelmed by these. We have a responsibility to work ethically, to do what we can and need to recognise that the 'problem' is political and social, and cannot be solved by broader education practices – let alone the practices of career counselling and career coaching. Neither can we 'blame' the social conditions of people's lives when pragmatism may dictate that a job now (any job that provides an income) is more attractive than time spent in education and training, which is often viewed as the 'solution' to inequality. Taken together, various cultural, social and economic influences will affect the 'choices' that individuals can make, and at times the very notion of choice is unsustainable. These wider influences present challenges for the career practitioner who must work within the systems of influence for their client or clients – whether this is a publicly funded employment service, a school, a community service or in a private or organisational setting.

In practice

In this section of the chapter I want to move on and consider how career counsellors and career coaches can work towards anti-oppressive practice. Before the text mentioned above, an earlier publication by Arulmani and Nag-Arulmani (2004) outlined the problems with the unthinking adoption of psychological and individualistic approaches to career development within collectivist cultures, citing their work in India and the region. The work of Mark Watson in South Africa has been mentioned in a previous chapter and in a recent article (2013) he supports their claim that individual decision making may not only be inappropriate in collectivist societies, it may also be subject to disapproval. Watson goes on to say, 'In terms of identity formation in certain African cultures the language of *I* is the language of *we*. What happens to the group happens to the individual and vice versa' (2013: 7).

Reading this reminded me of an encounter some years ago at a conference where a researcher from an African country was making a similar point. As I recall, she was discussing the traditions of a collective community and using the narratives of women who had formed a trading co-operative to sell traditional crafts beyond their immediate and 'normal' market. A member of the audience commented that none of the women used the first person singular (*I*) when talking about their involvement in the project. 'Well no' she responded, 'in such places there is no such being as *I*, in African villages you cannot survive as an individual: the country, the climate will not let you.' And of course this influence does not end once economies industrialise – develop – and become part of a globalised economy. Westernised conceptions of the role of work and the meaning of 'career' do not overtake a philosophically different attitude to work that is based in a spirituality and set of values that have a longer history than many Christian-based beliefs (Arulmani and Nag-Arulmani, 2004; Watson, 2013).

Activity 8.2

So in practice, what can we do to work towards an approach that is at the very least anti-oppressive? To begin with, try to define the term anti-oppressive practice. It may be helpful to think first about what would constitute oppressive practice and to acknowledge that there are subtleties here – oppressive practice may be unconscious and not overt.

Within the helping professions, anti-oppressive practice is an explicit recognition that oppression exists in even the most democratic of societies. Anti-oppressive behaviour attempts to remove or negate the influence of that oppression. As a starting point within career counselling and coaching, we have already acknowledged that what works for one person does not necessarily work for another. But more is at stake; we have also discussed issues of power and control and the constraints imposed, sometimes for 'good' reasons by state governance. Practitioners can be conflicted by the need to control, i.e. move people off an unemployment register, and the responsibility to care for the individual's or group's particular needs and interests. In the case studies below we have two contrasting approaches that illustrate the pressures, but deal with these in different ways.

Case study 8.1: Working for the client in busy practice

Peter has a full day ahead of him, working as an adviser in a Public Employment Office in a large town with a high rate of unemployment. As a publicly funded service they have targets to meet, but Peter wants to help the person he is working with, Tanja, who is originally from an Eastern state in Europe. It is important that Tanja understands the limitations of what he can do, so Peter mentions the policies that govern his work and refers to a particular form that Tanja needs to complete, using its abbreviated name. Once satisfied that he has covered all of this, he looks at the clock and says, 'I'm here to help. In order to facilitate the process of you initiating a claim on B361, I'll ask you questions and fill in the form for you. Let's get started on this and then later we can discuss the jobs that might suit you, going forward.'

Case study 8.2: Working with the client in busy practice

Jacques works in the same office and also has a busy day and is, similarly, aware of the targets he needs to meet. He has an appointment with Silvia (also from an Eastern European state) who he expects wants to discuss work, but first they have to engage with the paperwork. Jacques begins by ensuring that Silvia is aware of the time available today and checking the reason why she is attending at the centre, so that he is clear about her priorities. He then explains why they need to complete the form. He shows her the form and asks if it would be helpful to work through this together. Jacques has found that this helps him to assess the person's language skills without 'testing' them in a formal manner. He clarifies that they will then be able to spend time at the next appointment thinking about the work that interests Silvia, what is available and how to apply. Jacques looks at the clock and confirms that today they have 20 minutes, but they will book the next appointment before Silvia leaves. He asks, 'How does that sound to you Silvia, will this be useful?' Silvia says, 'Yes this will help me.' 'OK' says Jacques, 'and as we do this you can tell me a little about yourself, which will help me to get to know you a little and help us to complete the form.'

In the first example discussing issues in jargon is not helpful to the client and, in its effects, oppressive. In the second example, speaking plainly and clearly is helpful and enables the client to understand the issues and to be involved in the decision making process that affects their life. At the service level, anti-oppressive practice is about working with clients in client-centred ways in the development of the service and its practices. This collaborative relationship assists the individual or group to develop their own ideas about the level of involvement that is appropriate for them, in their context. There are factors, however, over which the practitioner may have no control where, for instance, the age, gender or sexuality of the practitioner might be perceived as oppressive by the client.

Before moving on to draw on the multicultural approach in counselling, it is useful to pause and see if the coaching literature might add to this discussion. In simple terms, career coaching has been described earlier as focusing on learning how to do things and paying specific attention to behaviour. In career coaching issues relating to diversity in a broader social context do not appear to be at the centre of the work. For example, an index search in the books already cited in this text for words and terms like equity, equal opportunity, social justice, inclusion and diversity, did not find references to any of these concepts. Empowerment gets a mention in one of the texts, but this is not analysed and the word is used so frequently now in many discourses that it is rendered virtually meaningless. My own view would be that as career practitioners we can enable, but we do not 'give power' to individuals or groups, although we can disempower or dis-able, as in the example above. Those working as career coaches in national and international organisations, and those working with private individuals, will encounter 'difference'. My search for literature on these issues was cursory and there will be journal articles on coaching that do analyse and theorise such concerns, but in consideration of time and word limits, the chapter will now consider principles from multicultural counselling that we can apply to both career counselling and career coaching.

The multicultural approach in counselling and psychotherapy: Usefulness for career counselling and coaching

As explained earlier, this chapter cannot make suggestions for working with specific groups, and we must always be aware of the problem of stereotyping when we think of fitting particular people into a preordained model, as this is also a kind of tyranny. Many of the theoretical approaches that are used in both career counselling and career coaching assume a high level of resourcefulness in clients, whereas individuals' capacity to effect change will be influenced by their social context. The multicultural approach within counselling and psychotherapy has produced work that encompasses the social, alongside the psychological. The work of Sue et al. (1996),

Ivey et al. (1997) and Monk et al. (2008) in counselling and psychotherapy, and Bimrose (1996) in guidance, supports both an integrated and multicultural approach that advocates the use of particular strategies as relevant to the client's needs. Jenny Bimrose (1996), who pioneered this work in the UK, pointed to the discussion offered by D'Andrea and Daniels (1991) of the four main approaches in training programmes for multicultural counselling in the United States. These remain relevant to the discussion and could be used to evaluate our positioning in terms of awareness and development of a multicultural and anti-oppressive approach. The approaches are explained in the case study that follows.

Case study 8.3: Assessing multicultural competency – four short vignettes

1. Culturally entrenched

Here a process model along with the core counselling skills based on active listening, genuineness, empathy and respect, are all that is needed to be able to work with the client. From a position of unconditional positive regard (UPR), practitioners are viewed as being able to rise above any cultural or social differences between themselves and the client.

Anya believes that her training is sufficient as UPR and impartiality were emphasised and these are core to good practice, and she says, 'I do not discriminate and I treat everyone the same.' She also thinks having a humanistic approach is enough, 'After all humanism believes that everyone can think and act independently and I facilitate that in the model I use in my careers work.'

2. Cross-cultural awakening

Here cultural differences are acknowledged but similarities are looked for to diminish difference in a liberal attempt to offer the same service across groups. The focus is on applying the same model and the same skills such as empathy and respect.

Tom believes that it is part of his role to help the marginalised individuals he works with understand how to operate successfully within the mainstream culture. The coaching approach he trained in highlighted the importance of demonstrating empathy and respect, aiming to see the situation from the client's point of view, which he says, 'may be very different to mine'. His goal is to equip his clients with the knowledge and skills they need, in order to motivate them to develop their career profiles.

(Continued)

(Continued)

3. Cultural integrity

This becomes more progressive in that a range of approaches may be considered that allows for cross-cultural communication skills, built on knowledge of different groups. In other words consideration is given to what works best for particular clients.

Bethany was introduced to a number of approaches in her training. 'We could not look at them all in depth, but I am aware that having only one way of working will not fit all of my clients.' As she is now working in a large multiethnic city, she is reviewing her approach, re-reading her course notes on verbal and non-verbal communication, and evaluating the models that appear to work best for the diverse clients who see her for career counselling.

4. Infusion

This would incorporate multicultural goals in all areas of a training curriculum. Multiculturalism becomes embedded into all areas in the training programme not just the skills related elements.

Jamaal was also introduced to a range of approaches on his training programme, but he says, 'We spent a long time thinking about the issues that underpin difference and diversity, across all the modules. Specifically we thought about our own world view and how that affects our relationships with our clients. And we examined a number of principles, or competences if you like, and reflected on these in terms of the development of our practice. We did this at various points on the programme. To prepare us for working with diverse clients in career counselling, we then set ourselves tasks to increase our multicultural understanding.'

Infusion does not mean that the practitioner attempts to merge with the client. It should be clear in the discussion that cultural competence on the part of the career practitioner begins by acknowledging the cultural values that inform their own worldview. This is needed to avoid a 'them and us' approach to diversity which sees some groups as 'other', or as people described in deficient terms, i.e. the disaffected, the disengaged, the difficult-to-help or non-English speakers, non-indigenous people. Of course, what we see in others depends very much on where we stand to look. Our particular stance needs to be understood in terms of its social and historical origins. We need to understand how the culture we inhabit informs our views about work and career, in order to understand how the dynamics evident in other cultures prepare individuals and groups for their engagement with their 'world of work'. Arulmani describes this as 'cultural preparedness' and outlines a model to explain how this 'works' within an Asian context (Arulmani, 2014). Leong and Pearce (2014) also write about integrative and culturally accommodating models when considering the need for indigenous models in vocational psychology.

Beyond competences and towards a way of being

To think about what, as individual practitioners, we can do to increase our multiculturally relevant practice, I am going to draw on previous work outlined in Irving and Malik (Reid, 2005) and in Reid and Westergaard (Reid, 2011). In both publications I adapted Sue et al.'s (1995) matrix that defines cross-cultural skills and competences for counsellors. The matrix organises skills and competences under the following headings:

- Awareness of own assumptions, values and biases.
- Understanding the worldview of the culturally different client.
- Developing appropriate intervention techniques and strategies.

The matrix is detailed and the original in Sue et al. (1995) should be referred to, but for our purposes here in the context of career counselling and coaching, the following is a summary, and can be thought of as principles that offer guidelines for practice. (I have substituted the term 'career counselling and coaching' for the word 'guidance' which appeared in the original).

   Practitioners who are culturally competent:

- Ensure they are aware of their own biases and limitations and are knowledgeable about how these affect the career counselling and coaching process
- Recognise the range of social variables that lead to cultural difference and are knowledgeable about the effects of oppression, racism, discrimination and stereotyping on themselves and others
- Understand differences in communication styles and their impact
- Are open about the career counselling and coaching process and actively seek clients' understanding about the purpose of the interaction and their views about ways of working together
- Actively engage in training and education opportunities to enrich their understanding and effectiveness for working with culturally different groups
- Are aware of the impact of negative reactions and treatment experienced by culturally different groups, and seek to understand this and not devalue that experience

- Understand how and why traditional and established approaches may be inappropriate and seek out research and other material that will enrich their understanding
- Engage in outreach work with clients outside of the normal work setting to broaden their understanding
- Respect clients' beliefs, values and views about what career counselling and coaching can offer and what their community can offer, and are aware of any conflicting values they may have
- Value the language of the client and do not judge a language or manner of speech as an impediment to the career counselling and coaching process, and will refer when their (practitioners') linguistic skills are inadequate
- Recognise that institutionalised methods of assessment may be unhelpful and create barriers
- Are aware of discriminatory practices at the individual, social and organisational level
- Make genuine attempts to advocate with, or lobby on behalf of, clients to overcome relevant discrimination
- Extend their communication skills so that they are not limited by a singular cultural approach
- Are open to alternative ways of helping, including using the resources of the clients' communities. (Reid, 2005: 178–179)

The above implies taking time to understand the client's philosophy of life, beliefs, values and assumptions and not rushing to apply what we might think would be the best approach. It may suggest that a career counsellor or coach from the same background as the client may be more effective, although resource constraints will often limit this as a possibility. And authentic listening takes time, but the effective use of time is a key element and its importance in work that aims to be multicultural and transcultural cannot be over-emphasised. In a later chapter a range of counselling skills are considered and empathy, amongst other advanced skills and attitudes, is of particular relevance here.

Empathy, an attempt to understand and share another's feelings and emotions, is easier to display when culture is shared, but difficult to achieve in cross-cultural communications. And a reminder here, the term cross-cultural does not simply refer to ethnicity, it also covers communication between different interest groups, as well as between adults and young people in any culture. Empathy is a way of 'being' with a client and not a skill that a practitioner switches on and off at the right time, but it is never fully achievable. As Arendt (1997) tells us, the one thing we all have in common is that we are all different in our uniqueness. So as practitioners we need to be alert to cross-cultural misunderstanding which can undermine the rapport building that is essential for empathic responses and anti-oppressive practice.

Although an interesting subject, it would be a Herculean task to learn all the social messages contained in body language across different cultures, but we can be aware of common problems (Ivey et al., 1997). These are outlined in the following general points and the case study:

1. **Misattribution**: we can assign the wrong or unintended meaning to non-verbal behaviour. This is of course a two-way process – we can also send the wrong signal.
2. **Misunderstanding the context**: 'rules' about behaviour in formal and informal settings can vary across cultures.
3. **Missing signals**: gestures and body language are often subtle and can be missed by a person from a different culture. (Similarly words may be the same but the meaning can alter with the use of pace, cadence and emphasis.) (Reid, 2005: 181)

Case study 8.4: Cross-cultural misunderstandings

1. **Misattribution**: Jo was irritated that his client did not maintain eye contact with him and thought she was disinterested in the discussion, but for Sha, Jo's 'staring' at her was both uncomfortable and rude.
2. **Misunderstanding the context**: At the career coaching conferencing that was taking place in one of the Arabian Gulf States, Brenda, who is British, offered her hand to 'His Excellency' after he gave the opening address. She was offended when he appeared reluctant to shake her hand and then surprised at the 'weak' handshake she received, but His Excellency's norms were different.
3. **Missing signals (gestures)**: Daniel used a hand gesture which to him meant OK, great, A1, but he did not see the look on his client's face. For Maria, the client, the gesture had an altogether different meaning which was offensive. **Missing signals (words)**: Jem was concerned that his client Prem, appeared to be getting frustrated with him as Prem raised his voice at the end of each sentence. When he spoke to a colleague later who had more experience of working with the group, the colleague explained that the difference in tone and tempo is a cultural norm, not necessarily evidence of increasing annoyance or frustration.

So, an important task for the practitioner is to be alert to their own body language, cultural values and beliefs. This helps in assessing the meaning of nonverbal and verbal cross-cultural communication and avoids making unwarranted assumptions.

In addition to the examples above, there can be variations in: how to sit (e.g. opposite, at an angle, side-by-side); the use of space and closeness; amounts of touching (and whether there is a ban on any touching); voice levels and the importance of time structuring (i.e. keeping to appointment times). If our practice involves working often with particular groups, then we would wish to be familiar with the expectations and norms for the group, but what else can we do to improve multicultural competence, cultural preparedness and avoidance of anti-oppressive behaviour?

Improving our 'stance'

The book has highlighted the importance of an awareness of the political nature of careers work and called for an exploration of how power shapes discourses within the field. But, back on the ground of practice, what other practical activities can practitioners engage with?

Activity 8.3

What practical activities to increase multicultural awareness would you suggest for a career practitioner at the training stage, but also for their continuous professional development? Make a list of your ideas.

Depending on the level of professional training, most courses will involve a period of placement activity. If placed in a situation with people who are culturally (in its widest terms) different, this can be used to increase self-awareness of a practitioner's own cultural values. It would be useful to reflect on the differences in an active way by recording impressions and assumptions, in order to learn from the experience. This can be through any means, for example a journal (written or verbal), and a discussion with colleagues. Such placement activity can be short term where resources and time are in short supply; thus a visit to an 'unfamiliar' cultural group can be used to find out about the group's views about the purpose and process of career counselling and coaching. This new or developed knowledge of the group can be shared **appropriately** with colleagues, through a presentation, or publication, or via relevant social media sites. Representatives of different groups can also be invited to speak to peers on a particular topic. All of these suggestions, and you may have other ideas and better ones, can be undertaken by those in training and by experienced practitioners wanting to refresh their understanding. The aim in all of this is to become a reflexive, anti-oppressive practitioner who thinks beyond the immediacy of practice, and can demonstrate a way of being that goes further than knowledge of relevant anti-discriminatory legislation and ethical codes, important though the latter are.

Reflection point 8.4

Looking back at the principles and the tasks suggested, what areas do you want to work on, for your own multicultural competence and cultural preparedness? How will you do this – could you draft a personal action plan?

In discussing multicultural principles and anti-oppressive practice we need, of course, to avoid labelling individuals, expecting certain behaviour due to perceived membership of particular groups. A person may belong to a number of social groups, and the categories that may be used for convenience are socially constructed. At the same time the most significant group aspect is likely to affect, positively or negatively, the career 'choices' of an individual. Across Europe, the new workforce arriving from Eastern Europe and elsewhere has different cultural experiences from previous migrants (who, for good or ill, may have shared a colonial past with their 'host' country). Career practitioners working with diversity in Western economies need to be open to new 'differences' and attitudes to work, and the meaning of career. For example, a doctoral student of mine recently talked about one of her interviewees who is a well qualified, political and economic migrant from Eastern Europe. She is delighted to work in an occupation in the UK that to me seemed menial, considering her qualifications and previously high professional status. I took a judgemental stance on this; but my student educated me. The job within the UK represented a freedom to choose and a livelihood that was denied to the person in their country of origin.

In conclusion, whatever we encounter, the theories and approaches we attempt to apply need to be appropriate and adapted to the individual and groups concerned – 'one size does not fit all', indeed we may be trying to use the wrong clothes entirely. Before working with diverse individuals, working effectively with difference means we have to acknowledge the 'otherness' of the other and of ourselves. This requires critical insight. Watson (2013), in looking at the influence of culture on career at the macro, meso and micro level, is critical of the importation of approaches into non-Western cultures. This includes approaches like career construction theory (discussed in a previous chapter) that are more nuanced towards difference, if, **in application**, such approaches underplay the social and the cultural; and consequently fail to engage with the 'local' meaning of career, work and employment.

For effective and anti-oppressive practice in such contexts, Watson suggests that 'career practitioners themselves need to critically deconstruct and reconstruct the career theories that may inform their practice' (2013: 11).

Chapter summary

In this chapter on working with diversity, definitions of the terms used have been offered and 'troubled at'. There are philosophical, cultural and ethical arguments that have been explored a little, in order to ground an understanding of multicultural principles for working within and across cultures. The multicultural approach within therapeutic counselling was drawn on and reference made to previous writings that have applied this to the careers field. A set of principles was defined as guidelines for the development of anti-oppressive practice in careers work. A number of tasks were then suggested that can develop and enhance our cultural preparedness and multicultural understandings. It was also noted that this chapter has paid less attention to career coaching, but upheld the view that the ethical principles discussed are important in all careers work. The next chapter considers career development in organisations, many of which will be operating on a global stage where transcultural understandings will be crucial.

Further reading

Arulmani, G., Bakshi, A.J., Leong, F.T.L. and Watts, A.G. (eds) (2014) *Handbook of Career Development: International Perspectives.* New York: Springer.
This is the most comprehensive text available to offer international perspectives on the issues raised in this chapter, but it is also full of practical innovations that are relevant across the contemporary field of careers work. There are 41 chapters and it is available as an ebook.

Biesta, G.J.J. (2006) *Beyond Learning: Democratic Education for a Human Future.* Boulder, CO: Paradigm Publishers.
There are many texts that can offer philosophical insights into what it means to be human, and the development of the rational and democratic citizen. Biesta problematises many of the accepted ways of thinking, and the discussion is useful when trying to think more deeply about what we mean when we engage in discourses about equity, social justice and inclusion. His 'field' is education, but the debate is relevant for careers work. It is a short book and will provide a 'way in' for those who want to understand more.

Irving, B.A. and Malik, B. (2005) *Critical Reflections on Career Education and Guidance: Promoting Social Justice Within a Global Economy*. Abingdon: Routledge.

This remains a very useful text for exploring the social influences on 'career choice and decision making'. It questions the long-held views on how to think about and practice career education and guidance. Alongside the academic discussion, each chapter provides examples of how to apply the concepts to practice.

To find out more about legislation that covers discrimination in the UK as outlined in the Equality Act 2010, go to: www.gov.uk/equality-act-2010-guidance (last accessed 22 April 2014).

Activity 8.1: My answers

Direct discrimination:

1. The employer is discriminating by denying training on the grounds of sex. All employees regardless of sex should be protected against potential injury.
4. The agent is discriminating on the basis of race.

Indirect discrimination:

2. Fluency in spoken and written English is unlikely to be a reasonable requirement for the job and would discriminate against someone who does not have this fluency, because of their race, ethnicity, or potentially an impairment that would not affect their ability to undertake the work.
3. This may disadvantage a sight-impaired individual who is not eligible to have a driving licence, and may not be able to produce alternative photographic identification. The store is discriminating indirectly.
5. This is an example of indirect discrimination as in effect it would discriminate against members of some religious groups.

9

Career development in organisations

This chapter will:

- discuss the role of the career counsellor or career coach working in organisations;
- list the social and economic benefits of careers work in and beyond organisations;
- consider the calls for realism and resilience in terms of career management;
- relate the above to a discussion on 'assessment' in careers work;
- outline approaches which explain transition management in careers work.

Introduction

The career practitioner may work within, or work with, organisations such as schools, colleges, universities, companies and other organisations (the latter could be public, not for profit or private). Outside of education, the career coach or career consultant (as discussed in earlier chapters) may work within a Human Relations (HR) department focusing on employees' career development, or they may be an independent career coach or consultant. Another way of describing this activity is to use the term 'adult careers work', although that begs a question about students as adults in higher education, whether they are 18 or over 21. However, in discussing career development in organisational settings in this chapter, the focus moves away from careers work with young people in state-organised educational settings (which are of course organisations), although many of the concepts are relevant when considering their career development (for example the concepts of work satisfaction and resilience). Within an organisation and in the wider society at the macro level, careers work has social and economic benefits. In this chapter the potential outcomes of careers work will be considered.

For many career practitioners, and particularly in an economic recession, emphasis is placed on practice that has a focus on 'realism and resilience' in terms of career interests and the outcomes of intervention, but this is a prevalent discourse that needs to be examined. Flexibility, adaptability, recognising that jobs are rarely 'for life' are all important issues, but what do we mean when we expect people to make 'realistic' choices – realistic on whose terms, and does this ignore or marginalise the concept of career satisfaction? The prevailing discourse that promotes a need for realism and resilience may shift the 'blame' for unemployment and underemployment onto individuals, despite the wider social and economic context.

Increasing 'employability' would be the aim of building resilient jobseekers and many interventions are preceded by a process of 'assessment' in order to enable this. Assessment, in different forms, takes place in a range of sectors, to identify the counselling and coaching needs of a client, but its use is particularly apparent when working in organisations within the 'adult' field of practice. A discussion on career assessment will be included in this chapter. The chapter will also outline ways to theorise work transitions, whether these are voluntary or forced.

The role of the career counsellor or coach within organisations

In a globalised market where the capitalist profit margin rules, it would be easy to be cynical about the motives of commercial organisations with regard to the career development of their employees. However, many large organisations, and small and medium-sized enterprises, do invest in the career development of their staff from the perspective of being a 'good employer', although this will be alongside a sharp focus on the business perspective. The interest will be around ensuring that relevant skills and expertise are available (the term 'talent matching' is often used), and are maintained and developed in order to sustain economic growth. Economic growth will also be a driver for government policy in terms of the guidance on career development work given to the education sector; albeit that guidance is not always backed up by sufficient dedicated funding in changing socio-economic times.

The career support that organisations invest in, from schools to global organisations, is, then, linked to broad government policy and the relationship between economic activity, systems of social security, and more tangentially perhaps, a concern for the health and wellbeing of a population. The career guidance counsellor has been viewed as the 'broker' operating between these systems and their clients (Killeen, 1996b). Watts and Sultana (2004) have suggested that careers services are expected to address three main areas in providing what can be described as both a public benefit and a private good (Kidd, 2006). These three areas are: meeting learning goals related to the effective education and training for increasing an individual's employability; meeting the demands of the labour market – in terms of matching people to jobs within the capitalist supply and demand system of employment opportunities that dominates in Western economies; and also meeting the desire for social equity (as discussed in the previous chapter). As Kidd (2006) points out, an organisation will also want people with the necessary skills as the market changes and want employees who, therefore, contribute to economic growth and sustainability.

Reflection point 9.1

What is described above is an instrumental approach focused on the needs of a particular type of economy. What might be lacking in this argument – what are your thoughts?

The above is a 'common sense' approach, but when we think beyond the surface rationale for this argument we can envisage many problems at the individual level. In the last chapter we explored notions of fair equity and social justice and I imagine your reflections touched on the criticisms of a neo-liberal approach that can ignore the reality of the lives of individuals in hard times. The degree to which career counselling and coaching can meet national economic benefits may appear limited, but the work can make a difference. Indeed, Kidd suggests (2006: 86), 'even a marginal impact on GDP would be enough to justify the modest level of public investment in career guidance and counselling'. At the personal level, within a publicly funded service or a commercial or private organisation, the social benefits can be significant.

Activity 9.1

Could you list the social and economic benefits of career counselling and coaching as you see them?

(My thoughts are at the end of the chapter)

One of the areas you may have considered in the activity is related to identity. Career counselling and coaching works with a person's self-concept and an adult's sense of self is often linked to their occupation. Theoretical perspectives on identity can be located in both psychology and social theory and others transverse both. We could argue that identity work is part of the role of the career practitioner, when people are considering who they are and who or what they might like to be, or do next, or in the future. These are complex matters, however, and are not reducible to personality types – we all demonstrate multiple identities or roles at work and at home. The literature around identity is vast and cannot be covered here, but our identities are shaped in and by the organisations within which we work. A fuller examination of the relationship between identity and work organisations would be an area of further study for the knowledgeable practitioner, and the work of Kenny et al. (2011) is a good read on this topic. A perceived loss of identity can accompany a difficult movement from education to work, from one occupation to another, from employment to unemployment and from work to retirement. These all constitute transitions and will be discussed later in the chapter.

Before moving on, it is also important to acknowledge that this discussion is focusing on Western economies which are often described as post-industrial, but in many other developing economies there will be a mix of industrial, post-industrial and traditional work. Work in the latter sector (possibly about 50 per cent of the world's population are involved in such activity) may be based on the land or sea, for instance, or local crafts and various barter arrangements in collectivist societies where the word 'livelihood' is more meaningful than 'career' (Arulmani, 2014). And the mix may go further where those working in pre-industrial occupations may also be using the internet to sell their wares (Arulmani, 2014).

So what is the role of the career counsellor or coach working in organisations? Well, it will depend of course on the sector and the organisation, who funds the work, the aims and goals envisaged in terms of outcomes and the wider, social, economic and cultural context. Whilst this makes the role difficult to 'pin down', it also suggests a level of fluidity which is beneficial. In other words, the role can be adapted to suit and a practitioner can choose to move between sectors. That is not as easy as it sounds as, inevitably, job mobility will depend on the current labour market, constraints in terms of qualification and experience, and the perceived advantages of any type of careers service, as understood by those paying for it (state or private). Career practitioners have to be resilient too – and this concept is discussed in the next section.

Realism and resilience

I imagine that one of the social benefits that you may have listed above would be that effective careers work can increase the likelihood of job satisfaction. As Yates (2014: 44) states: 'how happy you are in your job is determined by a combination of work factors as well as your personality and life events'. Work factors include how varied the work might be, your relationships with colleagues, the working conditions within which the job takes place; the manageability of the workload; the degree of autonomy experienced and the educational opportunities for development that are available (Yates, ibid.). Given that individuals will have different priorities, finding out their views on the above, what is relevant for them in work or when seeking work, can lead to useful discussions to identify what the client views as leading to career success – on their terms.

The theory underpinning personality traits and the match to occupations was considered in an earlier chapter. Yates notes that although trait/factor matching theory has a 'common sense' appeal, there is little empirical evidence to claim that when applied, it does increase work congruence or job satisfaction, with the exception perhaps of 'social types' finding increased congruence in a range of helping roles working with people. Citing the work of Dik et al. (2010: 49) she notes 'that avoiding "incongruence" is more important than finding congruence'.

Where does the above lead in terms of realism and resilience in career management? The need for 'realistic decision making' when it comes to further education, training and careers should make us question realistic for whom. In other words, what may seem realistic to a policy maker could involve full employment and contributing to the economy of a country, but for an individual living in an area of chronic unemployment and limited work opportunities a decision to engage in the informal economy, or to rely on social welfare payments, may be more realistic. Realism, then, can mean many things, but at the individual level it would mean making decisions based on what is achievable. The difficulty here is that we may not know what we are capable of, or may have distorted views about our abilities and potential. Clients may under- or over-aspire and the career counsellor or coach will need to take a skilled and careful approach when challenging apparent discrepancies in the client's thinking. The aim is to encourage and build confidence, not discourage and disable the client's thinking and planning.

A number of questions could be considered when evaluating the realism of a career goal, such as:

- How long would it take to achieve this goal – does the client have the time and commitment?
- What is needed in terms of qualifications and skills – is this 'doable' now or in the future?
- What are the resources needed to achieve this goal, including formal and informal support and financial costs?
- Is the goal congruent or incongruent with the client's interests and personality traits?
- How does it fit within the broader context of the client's life and their views about wellbeing for example?

- How competitive might this career goal be and what are the consequences if opportunities to achieve the goal are limited?
- Does the client have a view about the sustainability of this work, what some may refer to as 'future proofing'?

In order to find job satisfaction in a shifting career landscape, resilience is often required. Resilience in the job market can be defined as the ability to overcome the unexpected and to 'keep on keeping on'. The term suggests that the resilient person can 'bounce back' from the vicissitudes encountered in the attempts to find another suitable job when one is lost. Job satisfaction, or what has been described elsewhere as 'career happiness' (Bassot et al., 2014), may not be found if the person takes the next job available; that 'choice' can be severely limited when there is an immediate financial imperative. An individual's perception of what is 'good work' is often circumscribed by the material conditions of their life.

It is tempting to think of resilience as being a personality trait that some have and some do not. It is the case that some individuals have a greater propensity to remain calm in the face of a crisis, while others unravel. It is more useful and accurate, however, to think about resilience in terms of a process than a fixed trait; from this perspective people can learn to become more resilient (in a previous chapter, cognitive behavioural and solution-focused approaches to career development were discussed). Every individual, as part of the human condition, can demonstrate resilience and do so when they are not overwhelmed by, to the point of not surviving, a stressful situation.

There are a number of factors which assist resilience; the single biggest influence is likely to be the presence of positive relationships within the individual's family, whatever form this takes. Other factors include:

- a positive self-concept and self-efficacy beliefs (i.e. confidence in one's strengths and abilities);
- an ability to make 'realistic' plans (as in the previous section);
- effective communication skills;
- the development of problem-solving skills;
- the management of emotions and impulses that may be destructive.

These factors can be developed through education processes (for example a career learning and development programme in an organisation), and with the support of a career counsellor or coach.

Once again we should not make assumptions that resilience is demonstrated in the same way for all people. This will vary across time, cultures, community values and geographical locations and may not conform to the mainstream, societal view of how an individual should behave. In certain situations resilience, and indeed survival, may depend on a passive disengagement, and in work situations this type of resilience can be evident where bullying is experienced. How resilient a person can be needs to be balanced against the risks they perceive, real and/or imagined. 'Building resilience' has become a term that is ever-present, appearing in government-speak. The mantra goes something like this: in the need to grow a competitive economy, all citizens must be adaptable and build resilience into the development of their employability skills.

Part of the meaning of resilience is the ability to return to the original form – difficult, impossible maybe, when the changes within education, training and work have been extensive in recent years.

Reflection point 9.2

Read the definition of resilience below, taken from the web page of *Psychology Today* magazine. Think about individual words and the meaning they convey – what are your thoughts?

> Resilience is that ineffable quality that allows some people to be knocked down by life and come back stronger than ever. Rather than letting failure overcome them and drain their resolve, they find a way to rise from the ashes. Psychologists have identified some of the factors that make someone resilient, among them a positive attitude, optimism, the ability to regulate emotions, and the ability to see failure as a form of helpful feedback. Even after a misfortune, blessed with such an outlook, resilient people are able to change course and soldier on. (www.psychologytoday.com/basics/resilience, accessed 19 May 2014)

For me this is too perky. Linguists interested in discourse analysis would have a better way of describing the language here, but it seems relentlessly positive and underplays the very real circumstances that many people will be trying to manage in difficult lives. It takes us back to the notion that there are 'resilient people' and by extension non-resilient people, and that people who demonstrate resilience do so without being emotionally affected or experiencing stress. Importantly, if we do not examine the concept of resilience and the difficulties that the language can mask, we can shift the 'blame' for unemployment and underemployment solely onto individuals, who are just not trying hard enough – who are not capable of seeing 'failure as a form of helpful feedback'. As already stated, in order to work with clients appropriately we need to see the situation from their point of view. We gain an insight into the client's perspective by assessing the needs of a client when they 'present' for career counselling or coaching. In careers work, assessment can take many different forms and in what follows we will first consider a 'soft' approach to assessment, before moving on to assessment via formal testing (the latter being particularly prevalent in adult careers work).

Assessment in careers work

Assessment in carers work was discussed briefly in Chapter 5, but is returned to here in the context of adult careers work. What comes to your mind when you read the word assessment? For most of us it means being tested by someone else to see if we are 'good enough' to pass the examination, the entry test or the interview. In careers work formal testing does occur, but we can also think of assessment as an activity that is shared with the client – this is the 'softer' approach – where the practitioner works with the client to arrive at a better understanding of the current situation (Reid and Fielding, 2007). This can draw on wider sources of information, but the focus is on the individual's thoughts and feelings, to clarify these before moving on to think of future goals and ways of achieving them. Of course, we all make assessments about people when we first meet them and our initial impressions may be correct or turn out to be misguided. This is important to recognise; both that we make judgments and that they can be incorrect. Our assessment will be influenced by a number of factors depending on the context, our role, any existing knowledge about the individual, the expectations of the purpose of the meeting and our previous experience.

The counselling skills that are useful in the assessment of the client's interests and requirements are looked at in detail in the next chapter, but listening and attending, and asking open questions are essential in the initial meeting (and important throughout the work). A case study follows to illustrate this.

Case study 9.1: Assessing by listening and attending

Jacob is a career coach working in a global organisation. He has a post-graduate diploma in 'career and talent matching' and receives referrals from other colleagues in the company. Tony has been referred as he identified in his recent appraisal that he is looking to develop his career, but cannot see the possibilities of achieving this in his current post. Jacob is aware that Tony is a senior administrator who has been moved to another section during a recent restructure of the company. He thinks

(Continued)

(Continued)

Tony is probably unhappy with this move and is expecting career coaching to solve his issues. Jacob thinks a formal assessment test will be useful and will give Tony something tangible to take away at the end of the session.

When Tony arrives, Jacob resists the temptation to start the test too soon and after the usual explanation of the career coaching service, makes a conscious effort to slow down and ask Tony what he hopes to achieve from the work they will do together. In asking an open question at this point, Jacob avoids acting on his previous assumptions and establishes that he is interested in Tony's point of view. Tony says he is not sure what he expects, but hopes that he will be able to think about how he can progress further in the organisation and maybe find out if he is a suitable candidate for further study. Jacob asks Tony to say a little bit more about his current post and his thinking about further study. Contrary to what Jacob expected, Tony is not unhappy in his new position since the restructure, but wants to explore where the job might take him in the future. Jacob hears the excitement in Tony's voice as he talks about this and rethinks what the agenda might be for their work together. He summarises what Tony has said and wonders aloud what Tony's first priority might be for them to explore in the search for future career goals and their development – handing the development of the agenda for their work together back to Tony. An assessment test to think about career development may be useful at some point, but for now Jacob is finding out about Tony and his coaching needs through listening to Tony talk about his current situation and his interests.

For many career counsellors attending and listening to the client's story is the preferred way of 'assessing' the client's needs. That said, career assessment tools and techniques are now widely available via the internet and individuals can use them to self-assess their interests and suitability for a range of occupations. Early versions of such assessment programmes relied heavily on the trait/factor theory discussed previously (i.e. Holland, 1985) and such tests remain useful as part of a practitioner's 'tool box'. In the development of career thinking in a context of change, assessment tools and techniques (on the internet or using paper-based materials and games) are now more likely to pay attention to wider issues, such as values and social context. These may include, for instance, checklists and rating scales, card sorts, reflections on previous experience, responses to scenarios, and other creative methods such as games incorporating a variety of media, writing, using drawing techniques or collage (McMahon and Watson, 2015).

Kidd (2006) notes that the use of assessment tools is a subject that can cause controversy in careers work, depending on the sector the practitioner works in, their training and understanding of what is available. For example, practitioners whose training draws heavily on the discipline of psychology are likely to use formal tools (such as psychometric or 'personality' test) more than those whose training is more eclectic. As noted above, with the development of the internet, such tools are now easy to access by clients and no longer rely on an expert trained to use interest inventories or psychometric assessment.

Although there are benefits to open access to tests, clients may not always find it easy to work with the results of the test. Ideally a career counsellor would work with a client to prepare them for an assessment process, discussing the test, its aims and the type of information that the test will supply. However sophisticated an individual is in using the internet, the person may be confused with the results they receive and may seek help with the interpretation and application of the findings. Seeing such assessment tests as part of the process of career counselling or career coaching is vital (rather than all that is required) and, whether administered in or out of the counselling or coaching session, they can be a useful resource for discussion. Kidd suggests the following to help practitioners to assess the value of an assessment tool:

- Consider the attributes measured by the instrument and check with the client on their accuracy.
- Check with the client as to whether some attributes are over- or under-emphasised in the total picture.
- Discuss with the client whether some information from the assessment is only relevant to a certain stage or a passing stage in development.
- Check whether some information has been overlooked because it does not fit neatly with the rest.
- Discuss with the client how far the information takes account of the desired or future self as well as the present self.
- Help the client to think broadly about how the combination of characteristics relate to a broad range of occupations.
- Help the client to consider the lifestyle implications of the occupations identified by an instrument, including travel, income and working hours.
- Suggest ways to explore occupational options when they have been identified, for example, job shadowing, viewing videos, internships and part-time work.
- After some of this exploration has been carried out, offer a follow-up interview to help them evaluate what they have learned, and to decide whether to keep specific occupations on a short list or discard them. (Kidd, 2006: 111–12)

Examples of tools can be located on the internet by using a search engine and entering the words 'career assessment tools': examples include (accessed 19 May 2014) a UK government sponsored site at: https://nationalcareersservice.direct.gov.uk/tools, and a directory at: https://careerplanning.about.com. Having considered the activity of assessment, the chapter now moves on to explore the concept of managing transitions for careers work.

Managing transitions

The transition from employment to unemployment is an area which has generated research and theory that is useful when working with adult clients. Losing a job, being made redundant (literally, no longer needed – superfluous) can have dramatic effects on an individual's sense of their value, their self-concept. Adjusting to this status involves deconstructing views held about their place in the world and their relationships with others, and reconstructing a different view of self. Managing this process is not straightforward and will not be the same for all individuals.

Aside from the above example, definitions of transition focus on diverse features. For example, this could relate to any event that leads to a change in our relationships with another person, even when an anticipated event did not happen and the change did not take place (e.g. the cancellation of plans for a wedding or sharing a house together) – this may still be experienced as a transition. A transition may challenge our previous assumptions and patterns of behaviour, causing us to question, reflect on and change our view. This may occur in life when our role changes: for example, from living on one's own to living in partnership with another, on becoming a parent, or when experiencing bereavement. When a transition is disruptive (positively or negatively) this may have an impact on our personal identity – our view of self, and on our social identity – how others see us. At such times of crisis we may view the change as an overwhelming challenge or an unexpected opportunity to take our life in a new direction. But of course this is not an either/or situation, how we react will depend on a range of variables, both personal and social, and our capacity to manage the transition at that point of time. What might be stressful at one stage of our life is not at another, and our emotional response from one day to another may vary – depending on the current circumstances. Our 'character' or psychological profile, our experience of managing previous transitions and the support we can draw on, will all affect the process of moving through a transition. But where such variables are not fixed, these are areas that can be developed to help us manage change and transition.

Many authors have written about the significant changes in Western society and the risks to the individual's sense of identity (Beck, 1976) at this time of transition from a period of stability known as modernity, to postmodernity (Giddens, 1999); or what Archer (2012) refers to as late modernity and Bauman (2006) liquid modernity. For our discussion here we can draw on Archer's work when she speaks of the 'reflexive imperative' in the current changing times. In brief, her argument is that when norms are disrupted in rapidly changing society, individuals, specifically young people, are no longer socialised into following the behaviour patterns of the previous generation. She suggests that the imperative to be reflexive is proportionate to the degree of change that individuals experience in a reshaping society. This need for reflexivity (our internal conversations) is derived from an individual's concerns about their place in the social context and the 'finding' of their personal interests: the interplay of internal and external worlds. According to Archer (2012), reflexivity increases at times of transition, acting as a mediator between the constraints of structural determinism and the freedoms of personal agency.

Refection point 9.3

We have discussed reflexivity, structural determinism and personal agency earlier in the book. Are the terms clear to you or would it be helpful to revisit those pages at this point?

Where we have to make a decision about what to do next, this may become a turning point, where a life takes a different pathway. However, often we do not recognise this until we look back and reflect on the transition and recognise the changes that occurred. Turning points do not necessarily come with signposts and flashing lights, and are often fast-paced with moving goals. That said, in careers work there will be transition points that can be foreseen and preparing for these is often at the core of a career counsellor's or coach's work with clients. The practitioner will also be working with clients who are moving through a transition or have been immobilised by a significant change in their life. In my own practice when working with adult clients, it was often the case that an individual would want a career change as a solution to another, perceived as negative, aspect of their life. The case study below is an example of this.

Case study 9.2: Time for a new direction?

I was working in a community college with students from ages 13 to 19 and adult clients who were able to access career counselling, either as a participant in community education at the college, through a local authority bursary scheme or self-funded. 'Janet' had booked an appointment to discuss her desire for a career change and was

(Continued)

(Continued)

self-funded. Janet wanted to change her occupation – 'leave and find another job as quickly as possible' – but was not engaging in the initial exploration of her interests. Although I did not want to challenge her too early in the career counselling relationship, it was important that I understood the need for a change and the need for haste.

In response to my question, Janet said, 'I have been working as an accountant for years and I have now made up my mind that it is time for a change.' I asked what had led to her making this decision, at which point Janet became irritated with me saying, 'I wasn't expecting all these questions, I thought you would give me a test or something and then I could explore alternatives.' I apologised for not clarifying the process fully at the start of the interview and explained that in order to explore options that would be meaningful to her, I was trying to understand what had brought her to this decision at this point in time. At this juncture Janet stood up as if to leave and then sat back down and was clearly on the brink of tears. I waited and then Janet told me that her partner had died recently and unexpectedly, and now that she was on her own, she wanted to move on and change her life.

Janet was in transition, but probably not at the point where a career change should be rushed. The rest of the session was spent with me listening to Janet talking about the loss of her partner and how it had changed her self-concept, but also of her stated need to find a new direction in her life. We agreed that making a decision to leave her current job immediately was, in her words 'a bit hasty, now I've talked about it', but that she would come back for a career counselling session in a few weeks time.

Although we cannot generalize about how an individual may react to a transition, whether planned or unplanned, there may be certain emotional states in a transition that are recognisable. The model by Hopson (1981) reproduced in Figure 9.1 can be applied to a range of transitions, but it should be noted that the length of time an individual will stay in any one stage will differ from person to person, and from event to event.

Activity 9.2

1. Thinking back to Janet, where was she on the transition curve?
2. Reflect on a recent transition that you have undergone, maybe when you changed jobs or entered a training or education programme – try to plot the stages of that transition on Figure 9.1.

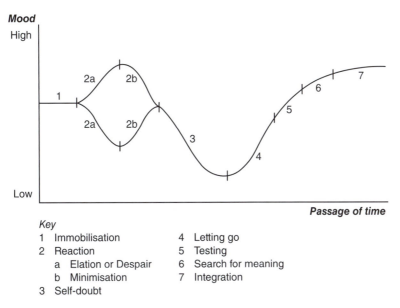

Figure 9.1   The seven-stage transition curve (Sugarman, 1986, adapted from Hopson, 1981)

The curve, without the words, is something that the practitioner can reproduce easily on a notepad and is a useful tool for showing a client that their experience is not unusual, that there are theories about transitions based on a 'predictable' pattern of reactions that can lead, over time, to life balance. This can be a helpful and hopeful conversation before a discussion on how to manage the transition. In saying this we would recognise that transitions are often non-linear and an individual will not automatically 'progress' from one stage to the next; but our aim is to, respectfully and mindfully, support the person's self confidence in the belief that a positive outcome is possible. Showing Janet the curve was helpful, she had moved beyond immobilisation as she was taking action by seeing me, but she was also experiencing some self doubt and reacting without reflecting on the implications of a 'hasty' decision. Janet did call in a few weeks later to say that she had changed her mind about leaving her current job, but was 'exploring other life-changing interests outside of work' and no longer needed the interview. I hope that she tested these out and found the new meaning in her life she was looking for. Integration in the model is the point reached when the individual is no longer in crisis and the current transition to a new 'state' is complete.

Throughout the book thus far and again in this chapter, attention has been paid to the social constraints that can affect career development and, here, a successful transition. Success can depend on aspects such as the buoyancy, or otherwise, of the employment market and the type of job opportunities available; plus the individual biographies of clients. Age, ethnicity, gender, class and disability for example may also affect outcomes. For instance, when working in a comprehensive school with a large sixth form, the majority of students went on to higher education; this was the norm and what the school and most parents expected. Mind you, this was often constructive procrastination, delaying entry into the 'adult' world of work, rather than a well managed and thought-through transition – which might be the aim of a career intervention policy. The same transition, or approach to 'decision making', would have been far less easy for many other young people living in another part of the same county in England where the expectations, opportunities and support were very different. We can apply the same thinking to work with adults in a range of settings, whether in employment or unemployment. A benefit of transition models is that they can be applied to any age group and provide a focus for discussing an individual's subjective experience of transition. This does not, however, remove a concern about 'all-encompassing' explanations that hide structural factors. The caution here then is to keep social variables in mind when thinking of theoretical models and interventions that may explain and also help with transition.

There are several transition theories and the cyclical model from Nicholson and West (1988) is well known within the literature on work role transitions. Any such model, whether linear or cyclical, suggests distinct stages and we need to recognise that these are interdependent and the outcomes of one stage will be influential on the development at the next stage of the model. And of course, people get stuck, fall back, drop out and thus experience frustration and failure; the latter threatening self-esteem and self-efficacy. Nicholson's (1990) model emphasises the career-related tasks that need to be addressed at each of four stages. These are:

1. Preparation – expecting and anticipating change
2. Encounter – developing an understanding of the new situation
3. Adjustment – finding ways of coping with the new situation
4. Stabilisation – becoming settled in the new situation. (Kidd, 2006: 44)

Nicholson makes note of the learning process that takes place when individuals manage career transitions and views this as preparation for the next transition – hence the cyclical nature of the model – and refers to this as 'recursion'. As mentioned above, any of the stages can be disrupted and change may be rapid, without the time for adequate preparation. Transition models of this nature can provide a useful starting point for understanding and describing what may be happening at a time of transition, but the practitioner will need to work from the client's view of what is happening to them. Transitions cannot be understood merely as rational decision making where the individual moves through stages from education to work, or from one occupation to another. More than ever in what has been referred to previously as liquid modernity (Bauman, 2006), managing a career is a fluid, social process. In organisational settings, depending on the levels of attachment to the organisation, individuals may draw on the support of career coaches or HR managers, but will also seek help from others who provide meaningful relationships, both in work and in their personal lives (Kidd et al., 2004).

An alternative model that pays attention to the subjective experience of clients is Schlossberg and colleagues's adult career development transition model (1995). The model has three parts:

1. Approaching transition: transition identification and transition process.
2. Taking stock of coping resources: the 4 S system.
3. Taking charge: strengthening resources.

The first part considers the type of change that is occurring, whether it was expected or not, the impact it may have and the position of the person in terms of where they are in the process. It pays attention to the individual's perception of the nature of the change, acknowledging that this cannot be generalised and will be unique to the individual.

In managing the transition, the aim of the second part is to think about the resources the individual can utilise. The 4 Ss are used to analyse:

- Situation: what is happening in the person's life now that is causing the transition?
- Self: what are their personal, psychological resources (this will vary)?
- Support: what help is available and how much – their social support (formal and informal)?
- Strategies: what strategies have they used in the past and what new strategies would they find helpful?

Finally in the third part of this model, individuals, having identified the above and drawn strength from acknowledging the helping forces they can draw on – their potential coping resources – are better prepared to take charge of the transition.

Understanding the concept of transition is important for career practitioners as many people seek help when they are dealing with transition. Transition is likely to be an emotional experience and can be stressful; helping clients to think about the transition in a structured approach can 'unpack' the situation with them. In terms of managing any related stress, this can clarify the aspects that the client can do something about now, what they might be able to do something about in the near future and maybe what is beyond, either their coping skills, or their power to affect change at this point in time.

Above all, the models outlined above (and more can be found in the literature) can illustrate to individuals that the emotions they may be experiencing are normal. This is not to underplay their significance, but can be helpful in reframing the situation when people are stuck and unable to see the situation from an alternative perspective. When transition is experienced as stressful, it can be difficult to 'see the wood for the trees': in other words everything is in the foreground and solutions (which can be hidden in the background) are not discernible. Recognising that transitional stress can occur, and working alongside a client to develop techniques that are meaningful for their psychological and social context, can aid the management of change.

In the section above, the focus has been on the difficulties that the client is likely to experience. But, transitions can also be positive turning points in a life and a career. Often there is a sense that people need to move on, make decisions and not spend too much time vacillating. Contrary to this view, Cochran (1997) advises that people should be given an opportunity for wavering, for taking time, for consideration of the options and for reflection. From this perspective, indecision is a good thing (providing it does not go on for too long, becoming disabling) and can help to smooth a transition, leading to positive outcomes.

Chapter summary

In this chapter the role of the career counsellor or career coach in an organisation has focused on work with adult clients. It has considered the social and economic benefits of careers work and recognised that these are not limited to work with adults, but are affected by the context and value placed on careers work and the resources available to increase its effectiveness. The chapter has taken a critical approach to the calls for clients to be realistic and resilient, whilst recognising the need for adaptability within changing social and economic times. In helping clients to manage their careers, it considered the first step, which is assessing the needs of the client from the client's perspective, before discussing the use of assessment tools. Finally, the chapter outlined theoretical approaches to managing transitions – an activity that is at the core of careers work.

The next chapter marks a transition in the book, where we move from a focus on understanding theory and concepts to the application of processes, skills and techniques in the practice of career counselling and coaching.

Further reading

Kenny, K., Whittle, A. and Willmott, H. (2011) *Understanding Identity and Organizations*. London: Sage.
This is a very accessible book that pays proper attention to the social science theory that will further an understanding of the development of the individual in organisations. It offers an in-depth discussion of the concept of identity for a contemporary and global employment context. Case studies are used to illuminate the text, along with illustrations at appropriate points.

Kidd, J.M. (2006) *Understanding Career Counselling: Theory, Research and Practice*. London: Sage. Recommended previously, but two chapters have particular relevance here: 2. Theories of Adult Career Development and 6. Assessment Tools and Techniques.

McMahon, M. and Watson, M. (eds) (2015) *Career Assessment: Qualitative Approaches*. Rotterdam, Netherlands: Sense Publications.
'Assessment' in this edited collection uses the term in a holistic sense, i.e. not only assessing the client's needs, but also assessing what type of intervention will suit the career learning preferences of the individual. The approach is constructivist, working alongside the client, and includes narrative and creative models. It also incorporates the qualitative use of quantitative career assessment.

Activity 9.1: My thoughts

An important benefit of career counselling and coaching would be the learning that takes place – the learning outcomes that emerge. These were described in an earlier chapter with reference to the DOTS model (Law and Watts, 1977) and they usually occur in the order shown below. This comes with the usual caveat about linearity and recognition that all of this may not be achieved in any one session: career counselling and coaching should be a process, not a one-off event.

- Self-awareness – the client has thought about their interests, their strengths and areas for development.
- Opportunity awareness – the client is aware of a wider range of opportunities that are available, what these require and how these resonate with their strengths and interests.

(Continued)

(Continued)

- Decision making – the client is better able to recognise that a decision needs to be made and has identified their mode of decision making, and explored alternatives, in preparation for establishing their goals.
- Transitions – the client has thought about what might be involved in making a transition and has some strategies for managing this and planning action steps.

If you took a broader approach to social and economic benefits your list may include the following:

The individual:

- makes a more informed choice;
- is better prepared to find work;
- is better suited to the occupation;
- finds job satisfaction.

Societal and economic benefits include:

- fewer 'drop outs' in the education and training market;
- efficiency in the job market (matching supply and demand);
- more economically active workers;
- less job turn-over;
- fewer skills shortages;
- less government expenditure on welfare benefits;
- greater equity through the promotion of equality of opportunity;
- raised aspirations via career support for individuals;
- increased social justice through raised ambitions.

And tentatively (as it is a big claim), more satisfied citizens and the reduction of alienation.

10

Models for structuring
career conversations

This chapter will:

- provide an initial framework for structuring career conversations;
- refer to other models that are useful for career counselling and coaching.

Introduction

This chapter 'signposts' a move in the book to a greater focus on the application of models, methods and skills. That said, it is not the aim of this text to separate theory from practice, and preceding chapters have taken care to offer insights into how theory is grounded in the work of career practitioners. To begin this focus, a three-stage model will be described that can provide the initial framework for those new to careers work. There are other models available and while not all can be discussed here, the chapter will indicate useful approaches for career counselling and career coaching. Once models have been discussed in this chapter, the following chapter will consider counselling and communication skills, plus techniques that can be incorporated into career counselling and coaching conversations.

Introducing a framework for careers work

I am going to draw, unashamedly, on the framework that has been developed in my institution and published by Reid and Fielding in 2007. This model has stood the test of time, but is also flexible, allowing for different and new approaches to be encompassed within its structure. The work of Rogers (1951, 1961) and Egan (2007), informs many of the models used in the counselling field, and Egan's *Skilled Helper* provided the structure for the development of our framework. Egan's work has been updated regularly and at the time of writing is now in its 10th edition (2013). It remains a core text for counselling but is premised on longer-term relationships than those that are, normally, available in career counselling and coaching. For the education and training of career practitioners we (Hazel Reid and Alison Fielding) reframed this into the Single Interaction Model (SIM), to reflect the more time-limited context that career practitioners operate within.

SIM offers an integrated approach, drawing on the theoretical ideas that inform the related tools and strategies that a practitioner chooses to integrate for their practice. This chapter will focus on *how* to use the model. As discussed previously in the book, integrated approaches are informed by a number of theoretical perspectives – for example, humanistic, behavioural, psychodynamic, multicultural and constructivist. The approach utilised in SIM has much in common with other models; however, there is a clear emphasis on the humanistic approach in counselling. Flexibility is essential and a cautionary note about the unthinking adaptation of singular approaches has already been made.

Reflection point 10.1

Think back to your earlier reading – what is the main criticism of the humanistic approach?

Later in this chapter other approaches will be mentioned, including the work of Arulmani and Nag-Arulmani (2004) who write from an Asian context, a part of the world where the domination of 'Western' humanist thinking is less appropriate. The other caution to bear in mind is that humanistic approaches assume a high level of individual agency, which can be severely constrained in many circumstances; thus we need to be mindful that an over-psychologised approach can mask the actual opportunities available for individuals to act independently. Finally, in many collectivist societies the notion of individual decision making is not understood or culturally relevant. In later editions of Egan's work, more attention has been paid to cultural relevance and the term 'The Skilled Helper' remains useful; albeit the word 'helper' has expert connotations. Overall, the model proposed (SIM) is *goal-orientated* and it is in the *action*, related to agreed goals, that career practitioners can reach *positive outcomes* in their work with clients (in all age groups).

EGAN Three-stage Model	**Single Interaction Model (SIM)**
STAGE 1: Current scenario	**STAGE 1: Negotiating the contract and agreeing an agenda**
• Story: the young person explains current situation • Blind spots: helping the young person to identify and be clear about problems and issues • Leverage: which are the most important issues to focus on during the remainder of the work.	• Introductions are made and the purpose is shared • Young person is helped to focus on their current situation and raise issues for discussion • Objectives for the interaction are discussed and prioritised • An agenda for the interaction is agreed.
STAGE 2: Preferred scenario	**STAGE 2: Developing issues and identifying goals**
• Possibilities: helping the young person to identify what they want and if it is possible • Agenda: translating possibilities into realistic goals • Commitment: testing out the motivation, considering the difficulties and choosing the goals.	• The young person is helped to explore the issues in greater depth • Possible options for the future are discussed • Through discussion, sharing of information and evaluation of possible options, realistic goals are identified.
STAGE 3: Getting there	**STAGE 3: Designing, planning and implementing action**
• Strategies: helping the young person to consider strategies for action • Best fit: which strategy is going to be most appropriate for this young person • Plan: turning strategies into a concrete plan for action.	• Identifying possible courses of action • Discussing and evaluating the benefits of particular courses of action • Agreeing specific action to be carried out.
Stages completed over a period of time, but each interaction has a beginning (stage 1), middle (stage 2) and end (stage 3).	*All three stages completed in a single interaction.*

Figure 10.1   Comparison of Egan and SIM

Source: Reid, H.L. & Fielding, A.J. (2007) *Providing Support to Young People: A Model for Structuring Helping Relationships*. London: Routledge, p. 14.

Applying the model to career counselling and coaching

The method in the Single Interaction Model is, like many others, based on a person-centred ethos. This is a collaborative approach, working alongside the client, but follows a flexible structure. The model, and the skills and strategies explained in the next chapter, can be applied in a broad range of contexts for careers work, including one-to-one and group interventions (working with groups is explored in Chapter 12). Indeed, anyone involved in a 'working with people' context will participate in a wide range of communication activities, even where not directly involved with clients. The model presented is, then, equally appropriate for a variety of situations: for example tutoring, facilitating, mentoring, supervision, youth support and other forms of coaching. Professional helping, of one sort or another, is often an iterative process. Clients may require career counselling or coaching over a short or longer period of time, and this need may re-occur at transition points or as their situations change. As explained, the Single Interaction Model (SIM) is informed by the work of Egan, but is adapted for shorter time-bound interventions. Figure 10.1 places Egan and SIM side by side, affording a comparison of the two models. Which model is used will depend on the time available and/or the level of support the person needs.

The purpose of the model is to assist the client to consider where they are at present (what brings them to the career practitioner), where they might like to be in the future (what are their interests, options and their goals), and how they are going to get there (what action will be helpful to assist them to reach their goals). The model progresses through three stages designed to help them to become aware of opportunities, to consider alternatives, to recognise decisions to be made, to identify the changes and choices they can make and so forth. The model reflects the stages of decision making, but acknowledges that, despite the staged approach, decision making is often not linear. Recursion occurs and this is normal and expected. Career practitioners also know that informal help, that is, advice from friends, family, colleagues and the media, will play its part in the process, alongside reflection on the individual's previous experiences. All of these influences will inform and shape decisions, choices and outcomes.

Activity 10.1

Think back to one or more career or educational decisions you have made, and make notes under the following headings:

- What was the decision you had to make?
- When was this – the context?
- Who or what helped you to make the decision?
- What information did you need?
- How did you make the decision?
- What would you say had the greatest influence on your eventual decision?

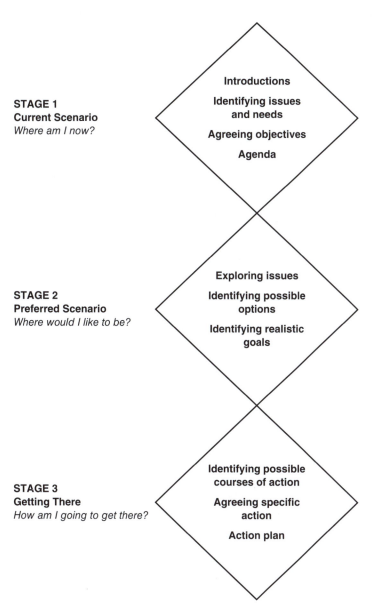

Figure 10.2   The three-stage model

Source: Reid, H.L. & Fielding, A.J. (2007) *Providing Support to Young People: A Model for Structuring Helping Relationships*. London: Routledge, p. 20.

In the activity above, the purpose is not to evaluate the decision made, but to think about the factors involved. Support offered by career practitioners does not operate in isolation from informal help; indeed, professional careers work may not be included in your list above. Informal help will have an impact whether positive or negative, thus, acknowledging the importance of the social context for the client is fundamental for effective careers work to take place. The benefit of a formal helping process is rooted in the presence of a skilled practitioner who demonstrates appropriate listening and challenging skills (and can access relevant information for/with the client). These skills, as outlined later, provide a reflective space for the client to think and explore ideas, before any information or advice is offered. The ultimate goal of careers work is that the person will learn from the process and be enabled to help themselves, whilst being supported through the process of careers counselling and coaching in order to construct their career future.

Before looking at each stage in detail, a simplified version of a three-stage model is provided in Figure 10.2. The diamond shape of each stage represents the need to explore – to move out – before moving in to focus at the end of each stage. In other words it depicts the process of *opening up* the discussion *then focusing*: moving from *the possible* to *the specific*, at each stage. Models, in words or diagrammatic form, help us think about that overall structure for careers work, but they are offered as tools to think with: a guide rather than a prescription. And it is worth emphasising that alongside providing a structure for a career intervention or interaction for the career counsellor or coach, the process reflects, in general, the 'normal' process of decision making. In the Reid and Fielding book referred to above, we trouble at words like helper and intervention, but we do need a shared language as this is more than an informal conversation or 'cosy chat' – 'It is not the same as talking to a friend but a professional conversation: what we describe as "talking with a shared purpose"' (Reid and Fielding, 2007: 1).

Of course, people get stuck in the process of career decision making, hence the role of the career practitioner. Further, the amount of time spent in any one stage will depend on the individual's particular needs. How advanced a client is in the process of assessing their own situation and identifying their options and goals will vary, and will depend on a number of psychological and contextual issues. An early task for the career practitioner, in terms of a staged approach, is to assess where the client is, so that they can provide the help that is most relevant, in order to avoid moving on too quickly ahead of the client's readiness. We can refer to this as making a space for the client to tell their story. The practitioner is listening carefully and should also be alert to how stories 'tell the client' – in other words what socially produced narratives are evident in the stories the client tells about themselves. Are their stories over influenced by structural issues such as class, gender, ethnicity, sexuality and so on? Young clients in particular often arrive for 'help' with narratives that are told about them by (more powerful) others, which will not be the whole story of their life and/ or their potential. The attentive practitioner will be aware of this, not to be confrontational, but to ensure that the conversation is relevant to the wider circumstances of the person's life.

The three-stage model of helping

In what follows the different stages and steps that make up the whole process, as shown in Figure 10.1, are explained further. What is offered here is a summary, and the reader is directed to Reid and Fielding (2007) where the detail of the Single Interaction Model (SIM) can be found in Chapter 7. The stages in Egan (2013) could also be consulted (although it was the 2007 edition that was used in the development of SIM and is referred to below).

Stage 1 SIM: Negotiating the contract and agreeing an agenda (Reid and Fielding, 2007; current scenario: Egan, 2007)

- Introductions are made and the purpose is shared.
- The person is helped to focus on their current situation and raise issues for discussion.
- Objectives for the interaction are discussed and prioritised.
- An agenda for the interaction is agreed.

At this opening stage the client is helped to assess their current situation. Whatever the context, this is likely to progress to identifying their current thinking in relation to future plans (or lack of plans), which may be educational or vocational, or related to other needs. It will include an opportunity to tell their own story, in other words 'where they are at the moment'. At the start it involves welcoming the client, introductions and clarifying the client's expectations of the purpose of the interaction – what they hope to achieve in working with the practitioner. It is important that this is a shared process and is not about the practitioner 'telling' the client what is going to happen. This sharing is achieved by using counselling skills, specifically at this early stage those of rapport building, using open questions and attentive listening and summarising. It is useful to clarify confidentiality and its limits, as applicable, once rapport is established. With introductions achieved, a shared idea of the purpose of the interview and clarity about the time that is available (for this and any subsequent meetings) follows. A good question to use (adapted from Savickas, 2011) can be 'How can I be useful to you today as we work together to think about your future?' Previous to offering this question it should be clear that the client is there to work collaboratively and will not be told what to do. The 'how can I be useful' question sets the tone for the work and also avoids the expert position of 'I am the expert, here to solve your problem or issue'. Of course this will need to be adapted as the intended meaning may not translate into other languages, but it works well in English.

The aim is for the practitioner to help the client to identify their career needs; if stuck, a question such as, 'So what brought you here to talk with me today?', can be useful. In a school situation a response might be 'my teacher', or 'the bus' – but that tells you something! Providing opportunities for the client to talk helps in the assessment of need, without using a test. You will begin to get a picture of their circumstances (where they are now) and their awareness, or lack of awareness, of the options that are open to them, and at what point in a transition they are currently. It is important that enough time is given to each step in Stage 1, particularly where the client appears resistant (i.e. as above, the young person who has been sent to see you), confused, or lacking in knowledge or understanding of the choices available to them. Although you may have worked hard at building rapport they may not trust you. A client that responds to all your wonderful open questions with 'I don't know' probably does know, but they don't trust you enough to tell you yet. This can be a sign that you need to slow down and stay with asking questions about what they do know, rather than the things they are unsure about. So, for example, remembering this is about finding out where they are now (their current scenario) open a conversation about their interests and the things they do away from their current education, training or work (Savickas' questions can be useful – see Chapter 7). A useful approach sometimes is to find out what they think 'other people' do in terms of the options available – this works well with young people who can be overwhelmed by the options that might be available, or if they cannot see that there are any options for them. If what the client says appears to be unrealistic in terms of what they are able to do or achieve, this early stage of the interview is not the place to challenge this; the aim is for clarification of their situation and related ideas at this point.

If a client seems very clear about their interests there can be a tendency to rush into exploration and information giving, Stage 2 – don't! A response can be, 'You have very clear ideas about what you want to do which is helpful – before we explore these further, let's just clarify a couple of things so that I can be sure I am on the right track.' You do not want to shut down the enthusiasm, but it is important that you summarise to check your understanding of the client's story so far. You can then agree the content for the interview and be sure that the client understands the contract of working together. So, before moving to Stage 2 you offer your understanding, check this with the client and, again, ensuring this is a shared process, you can say, 'So having clarified what we are going to focus on today, where would you like to start?' That done, you have negotiated a contract (the way of working together) and agreed an agenda (the content that the client wishes to focus on), and handed the next step back to the client.

A tendency for practitioners in training is to rush Stage 1 as the need to 'get an agenda' becomes the focus, whereas a key aim of Stage 1 is about building a relationship and clarification. Without the relationship the rest of the interview is likely to be superficial, and it may be that at the end of the interview the client will say something like, 'What I really wanted to talk about was working in the circus', or 'going back-packing in Australia', or 'I was thinking about going to university, but I guess I am too old', or 'Actually, what I really want to do is leave my current job', and so on.

Case study 10.1: Negotiating the contract and agreeing the agenda

Emma is in her first term in year one at university on an undergraduate programme for primary school teaching. She books an appointment to see the career counsellor Jai who works for Student Services within the university. Jai has a professional but friendly approach, and spends time with the opening introductions, clarifying the time they have (50 minutes for this interview) and so on. He asks Emma what she hopes to gain from the interview. Emma is unsure and says she is 'just so fed up with her course'. Jai probes a little and says, 'Tell me a little more about the course and the reasons you are fed up with it,' but Emma appears unable to be specific. 'It's all horrible and I want to leave,' she says, on the verge of tears. Jai does not immediately assume that what they need to talk about is leaving or an alternative to her current course, but decides to get to know Emma a little better first. He changes direction and signals this to Emma, ensuring that she knows he has heard the topic she raised at the start:

'I can see that you are upset Emma and we will come back to how you feel about the course and what we can do about that, but first I'd like to get to know you a bit better, tell me something about your life outside of the course work – what do you like doing?'

Emma talks a little about home, which is a long way away, and how she misses family and friends. Jai adopts the 'tell me a bit more' approach. At home she has many interests and really enjoys cooking and being out and about hill walking, which she does with friends in a club. 'But there aren't many hills here in the city,' she says with a small laugh. Jai asks about friends at the university and Emma says she hasn't really made any yet and he wonders out loud what attracted her to a city campus university, 'I thought it would be fun – it's certainly different,' responds Emma.

Jai is beginning to question whether it is the course or maybe being away from home and not finding good enough friendships yet that might be the real issue here. He has avoided running with the first topic presented to him and thinks, now is the time to clarify the issues. He summarises what he has heard so far and then moves on:

(Continued)

(Continued)

'You were clear that you do not like your course – it's all horrible, you said, and I'm also hearing Emma that you are missing home, family, friends, cooking and the hill walking. Before we talk about the course, tell me something about choosing primary school teaching for higher education.' Emma says, 'I've always wanted to be a primary school teacher, I love children and I really enjoyed the work experience in my local primary school.' Jai listens and reflects back some of Emma's words, 'You always wanted to be a primary teacher and you really enjoyed the work experience. So, I'm wondering why this course is not meeting your expectations and I'm also concerned about how you are feeling about being away from home. What do you think is upsetting you the most at the moment Emma?' Jai wants to be sure that alongside the topic Emma presents with, he is also providing her with an opportunity to explore related issues.

Emma looks thoughtful and says she thinks it is both. 'OK', says Jai, 'What do you think about spending some time exploring both points – your dislike of your course and missing home?' Emma agrees and Jai says, 'We have about 40 minutes Emma, where do you want to start?'

With some clients, where ongoing career counselling and coaching is available, it may take several sessions of rapport and trust building to achieve an agenda at the end of Stage 1. Even so, each meeting will have a structure: a beginning – Stage 1; a middle – Stage 2; and an end – Stage 3 (Culley and Bond, 2011). And, returning to the point that this is a framework into which other approaches can fit, if you go back to the narrative career counselling model outlined in Chapter 7, you will see how the opening questions resonate with Stage 1 of SIM.

Stage 2 SIM: Developing issues and identifying goals (Reid and Fielding, 2007; preferred scenario, Egan, 2007)

- The person is helped to explore the issues in greater depth.
- Possible options for the future are discussed.
- Through discussion, sharing of information and evaluation of possible options, realistic goals are identified.

At this stage in the process the client is encouraged to explore potential options and identify possible future goals that are appropriate for them. Goals can be small or large, immediate or longer term – it will depend on the circumstances. They may relate to targets or achievements along the way, before reaching the future or final goal. As outlined in a previous chapter when solution-focused work was examined, achieving small short-term goals can engender a sense of agency: a relatively small success is motivating, enabling the individual to move towards larger and long-term goals in and for the future. So, together the aim is to consider options and goals that are most appropriate and relevant, in relation to the client's values, abilities, aspirations, resources, context and needs.

As in Stage 1, before moving to Stage 3, there is a need to focus at the end of Stage 2 and work towards agreed and explicit goals. We should remember that this remains a learning process and is rarely linear, but during Stage 2 the client can be introduced to a number of strategies for exploring options and making choices. Horizons change for people on the move (Hodkinson and Sparkes, 1997) and when working with a client over a period of time the goals will change, but progress and positive outcomes remain the aim. The skill of summarising is important throughout the interview, but is always essential before moving to the next stage – for checking understanding and ensuring deeper reflection.

Case study 10.2: Developing issues and identifying goals

Emma decides she wants to think about missing home first, 'but it's really important that I sort myself out about the course'. Jai agrees and says, 'Tell me some more about the cooking and the hill walking first.' He had noticed Emma's energy when she talked about this and wants to stay with that energy for a bit longer. Jai wonders if Emma has looked into the activities offered at the university and Emma says she had a quick look at a leaflet but has not followed anything up yet. Emma talks about going out with her friends at home too, and how important family is to her. He asks about her accommodation and Emma says she has her own room in halls of residence, with a shared kitchen and the students nearby seem all right but she's not sure. Jai says, 'How do you think you might break the ice with them?' Emma says she is not sure, but will think about it some more. Jai senses that it is time to move to the issue of the course. He summarises their discussion about missing home to check he has understood this and for Emma to hear and reflect on what has been said so far, and then asks if Emma would now like to discuss the course – she does.

'OK, so tell me about the work experience first, what made it enjoyable?' Emma talks about the work experience with enthusiasm and Jai is convinced that she understands what is involved in primary school teaching and that her interest is genuine.

(Continued)

(Continued)

He moves on, 'So, what were you hoping the course would be like before you started here, Emma?' Jai begins to explore more deeply and uses appropriate challenging skills, so that they are both clear with regard to what is problematic with the course.

During this discussion Jai uses questioning in a way that keeps the rapport, but gets to the heart of the issue, 'I'm a bit confused, Emma. From all that you have said, the course is offering what you expected but clearly you are not happy and I'm wondering why that is.'

Emma thinks and Jai waits for her to gather her thoughts. 'Well,' says Emma, 'I just feel so lonely and I probably look miserable all the time which is probably not good for getting friends [sighs]. I'm pathetic; I find it difficult to engage with the course and I just go back and stay in my room mainly.'

Jai responds, 'You are being a bit hard on yourself, it is normal to feel a bit lonely, isolated sometimes when you first come away from home to university – particularly when you have friends and fun at home and have not found friends or fun here yet. Can I be clear then Emma, is it still leaving your course we are talking about, or leaving the university, or something else?'

'No, I don't want to leave the university and I've always wanted to be a primary school teacher, but there is no course nearer to home [pause]. Thinking about it now, talking with you, I guess it is the loneliness that is the main issue, not the course,' says Emma.

They continue to clarify this and then work towards goals to address the loneliness, thinking about the importance of making new friends and finding out more about activities that she could join – and ways of staying in touch with home. Jai summarises what they have talked about in Stage 2 and checks that they are still working on the issues that are important for Emma. He notices that she has been looking more hopeful, although sees that she is now frowning. He feeds this back to Emma and she laughs and says, 'Sorry I had drifted away there for a second – I was thinking about what you asked earlier about breaking the ice – I'm really good at making cakes, I could try that maybe?' 'That would work as an ice breaker for me!' says Jai, smiling.

Stage 3 SIM: Designing, planning and implementing action (Reid and Fielding, 2007; getting there, Egan, 2007)

- Possible courses of action are identified.
- The benefits of particular courses of action are discussed and evaluated.
- Specific action to be carried out is agreed.

Having identified goals, the work moves on to think about the action that can be taken, action that enables the individual to achieve the goals that have been identified in Stage 2 of the process. What is important here is that a range of action steps are identified and that the client selects the action that seems most appropriate, and within their capabilities for the goals (small or large, short-term or long-term) that have been agreed. For some clients, who have less agency, some agreed action will also be undertaken by the practitioner. Working collaboratively, the practitioner and the client will design an action plan, usually, but not always, recorded. Depending on the contract, there may be a follow-up career conversation where implementation and adjustment of the action plan is discussed and agreed.

Nearing the end of the interview there can be a tendency to rush Stage 3, but time needs to be invested in ensuring that the potential action is evaluated – the skill of challenging is often required. There is a danger at this point that the practitioner can 'take over' and start telling the client what to do, but the work needs to remain person-centred and open questions are still relevant. In this way there is a greater chance that the client will 'own' the action and be able to carry it out.

Case study 10.3: Designing, planning and implementing action

When they move to the final stage of the interview, Jai is keen that the action they agree comes from Emma, rather than from a list of things he thinks will be useful. Emma makes suggestions based on what they have discussed, and Jai encourages her gently when her response is a bit vague. 'So when you say you might find out about clubs and so on, what would stop you doing this, Emma – am I hearing something getting in the way?'

'Well,' says Emma, 'The leaflet I had was all about debating clubs and other highbrow stuff – not really me.' Jai clarifies that there is a much wider range of activities than this and they agree to pick up information in reception when they have finished. They agree on one or two other ideas and when Emma will be able to take action.

Jai thinks they have probably worked hard enough today and checks with Emma if they have covered what she needed to discuss. He returns to what she said at the start of the interview and asks Emma to reflect on her feelings now and what they have achieved during the session. Although Emma feels more positive about the course and thinks her dislike is about being away from home and not the higher education choice she made, Jai clarifies that if this turns out not to be the case, she can come back and see him again. Emma says she will. 'And you don't have to bring cake,' says Jai.

You might be surprised that the case study to illustrate the use of SIM was not about a 'straightforward' need to explore a career option or decision: this was deliberate. It was designed to emphasise that career counselling is complex and not about giving information and advice. Often the presenting topic ('the course is horrible and I want to leave') can mask a deeper issue which needs to be explored.

A further note on applying the model

It is worth repeating that the length of time spent on any one stage of the process will depend on the client's needs, the context of the work and the amount of time the practitioner is able to commit to the work. Assessing need is a diagnostic task that is more or less formal depending on the circumstances (as discussed in a previous chapter). A well-known model of assessing needs is provided by Maslow. A consideration of this here can remind us not to work with a client above or below their current position, in what Maslow termed the 'hierarchy of needs'; a summary follows.

Maslow's (1970) theory of motivation and personality states that there are human needs and motivations which are universal, and which can be seen to follow a pattern as each need is satisfied, within a 'hierarchy of needs', depicted in a pyramid diagram. At the base, the first level, there are physiological needs. This first level refers to the essential requirements which must be satisfied if we are to survive, such as hunger or thirst. When these baseline needs are met, others emerge. Once the physiological needs are satisfied, social requirements, termed safety needs, must be satisfied: these include shelter, security, stability, dependency, protection, and the need for structure. Following the satisfaction of the safety requirements, at the second level, the need for love, the giving and receiving of affection and belongingness emerges. Next, esteem needs emerge, when satisfied, leading to feelings of self confidence, self worth, capability and adequacy. Finally, at the top of the pyramid, 'self-actualisation' needs emerge, and if satisfied result in self fulfilment and the ability to become what one is capable of becoming. The theory does not assume that individuals will reach the stage of self-actualisation, but Maslow stated that humans have an innate drive to reach this point. Once again we can critique this as being a Western ideology, but Maslow's theory goes some way to link the individual to the social structures they inhabit. In other words, it is a theory that moves away from psychological perspectives that pay inadequate attention to the social context.

At the beginning of the chapter, SIM was described as an initial framework. In the training of career practitioners, who may go on to work in a range of settings, experience suggests that this framework provides a useful structure that the career counsellor or coach can adapt to include and incorporate a range of approaches. It remains important that the career counsellor or coach understands the model that they wish to apply, and its theoretical underpinnings, but the framework offers a good foundation for that development.

Reflection point 10.2

The model presented (SIM) as illustrated took place in a one-to-one setting. However, it may be the case that the client is not used to making decisions on their own, whether or not this is a cultural norm. Think for a moment about how the dynamic in the interaction changes if a parent or significant other is present? Does the model still work? What would be different?

Novice practitioners may worry about the presence of a parent or partner in the career interview. Yet, they can be a useful resource, in terms of adding relevant information, providing support and working with the client to make action happen. As appropriate to the cultural context, the career counsellor will need to use their skills to ensure that it is the client's interests that are the focus when a parent or partner is involved. In my own experience, the normal response from a parent present in a career conversation is, 'Thank you, I wish I had had this help when I was making career and educational decisions.' I once interviewed identical twins with both parents present: it took more time, but was successful. Without doubt it was challenging, but it was what the family wanted – insisting that I interviewed each twin on their own would have alienated the 'group'.

Alternative models

Although a detailed model has been provided in this chapter, a career conversation can follow a simple beginning, middle and end structure as advocated by Culley and Bond (2011). In his work on practical counselling and helping skills, Nelson-Jones (1997: 41) uses a five-stage DASIE lifeskills model. Depicted in the shape of a daisy, the five stages are:

- D – develop the relationship and clarify the problem(s)
- A – assess and restate problem(s) in skills terms
- S – state goals and plan interventions
- I – intervene to develop lifeskills
- E – emphasise take-away [the benefits] and end.

Nathan and Hill (2006) utilise a three-stage model where 'client' tasks and 'counsellor' tasks are identified for each stage. The stages are:

- screening, contracting, exploring;
- enabling client's understanding;
- action, outcome and endings.

Nathan and Hill state that there is a relationship between career counselling, career guidance, personal coaching and career coaching, but that their text has a focus on the career aspects in a client's life. They note that:

> People coming for career counselling are often unclear about their career direction. Coaching aims to enable people to become more effective in their current careers. There is overlap, but there is also a distinction. (Nathan and Hill, 2006: 2)

As in this text, they suggest that the boundaries are not as clear as we may think. For example, when working as a career counsellor in a public service, independently or in an HR role within an organisation, there will be many occasions when career counselling (and coaching) may overlap with personal counselling. And career coaching may also be about coaching clients to be successful in obtaining a job.

Activity 10.2

Issues may not be obvious at the start of an interaction and they may not be the stated or even conscious reasons that the client has sought career counselling or coaching (with or without an explicit topic). What could be the personal concerns that emerge in career counselling and career coaching? List these and compare with my list at the end of the chapter.

The work of Julia Yates has been referred to earlier in the book as a source for career coaching. Yates (2011) uses the GROW model from the field of coaching (Alexander, 2006; Whitmore, 2002) as a framework for career coaching interventions. The roots of the model are located in behavioural psychology. Yates suggests that it is a straightforward approach that is easy to explain to clients, when doing so is beneficial. There are four stages to the model which are summarised below:

1. **G**oal – identifying what the client wishes to achieve during the session.
2. **R**eality – exploring the goal further by an in-depth understanding of what is 'going on' for the client right now.
3. **O**ptions – generating options and then analysing and evaluating them logically, but also instinctively (this then balances the evaluation which combines the rational and emotional views of the client).
4. The **W**ay Forward – agreeing steps related to goals and the planning of action.

Yates notes, as in other models described here, that it is the client who takes responsibility for the content of the interview, whilst it is the practitioner's responsibility to manage the process. Agreed action, beyond the interview, in any model needs to be 'doable' – SMART (specific, measurable, achievable, realistic and time-bound).

The final alternative that there is space for in this chapter, derives from Arulmani and Nag-Arulmani (2004) who have developed 'a systemic approach to career counselling that is theory-driven and based on research findings from the Indian context' (2004: 119). Although it is a culturally sensitive model developed through their work in India and the region, that should not lead us to suppose that it is only relevant in that part of the world. With global migration many practitioners need a range of approaches that pay attention to culture and the potential needs of clients whose value base is more collectivist in ethos, rather than Western/individualist.

The model has a focus on a number of developmental tasks and is described as the career preparation process model of career counselling. In summary, it asks the career counsellor to pay attention to the following aspects when thinking about the career preparation of the client: (a) the role of the significant other(s) within a particular community in terms of the client's aspirations; and (b) the socio-economic status of the individual and the career beliefs that will govern their action (linked to the previous aspects, this includes what they think is possible in terms of aspirations). Based on a number of propositions derived from the key aspects above, the client's self-efficacy beliefs (coupled with their socio-economic status – SES) are shaped into valuing earning or learning, sooner or later, in a career development life span. Those with lower SES seek work at the earliest opportunity, while those with higher SES are more likely to have higher self-efficacy beliefs and seek further education. As discussed in an earlier chapter, self-efficacy is the extent or strength of a belief in one's own ability to complete tasks and reach goals (Bandura, 1977).

There will be many shades of variation and the summary above reduces the complexity of the theory and approach, but it alerts us, once again, to the need to consider socio-economic status. For example, Appadurai (2007) highlights that barely 20 per cent of the world's population has the luxury of making choices when it comes to career. SES may have a greater influence not only on the opportunities that might be available, but also on how clients value the options that are presented to them by a career counsellor or coach (in any context where they have relatively low socio-economic status). In collectivist societies this difference is likely to be even more acute. In the career preparation process, Arulmani and Nag-Arulmani state that alongside paying attention to the individual's physical, cognitive and social maturation, 'social cognitive factors and social learning experiences **concurrently** influence this process' (2004: 128 – my emphasis).

Refection point 10.3

You do not have to share this reflection with anyone else – but have your self-efficacy beliefs affected the choices you have made at any time? Look back at the activity 10.1 and think about this some more.

Chapter summary

In the move to more practical matters, this chapter has provided an initial framework for structuring career conversations – the Single Interaction Model (SIM). It was noted that this work derives from the counselling work of Egan (itself an integrated model) and has been adapted for work of a shorter time span. By referring to the framework as a single interaction model, we should not think it can only be used once with a client. Its adaptation was specifically for careers work and, as we will see in a later chapter, it can also be used for shaping group work. SIM has been used successfully for a number of years, but there are other models which are also useful and some of these have been outlined within the chapter.

Further reading

Arulmani, G. and Nag-Arulmani, S. (2004) *Career Counselling. A Handbook*. New Delhi: Tata McGraw-Hill Publishing.
As noted in the chapter, this book offers a model that is culturally tailored to so-called 'developing economies', but its value is not limited to this. A range of theory is used and adapted, and the text will be useful in any multicultural or transcultural setting.

Nathan, R. and Hill, L. (2006) *Career Counselling* (2nd edn). London: Sage.
This is a practical guide that is very good at describing relevant tools and techniques useful for careers work. Of particular interest in this second edition is the content on providing career counselling within organisations.

Reid, H.L. and Fielding, A.J. (2007) *Providing Support to Young People: A Model for Structuring Helping Relationships*. London: Routledge.

Chapter 10 and the next draw extensively on this text which was written for a variety of professionals working to support young people. Although aimed at the youth sector, the skills and the framework apply to work with adult clients. It is full of practical help and case studies to inform the development of effective careers work.

Activity 10.2: My responses

These draw on those listed by Nathan and Hill (2006: 3) and include 'redundancy, retraining, relocation, retirement, relationships at work, promotion, career breaks and stress'. Your list may have a different focus if for example you work with young people, and may consist of other concerns related to educational achievement or failure, peer relationships, family circumstances and other challenges associated with the age group of the client. The list can be even wider and include, for any age group, financial concerns, housing, health, bullying and so on. There are boundary issues and we need to understand the limits of our expertise and know when to offer a referral, but the point is that the wider context of a client's life will have a significant influence: the need for counselling skills (discussed in the next chapter) to manage career conversations should be clear.

11

Developing skills and techniques for career counselling and coaching

This chapter will:

- discuss the significance of non-verbal communication;
- explain 'basic' and advanced counselling skills;
- refer to a number of techniques that are useful for careers work.

Introduction

In the previous chapter, ways of structuring career interviews were explored; this chapter outlines the skills that are essential for effective careers work. Alongside the use of 'basic' and advanced skills, a number of techniques will be referred to that can aid reflection and action for both the practitioner and the client. Before discussing either of these aspects that are, largely, associated with talking, it is important to consider non-verbal communication and revisit the 'core conditions' of empathy, respect and congruence.

Non-verbal communication

In Reid and Fielding (2007: 69–70) a categorisation of non-verbal communication is offered.

Dimension	Example
Proximity	Closeness, distance, ability to touch
Posture	Leaning forwards or backwards Tense, rigid, relaxed, facing, turned away

Dimension	Example
Facial expression	Expressive, blank, smiling, frowning
Gaze	Staring, avoiding eye contact
Gesture	Amount, variety
Touch	Intimate, aggressive, avoidance

Communication is two-way of course and while observing the client's body language, we also need to be aware of the messages we send via our own non-verbal communication. And, as argued earlier in the book, we need to be mindful that body language varies across groups and cultures; as one example, avoiding eye contact conveys a different meaning in different cultural groups. In a Western context, each person looks at the other for around 50 per cent of the time, but 'mutual gaze' occupies only about 25 per cent of the time, during 'looking while talking'. However, this is not sustained eye contact, but glances that last about three seconds and mutual glances of about one second (Reid and Fielding, 2007); and we should note that sustained eye contact in any culture can be rather threatening.

Non-verbal messages can tell us many things and may conflict with the words that a client is using. For example, in evaluating the action that is being agreed in Stage 3 of SIM, a client may say, 'I could try to go to the college open day,' and at the same time frown and look away. We should at that point wonder if they are committed to this action. The verbal message is 'I will try', the non-verbal message is 'but I'll fail'. Our response could be, 'You say you will try but I'm picking up that it may be difficult. What would stop you going?' It may be that they are unsure of the location of the college, or that they had a previous negative experience, or they do not like using public transport or, more prosaically, this is the practitioner's idea of a good plan and the client is simply not interested enough. Para-verbal communication will also affect communication and refers to the sounds we make as we listen, which can be encouraging or not; for instance 'Ah' can indicate understanding, whilst a sigh might suggest irritation or boredom.

Other considerations with regard to non-verbal communication might include awareness of habits that may affect the relationship. For example, a practitioner who constantly clicks a pen or repeatedly gets up to find or look up information will not achieve rapport. The taking of notes can also be a barrier. From the client's point of view, the notes can seem more important than what they have to say and may cause them to withdraw their engagement. If note-taking is required, notes should be minimal, explained to the client so that they know why notes are being taken and if a record is kept, a client should be advised how notes will be stored. Note-taking should also be visible, so the client can see what is being written and the end result shared (i.e. they should have a copy).

Activity 11.1

If you are on a training programme for counselling skills you should have opportunities to practise, but it can be useful to practise in other social encounters. The next time you are with a friend, try to notice how many times you interrupt each other. To emphasise the importance of appropriate non-verbal communication, you could try the following. With a colleague or friend, ask them to tell you about a recent event, holiday or outing. As they speak, do not interrupt but keep your face straight (no smiling), look away repeatedly, sigh, fiddle with a pen, nod occasionally but do not engage with the story. They will soon 'dry up'. Swap and place yourself on the receiving end of unhelpful, non-verbal communication and then discuss how it feels.

Before moving on, it is important to remember that the use of any skill is taking place in a professional and respectful relationship. To be effective the practitioner will demonstrate the core conditions of empathy, congruence and unconditional positive regard (UPR) (Rogers, 1961).

Reflection point 11.1

What is your understanding of the sentence: 'To be effective the practitioner will demonstrate the core conditions of empathy, congruence and unconditional positive regard'? The core conditions were discussed in Chapter 5 – if your thoughts were unclear reread this section in Chapter 5 now, before continuing.

'Basic' counselling skills

I always struggle with the word 'basic' to describe these important skills which provide the essential foundation for effective work. 'Basic' in its true meaning suggests essential, fundamental, but in everyday speech might suggest something more minimal – hence the scare quotes. 'Foundation skills' does not appear grammatical and foundational is also problematic, so take from this discussion that basic skills are vital, crucial, central and so on.

Attending and listening

Attending and listening skills are fundamental for effective helping to take place and their importance cannot be over-emphasised. We have all experienced the feeling that we 'have not been listened to' at some time. This may make us feel dismissed, misunderstood or not accepted and can affect our self-esteem, as well as our confidence about our thoughts and feelings. (Reid and Fielding, 2007: 70)

The activity above is a demonstration of 'not being listened to'. Attending and listening skills are relatively easy to describe but do require practice to use effectively; in other words we cannot assume that we are 'naturally' good listeners. In normal conversation we interrupt, make comments, tell our own related stories, but listening and attending in a counselling interaction is very different. Drawing on the discussion so far, an experienced practitioner will demonstrate the following verbal and non-verbal skills (Reid and Fielding, 2007):

- *Verbal following*: comments that follow directly from what the speaker is saying, following what is being said by asking related questions and making comments, using para-verbal sounds, but without changing the subject or expressing judgments. In reflecting back in this way the practitioner demonstrates understanding, gains clarification and acknowledges that they have heard what the client has said, whilst staying with the client's agenda.
- *Non-verbal*: aspects of attending and listening are also demonstrated through body language and give other feedback signals to aid communication between the speaker and listener.
- *Posture*: adopting an open and relaxed posture gives the impression of having an open mind, helping to put the person at ease.

Activity 11.2

To follow up on the previous activity it would be useful to practise attending and listening skills for 'getting it right'. This time use appropriate body language, non-verbal and para-verbal signals, avoid interruption, but use 'verbal following skills', maybe using the phrase, 'Tell me more about …' to encourage further exploration. Again, it is always useful to be both the talker and the listener to experience how it feels from both perspectives, so swap roles and then discuss.

Questioning skills

Questioning skills are aimed at helping the client to reflect on their reasons for seeking career counselling or coaching; they will involve short and longer exploration and are used for checking and clarification. There are several types of questions, used for different purposes and outcomes. Questioning is a fundamental skill and the types need to be understood. The following is adapted from Reid and Fielding (2007: 72–3):

- *Open questions* – these are questions that are difficult to answer with just 'yes' or 'no'. They provide an opportunity to explain the issue and to describe thoughts, feelings and experiences. Open questions tend to begin with 'how', 'what', 'where' and may include 'why' questions; although care needs to be taken with 'why', as it can be over-challenging if used too early in the relationship. 'Why' can sound like 'come on – justify yourself'. Using the right tone of voice with, 'Tell me what…' or 'Tell me how'… is more collaborative than, 'Why do you…?' But there is a place for 'why' questions, and when used, they can be softened by asking, 'I'm wondering why…' or 'Tell me why…'. Of course, 'Tell me' is not a question: it creates an opening, as it is an invitation rather than a command for information.
- *Closed questions* – in contrast to open questions, they tend to demand 'yes' or 'no' answers. They begin with 'do you', 'have you', 'would you', 'can you' and so on. If a person is shy or reticent then the safest answer is 'no', to close down the questioning and avoid giving a 'wrong' answer. Closed questions are useful if you need a straight 'yes' or 'no' answer, but open questions are better for exploration and they avoid a 'testing' approach.
- *Leading questions* – these suggest that the practitioner already knows the answer and the client may find it hard to disagree, and thus leading questions increase any power imbalance in the relationship. They are very limiting if not misleading, close down the desire for a collaborative approach and are best avoided. We are often unaware that we are 'leading' and 'putting words in other people's mouths'. Every leading question comes with a value judgment from the practitioner, e.g. 'You wouldn't be interested in that, so what else …' (i.e. I have decided that option is not right for you).
- *Multiple questions* – these confuse people by demanding several responses at once. A variation is marathon questions; these are so long that by the time the question is ended no one (including the practitioner) really knows what was being asked in the first place.
- *Double questions* – present only two 'either/or' choices, and restrict instead of widening options. They can be useful when asking the person to compare and contrast ideas, but not when the intention is to open up ideas about potential options or courses of action.
- *Hypothetical questions* – these are useful to help a client to think about a possible option or goal, or the implications of that goal for their circumstances. They often start with, 'If you were … what …'

- *Supplementary questions* – these are used for reflecting back and clarification and require careful listening and attending.
- *Restatement* – this is a summary in a questioning form or tone that helps to reflect the client's message back to them and is useful for checking understanding. Sometimes restating one word that the client used with emphasis can be very powerful, enabling them to think about why the word was important in the expression of their view.

Using silence

Alongside active listening and questioning skills is the skill of using silence. Used sensitively this can encourage the client to reflect more deeply and expand further. In normal conversation we rarely use silence, but usually fill up the empty spaces. In career counselling and coaching conversations we need to give the person time to think – particularly when we ask a question that may be challenging. It takes experience and confidence to resist the temptation to rescue the client when there is a silence. Indeed, we might think of this skill as an advanced skill, but it is one we need to practise from the start. So, avoid 'leaping in' too quickly; use silence and if the person is struggling too much to respond, it will be more fruitful to think about the question that you just asked. Rephrase the question, for example, 'Hmm, that wasn't very clear so let me put that another way' or, 'I didn't express that very well, let me try again.' In any conversation, using silence appropriately and more often can be enabling for others, but clearly overdoing this has the opposite effect.

Rapport building

Rapport building skills are essential when working alongside the client, to create a working alliance of openness and trust. Self-presentation (for example, how we appear to the client, how we greet them, our use of non-verbal communication) is important and the practitioner should demonstrate UPR (Rogers, 1961). All the aspects of communication, verbal and non-verbal, discussed above will, if used effectively, enhance rapport (or undermine it, if not). Using the client's name during the discussion is an obvious way of maintaining rapport. Something to avoid is the continuous use of 'you', as in, 'What do you need to do/think about?' Using 'we' is more collaborative, and using 'other people', can take the pressure off the intensity of using 'you' all the time. Building rapport is vital at the start of the conversation, but has to be maintained throughout the relationship – through the use of the basic skills. Summarising is another important basic skill which signals that the client has been heard and that the practitioner is working to the client's agenda rather than their own.

Summarising

Summarising 'sums up' ideas, thoughts and feelings, but summaries are not used merely as ending points or conclusions – they should be used appropriately throughout the discussion. Summaries clarify understanding, provide focus and a sense of direction. They reflect back what has been said and the agreed action to be taken, both within and beyond the interview. They can be a powerful way of providing an opportunity for the client to reflect and question their own thinking. When the client hears their ideas reflected back to them, via a summary, this can be affirming; particularly if they have not had a chance to verbalise their thoughts previously.

Summaries are essential prior to focusing between stages in an interview (see Figure 10.2). For example, at the end of Stage 1, they are a means of drawing the initial, exploratory discussion together, and identifying clearly the agenda and issues for further discussion. They help both parties to think about where to start, or where to go next, and indicate the direction for the remainder of the work. Summaries also provide an opportunity to renegotiate the content of the discussion, where needed, which helps to ensure flexibility and maintain rapport – the working alliance. They are very useful when the practitioner, 'loses the thread'. If you are not sure where an interaction is going, the client is probably also lost. A summary helps to get you both back on to the agenda. If you are really lost, be honest and say, 'I've lost the plot a bit here, what did we say earlier that we wanted to focus on…?' or, 'How did we get to this point…?' or, 'We have moved away from our original discussion, let's remind ourselves what that was and think about what might be relevant now?' If the client is engaged, they will be able to work with you to regain an appropriate focus. The metaphor often used with student practitioners is: when you are stuck in a hole – stop digging, use a summary to climb out of the hole and get back on track with the client. And it is often very useful to invite the client to summarise, particularly at the end of an interaction; albeit that needs to be managed in a collaborative way and not introduced as a test of all they can remember.

When first using the skill of summarising it will feel like you are merely repeating what has just been said and you will question its usefulness. With practice you move from repetition to reflective summarising skills and will clarify understanding, achieve focus, 'signpost' what has been achieved and what happens next. A final point here, when there is more than one interview, it is sensible to begin with a short summary of the previous work and a review of any agreed action.

> # Reflection point 11.2
>
> Before looking at advanced skills, review your understanding of the chapter so far – what skills might you find more difficult, why, and how can you work to improve your competence in the use of that skill? It is always useful to note your reflections – in a way that is useful for you – and return to them later as your skills develop.

Advanced skills

The skills already discussed provide the foundation for a collaborative working relationship for career counselling and coaching and are used throughout the work. The skills of information sharing and challenging are advanced skills, and are essential for the exploration in Stage 2 of a three-stage model, and for evaluation and action planning in Stage 3.

Using information

The world is awash with information which we might assume is readily accessible. Careers information is widely available on the internet, but in most cases this comes without any discussion of the relative merits of alternatives. Although it is not a career practitioner's role to decide what is 'good' or 'bad' about any career or educational opportunity, it can be part of the role to help the client to make sense of the information that is available. Gathering, providing and sharing information are all important aspects of careers work, but need to be understood separately.

In the opening stages of the work, the practitioner will be gathering information from the client to aid the initial exploration and clarification (albeit that they may have some information before meeting the individual). This continues throughout the process as new issues and ideas emerge in the work. This is not about 'surveying' the client, however, to gather as much information as possible. It is a thoughtful process to assess what information is needed and why; and this work has to be undertaken within data protection regulations.

Information sharing is a two-way process where both parties contribute. The client is 'knowledgeable' and it is part of the practitioner's role to assess what they know already and what access to further information they may have. The aim of sharing information is to build a clear and full picture without jumping to conclusions about a client's lack of knowledge. When trying to assess the client's knowledge and understanding it is useful to ask questions that stay with their knowledge – in other words, look for the 'spark' or 'hook' that will get or keep the client engaged in the discussion. All too often the novice practitioner will rush to the next question on the list in their heads, instead of staying with the interest, and the client's energy. The advice is to explore the interest first with (again that useful phrase), 'Tell me more about …' to avoid the rush into exploring what else they may need to know. And useful to stress once again, avoid the 'What do you know about…?' question (often repeated), as on the receiving end it sounds like, 'I'm the expert and I know, but I'm going to test how much you know.'

On that point, student practitioners often worry that they will not know the information that a client needs. It is not possible to know everything and information changes rapidly, so what we think we know may be out of date in any case (and when we do think we know, it is not our place to overwhelm the client with our great store of knowledge). The best approach is to be clear about the information that is needed and then discuss ways of finding out. For example a useful response might be, 'I'm not sure and I don't want to give you misleading information, let's think about what we need to know precisely and how we could find out.' Whether or not it is the practitioner, the client and the practitioner, or the client on their own who finds the information will depend on the circumstances.

The ultimate aim is for the client to be enabled to discover information for themselves, not to have it provided for them, in order to increase a sense of ownership in the information seeking process. This is likely to be more motivating when we are adding to a person's knowledge with information that we have both agreed is relevant to their needs. Providing or discovering information can affirm or disprove a client's beliefs about what may be possible and the latter can be quite challenging. New information might suggest that current ideas have unexpected implications, good or bad, or that a service, education and training route or qualification they thought would be available is not. Many clients, depending on their circumstances and needs, will require support to interpret the information, to explore the implications and relevance for their context.

Activity 11.3

Information gathering and information sharing is an advanced skill that requires practice in order to be used effectively and in a collaborative manner. To summarise the above discussion, note down four points on providing and sharing information that you think will inform helpful practice. You'll find my summary points at the end of the chapter.

Challenging

The aim of challenging is to help the client to reflect, evaluate and increase their awareness and understanding, in order to gain a new perspective on a particular idea, thought, behaviour or feeling. Challenging, used sensitively, can help the client to recognise any barriers that are preventing them from identifying and achieving goals, whether these are externally erected or self-imposed. The advanced skill of effective challenging is one that is acquired with experience. A wrongly exercised challenge can do more harm than good; but such cautionary remarks can prevent a student practitioner from using a challenge where it is required. An interview that avoids challenge at all costs (because using the skill is 'too challenging'), becomes a superficial interview that achieves very little. Within a working alliance that pays respectful curiosity to the client and their story, a well timed challenge is illuminating, but it needs practice to make it effective. Westergaard notes that challenging 'is not a natural conversation skill. It is used when:

- There is a discrepancy between words, thoughts and actions;
- Consequences need to be thought through;
- Realism is an issue'. (2011a: 53)

Challenging too soon in the relationship will damage rapport and destroy trust. So how do you do it effectively? Some of the skills already discussed can achieve an effective challenge, i.e. via an open question, a follow-up question, reflecting back a word or phrase, a summary, use of a hypothetical question, through the use of empathy and congruence, and through sharing information. If challenging is for you a new skill, or one you have difficulty with, you will want to explore other texts to gain a greater insight into this powerful but most effective tool (see the list at the end of the chapter). The ultimate aim of challenging is to be helpful, not to make the client 'face reality', but for them to learn to reflect and self-challenge. When using the skill of challenging it is important to keep the following in mind. A challenge needs to be:

- constructive and relevant to the discussion;
- framed in appropriate, clear language;
- well timed;
- sensitive, but not endlessly tentative or apologetic;
- positive in its effects, not judgmental. (Reid and Fielding, 2007: 80)

Challenging the client without sensitivity is like using the 'why' question inappropriately – it can become a very blunt tool. To 'soften' a challenge it can be preceded by the words 'I'm wondering' at the start. Other useful phrases are:

'Something I don't quite understand is…'; or 'Maybe I got this wrong, but earlier you said… I'm wondering now how that fits with …' In these examples the challenge is presented to the client for them to work with the practitioner, in order that understanding can be shared. If the client does not understand the relevance of the challenge, then the practitioner should be open and explain, 'The reason I asked that question is…'

Immediacy is also a challenging skill but is used for a different purpose. A client may be challenged about what they are saying about their thoughts, feelings and actions in relation to issues that are outside of the career conversation with the practitioner. Immediacy would be used when something is not right within the interaction. For example, a client tells you they are 'desperate to see you' and you offer them an earlier appointment than you had originally suggested. However, when you meet they appear withdrawn and are not engaging in the conversation. This happened to me with a student who wanted to discuss her higher education choices. Using immediacy I sought to find out what was wrong in the 'here and now': 'I know you were "desperate" to see me, and yet you don't look comfortable and are not finding it easy to talk to me today – I wonder why that is?' The student then told me that she was in fact suffering with a migraine and felt sick, but knew I had booked her an appointment in my lunch hour so wanted to come. It was then clear that she was not feeling well, so I offered to continue or to rebook for another appointment as soon as was possible for both us – she took the latter option. Ignoring a problem in the interview does not make it go away and using immediacy can bring the issue to the fore and solve the immediate problem. It is a useful skill if the client is displaying any emotion which is having a negative impact on the interview.

In the case study that follows, note the way the practitioner uses both challenge and immediacy, in order to stay with the client's agenda and to explore the issue in more depth. The case study also illustrates a number of other skills, including summarising, using silence and information sharing.

Case study 11.1: Building a working alliance

Dom is a human relations practitioner who also works as a career coach in a large health trust that manages four district hospitals, two of which are teaching hospitals. Gillian is a senior practitioner who has been referred to him by her line-manager, as targets that were agreed at her annual appraisal in the previous year have not been met. The line-manager is concerned about Gillian's commitment to meeting the targets and thinks a conversation with Dom will be helpful. At the start of the interview Dom works hard to build rapport, explains that his role is to be useful to Gillian, uses open questions and tries to encourage her to identify what she would like to get from the session. He asks her about her work and although Gillian is polite, her responses are brief and non-committal and after about 15 minutes, she begins to look cross. Dom emphasises that he is meeting with Gillian to discuss her views about her role and the appraisal and what she wants to happen next, but at this point Gillian responds angrily with, 'This is just ridiculous!'

Dom needs to address Gillian's anger and using the skill of immediacy says, 'I can see that you are angry Gillian and I wonder what I have done to cause this, tell me – what is ridiculous?'

'Oh it's not you,' sighs Gillian, 'I can see you are trying to be helpful, but I'm really angry with my line-manager for sending me here. If they had spent time listening to me, they would know what the problem is, but all they care about are these wretched targets!'

Dom responds, 'OK, so tell me now what the problem is Gillian.'

Gillian's anger has dissipated somewhat as Dom has not ignored her emotion. She tells him about what she views as a lack of support for her role, the high staff turn-over in her department and the 'unreasonable targets' that were set in the previous year. Dom does not interrupt and pays close attention to her story. Gillian feels she has been heard and her mood changes – she is still angry with her manager, but no longer cross with Dom. 'Don't get me wrong, I love the work with patients, it's just all the paperwork, the red tape and the targets that drive me nuts,' says Gillian. Dom summarises what Gillian has told him and checks that his understanding is correct, 'What I'm hearing, Gillian, is a love for the job when working with patients, but frustration about the paperwork and the targets. But it sounds like something needs to change for you to balance the work – what do you want to change?'

Gillian laughs, 'Get rid of the targets! Well, I know they are there for a reason, but really! I guess I should have made more of a fuss last year when my individual targets were set, but I was too busy and couldn't be bothered.'

Dom responds, 'So, I'm wondering then is the issue something to do with communicating this frustration about "unreasonable targets" to your line-manager in a way that can be helpful for both of you?'

Gillian looks thoughtful and Dom waits for her reply. 'Well, I cannot ignore the targets they are externally set for the hospital trust of course, and the ones I get are unreasonable – but it's no good me just accepting them.'

'No good just accepting them.' Dom reflects back Gillian's words and then asks Gillian what would be useful for them to focus on now for the rest of the session. She suggests, 'Maybe thinking about how I can renegotiate my targets.'

(Continued)

(Continued)

As they continue the interview they discuss the bigger picture first. Dom asks Gillian, 'Tell me about the purpose of the targets, Gillian, for the trust and for your department and a little about how these are set, so that I can understand better.' They then move on to explore the goal of renegotiating Gillian's individual targets with her line-manager, and the benefits of being assertive and avoiding being either passive or aggressive. Gillian is engaged in the conversation but when they move from goals to possible action she looks troubled. She says she is not sure when she can get to see her line-manager. Dom notices this.

'We've been talking about how to renegotiate your targets and how to discuss these with your line-manager, but I'm picking up now that this might be difficult. What's stopping you from committing to this action Gillian?'

'To be honest,' says Gillian, 'I'm not sure he will listen and it may all be a waste of time.'

'Well, that is a possibility, but I'm wondering, what is the alternative in your view?' asks Dom.

'Hmm, I do nothing, it gets worse – I leave, which I do not want to do.'

'We could think about this some more if you want to?' offers Dom.

'No,' says Gillian, 'I just need to get on with this and sort it out.' They then move on to agree specific action that is time bound. Before Gillian leaves, Dom asks her what she thinks they have achieved through the discussion and Gillian replies, 'I cannot avoid targets, but at least I can make my views heard in a way that is likely to be more productive. I do love my job, I don't want to leave and every job has its frustrations, but I need to take some responsibility and work towards making the targets more reasonable.'

Techniques useful for careers work

A number of techniques have already been discussed in the book in earlier chapters, but this chapter will outline others that are effective. The purpose of any technique is to enable a client to self-challenge, clarify issues, generate new ideas where needed and to prioritise goals and action. It is useful to be familiar with a range of techniques, as some will be more appropriate than others, depending on the client and the context. In that sense, techniques are part of the 'toolkit' that a practitioner can use. It is salient to keep in mind that if a technique works, you should carry on using it and if it does not, try something else. That is not advocating for a dizzying array of techniques used one after another until something works – it is always important that we understand, practise, use carefully and evaluate our application of theory, skills and techniques.

The following techniques can help the client to clarify, make sense of, or compare ideas and issues that they wish to address, in order to move forward in their thinking. You may already use many of these ideas in your own decision making and planning, for example a 'thought-shower' list of possibilities for action. Other ideas that you are not familiar with, you could add to your 'toolkit'.

'Imagine' is a very simple technique; useful when working with people who lack confidence or assertiveness, or when ideas are vague or unrealistic. To encourage more focused thinking the practitioner asks the client to imagine what it would be like if the ideas were more 'concrete'. The client would be encouraged to describe what it feels like if they were in the new position, where changes had been made and ideas were clear and implemented. If that is not possible to imagine, then the focus can shift to identifying what the problem areas really are, so that these can be discussed and solutions worked on; this will constitute a move forward for the client. Using the imagine technique can be a confidence building exercise, which makes a previously insurmountable problem more manageable. Closely related to this technique is the use of the 'miracle question' which was discussed in an earlier chapter, for example:

'If you woke up tomorrow and you could do the course/job of your dreams, what would that course/job be like?' The follow-up questions then 'search for the detail' to assist the client to reflect further.

'Contrast' is a technique for assisting clients with choices, changes or confusion in order to gain a sharper focus. It works by asking the client to compare whatever issue they are focusing on, with something that is significantly different or opposite. For example, by comparing a city to a 'green field' university campus, staying in a school sixth form or moving to a further education (tertiary) college, applying for different courses or job opportunities and so on. It can also help the client to identify aspects that are hindering change and to consider whether these aspects are less of a difficulty than not making changes. So, for instance, a client may describe what it would be like to have taken action on an option and 'compare and contrast' this with not taking any action; in the latter position, circumstances do not change and remain as they are at present. Alternatively, contrast can be used to consider two or three different, but possible scenarios, through the use of hypothetical 'If you were … then what …?' questions. It is similar to the 'imagine' technique, but used as a means of clarifying thoughts towards alternative options and potentially towards making a choice.

'Gaining figure-ground perspective' is useful when the client is faced with choices and is not sure what to do. The aim of gaining figure-ground perspective is to try and identify the issues or factors that 'stand out' – gain figure ground – from the entirety of their lives (or the rest of the picture). A metaphor that relates to this is when the client 'cannot see the wood for the trees': in other words there is so much going on they cannot focus on what might be most important for them. So the story that is first presented is somewhat muddled – a picture in which nothing stands out as a major focal point. The role of the practitioner is to work collaboratively with the client, within their context, and separate the 'figure' (the central issue of concern that figures in the foreground) from the 'ground' (the details around the issues which form the background). It will not be possible for the client to gain a new perspective until the central issue that is causing a 'problem' has been identified. Via summarising, reflecting, and when appropriate 'sharing a hunch' and saying what you think might be the case, this technique can be a useful way of looking at the situation in order to gain clarity. But, this is exercised in a sensitive and tentative manner, in order to see whether the client shares your perception or not. This technique helps both parties to look at the 'problem' as something that is separate from the client as a person (White and Epston, 1990).

A balance sheet can be used as a decision making tool. The aim is for the client to 'weigh up' the advantages and disadvantages of any idea or plan that is being considered. As a technique it can be used as a method for comparing choices as well as a means of identifying, or increasing awareness of, the consequences of a possible decision. Balance sheets can be very simple, for example, two columns headed 'advantages' and 'disadvantages', or 'for' and 'against'. A more complex balance sheet might involve the pros and cons of two or more options. It is of course the client who identifies the advantages and disadvantages in order to assess if one outweighs the other, and to get a balanced picture of the option. The practitioner may share information if they see a gap in the knowledge that needs to be considered. A case study using a simple balance sheet technique, which is then extended, may be helpful to illustrate this.

Case study 11.2: Three techniques to aid decision making

When working with young people who were considering a career in the armed forces, it was often the case that the inherent danger did not appear in the 'against' column (i.e. they may be injured or killed). My approach would be to, sensitively, frame a challenge, such as, 'We have identified the advantages and the variety, the training and all the exciting things, but I'm wondering what else might put some people off – if for example you had to fight in a war zone?' The answer would identify the potential disadvantage, the danger, and would often receive the follow up response of, 'Well, I'd be trained for that.' But I would be reassured that having shared this information the client had understood the risks, alongside the benefits. When working with a young person, or with a client who may have difficulty accepting there may be disadvantages, it can be useful to talk about 'what's really good' and 'what may put some people off' a particular option.

Having shared a balanced list of advantages and disadvantages, the exercise can be extended to a thought-shower list of the personal qualities and evidence that a selection panel would want to see in an application or at an interview. This works for other education, training and career ideas and is very useful for any option that is likely to have competitive entry. The next activity might be thinking about what the client does now, or could do in the future, that would, therefore, increase their chances of being accepted; because they would be able to demonstrate their interest and suitability as a candidate. At the end of the interview, clients would often ask if they could keep the piece of paper that we had used – the answer was always, 'Of course, it's your interview and these are your thoughts.'

This three step technique works well in a group interview, where you have a small number of clients all wanting to explore a particular career, training or education option. But more on working with groups in the next chapter.

'Force-field analysis' also requires pen and paper (and, it is worth mentioning here that pen and paper exercises can mitigate any pressure built up through too much eye contact and questioning, provided their use is collaborative). The aim of this technique is to identify the positive forces (factors related to particular people, circumstances or resources) that will assist action, and the negative forces (again, factors related to particular people, circumstances or resources) that constrain action. In other words, what will help and what will get in the way. Identifying these positive and negative forces helps to evaluate potential goals and action, and work towards outcomes that are more likely to be 'successful'. In this way the client is forewarned of the constraining forces and aware of the helpful resources, before they embark on any action to reach their goals.

There are other techniques that can be utilised from counselling approaches, as discussed in previous chapters. For example, from solution-focused work: exception seeking, scaling, small steps for achievement, using compliments, searching for the detail and so on. Questions that search for meaning in the client's life were discussed in the use of narrative career counselling, and techniques from other approaches outlined can also be integrated as appropriate.

It is important to approach all of these techniques as shared activities, not as a test of the client's knowledge or a way of demonstrating the practitioner's expertise, but as a strategy to aid joint thinking. To use techniques successfully requires a mixture of familiarity and practice. In other words, you need to be familiar with the method so that you can use it with a certain degree of confidence and you need to experiment with using strategies in practise. The aim is to identify the techniques that you feel most comfortable with but that also, and more importantly, work best for individual clients in particular circumstances. With any advanced skill or use of a technique, timing is critical; alongside a developed understanding of the purpose of using the skill or technique, in unison with that ongoing 'watchfulness' with regard to its usefulness and relevance for the client.

Chapter summary

This chapter has considered the development of skills that are essential for effective communication in career counselling and coaching and has outlined techniques that are useful, as tools for the practitioner's toolkit. It looked at non-verbal communication and highlighted the importance of the messages we give through body language; and once again, raised a warning flag with regard to cultural difference. It explained the 'basic' skills that are essential for career conversations to be effective within a relationship built on unconditional positive regard, and went on to examine the advanced counselling skills required for purposeful work. It ended by referring to a number of techniques that, when working alongside the client, are helpful for the development of critical reflection on the options and decisions that a client is working towards.

Further reading

Culley, S. and Bond, T. (2011) *Integrative Counselling Skills in Action* (3rd edn). London: Sage. All the books in the Sage 'In Action' series are very readable. This is excellent and will provide further insight into the essential skills for counselling interactions.

Nelson-Jones, R. (1997) *Practical Counselling and Helping Skills* (4th edn). London: Cassell. The focus in this text is the development of lifeskills in order to promote change. Although the book's main focus is on counselling in the broad sense, the work details counselling skills and includes numerous practical exercises that are appropriate for careers work.

Reid, H.L. and Fielding, A.J. (2007) *Providing Support to Young People: A Model for Structuring Helping Relationships*. London: Routledge.
Chapter 6 in this text is useful here. Although aimed at the youth sector, the skills and techniques discussed apply to work with adult clients. Case studies and developed examples will extend the reader's understanding.

Westergaard, J. (2011a) 'Exploring person-centred principles and developing counselling skills', in H.L. Reid and J. Westergaard (eds), *Effective Counselling With Young People*. Exeter: Learning Matters.
Westergaard's discussion on the development of counselling skills is deeper than can be covered in this chapter and draws further on the counselling literature. Case studies exemplify the use of a range of relevant foundational and advanced skills.

Activity 11.3: My summary points

Practitioners need to:

- check the client's understanding of the information that is being shared, or what they are finding out during the process;
- work collaboratively with the client to obtain their views on how the information can be applied;
- be attentive to the client's reactions to the information that is being shared or discovered; observe their body language and ask them about their views or how they feel about what they are finding out;
- avoid overwhelming the client with information – we may be assuming they do not know already, and if too much information is given the client will not be able to absorb it and will not remember.

12

Supporting career learning and development in a range of contexts

This chapter will:

- explore the term career learning and development;
- consider the benefits of knowing about the labour market;
- discuss the significance of networking skills;
- list the advantages of careers work provided in group settings;
- introduce the three-stage model for structuring group interventions;
- emphasise the importance of a policy for learning and development in organisations.

Introduction

'Careers education' does not just happen in schools. In this chapter, the more nuanced term of 'career learning and development' will be introduced for a range of contexts within which people are supported with their learning about self and career. One distinction between career guidance and therapeutic counselling is the need for occupational information and labour market intelligence. The data are widely available, and in the previous chapter the sharing of information effectively in one-to-one interactions was considered in order to enhance clients' autonomous career decision making. Labour market intelligence is a more active term than labour market information and this distinction will be examined in the discussion. Useful information to support career learning and development is not limited to objective data sources such as job descriptions, educational and training routes into occupations, vacancy information or examples of CV writing and so on. To advocate on behalf of clients, when appropriate, career practitioners also need good networking skills, to work in partnership with other helping agencies and opportunity providers. Thus, in a fluid labour market, practitioners need more than one-to-one counselling skills to work effectively with clients; these skills, which are also essential for the development of their own careers, will be mentioned.

One particularly important area for skill development is the ability to offer career counselling and coaching in group settings: this is the focus of the second part of the chapter. Often this can be seen as a way of saving on costs and meeting the needs of many in a single session, but there are other advantages in learning about self and career in a group setting. A process for applying the three-stage model, described in Chapter 10, for group work will be outlined, with a focus on planning and negotiating a contract with a group. The chapter ends with an acknowledgement of the importance of a specified approach to learning and development within organisations.

Career learning and development

Barnes et al. (2011) explain that the term 'career learning and development' (CLD) is a better fit with the contemporary world of work than outdated notions of careers education, which were often based on a matching approach derived from positivist psychology.

Reflection point 12.1

Before we go further, what does the term careers education mean to you? Did you have careers education lessons at school? What did these cover and, looking back, what was your impression of the usefulness of these?

Your response and recollections will depend on where and when you went to school. My guess is that in terms of usefulness the reflections will be mixed, according to how organised, innovative and engaging the programme of careers education was in your school (if you had such a programme). There has been a long debate as to whether careers education should be a standalone topic or integrated within other subjects, and there are arguments for and against both of these options. Often the value of careers education 'lessons' is questioned because it is not linked to a curriculum subject that is examined, leading to a formal accredited qualification.

However, schools that value independent learning, civic participation, aspirational development, diversity (in terms of opportunities beyond school) and entrepreneurship are more likely to see the contribution that career learning and development can make to the whole school curriculum. Within and beyond the school, learning about self and learning about career take place in a social setting, and knowledge about both is constructed via interactions with others. The others here can be teachers and other professionals, peers, family and communities, and the learning is shaped by social circumstances, individual psychology and ongoing experiences in a changing context.

The settings within which this takes place also vary. Within schooling, careers education suggests a programme of teaching for learning about career (from the 1990s often with the 's' dropped to highlight that this is about an individual being educated for their career pathway, rather than information about all careers). The scope of such career education in the UK varied, but input for school students was located within personal, social and health education lessons as a statutory require-ment. That requirement is no longer in place, but the need for learning about self and career, and preparing for future options in education, training and work, would be recognised by the majority of schools. The difficulty in times of austerity is the com-petition for limited resources; however, the value of career learning and development should not be underestimated. Schools are expected to support young people in their transition to adulthood and providing a career learning and development programme within the curriculum can be an effective way of achieving this. A narrow approach which views the provision of career information via the internet, plus the occasional inspiring employer to give talks to students, is unlikely to be adequate to meet the needs of young people in what can be a mystifying world of opportunities. Where schools operate with a career practitioner offering one-to-one interviews, but without a career learning and development programme, this may be considered insufficient. A school career counsellor explains in the case study that follows.

Case study 12.1: The benefits of a programme of CLD

Katie is an experienced career counsellor who has worked in a number of senior schools, with students aged 11–18. When asked about the value of career learning and development as part of the curriculum, she responded with the following:

'It is immensely valuable. I used to work with school students from age 13–14 onwards, in lessons, as part of their preparation for making choices throughout their school life, and then again when making transitions from school to college, training or work. So, I would hold sessions about their choices for examination subjects, and the implications for future education and careers at each appropriate stage. These were always interactive sessions where the students would learn about general information and then through various exercises, they would then apply the knowledge to their likes, abilities and their own situation. We would also have days off the normal curriculum, where there would be intensive activities learning about the world of work, preparing for the future, thinking about how to make decisions. We'd have visiting speakers but not just to talk **at** students, they would organise activities – it was fun! That full programme does not happen currently. There is a view by non-experts that guest speakers are all you need to inspire young people – that is not enough in my view and there is no guarantee that invited speakers are going to be inspirational or impartial. And they may not be good at engaging with young people in any case.

So, I now find that when I see students on a one-to-one basis I spend half the time explaining all the things that I used to work through with them in whole group sessions – when career learning and development was part of the curriculum. It is not a very good use of time, and of course cuts down the amount of time that I have to work alongside individual students discussing how that information is relevant for them. If they had spent time on this before the one-to-one interviews, we could work at a much deeper level and I am convinced that would be more useful for them.'

What the case study above suggests is a need for a planned curriculum for career learning and development tailored to suit the needs of students at the various transition points. Bassot et al. (2014) offer a practical guide for developing such programmes for young people aged 11 to 19 in education. Ideas about self and one's place in work, and in community, change over time; as acknowledged when discussing developmental career theory in an early chapter in the book. Moving on from the DOTS model (Law and Watts, 1977) described previously, Bill Law offers a career learning theory (1996) which he continues to develop. He states:

> Notions of career planning based on a once-and-for-all (or even once-in-a-while) review of the options and priorities are weak because both the options and the priorities will change… All this argues for supporting people through a lifelong process of career-related thinking and rethinking, action and new action. (Law, 1996: 46)

Law's previous work on community interaction theory (1981) pays attention to people's encounters with others, in context, in attachments, where social interactions work to construct, in both limiting and/or liberating ways, notions of self and possibilities. Law draws on the work of Krumboltz (1994) and others (for example, Gottfredson, 1981) in the development of his career learning theory. The aim of career learning theory is, in its application, to 'take people to a point where they can recognise the difference between evidence and rhetoric, fact and opinion, argument and leverage' (Law, 1996: 66). There is insufficient space here for a full description of the career learning process described as *sensing*, *sifting*, *focusing* and *understanding* and how career learning and development programmes can be shaped around the theory. For a deeper discussion and understanding, Law's 'career learning cafe' website (www.hihohiho.com) will update you on his latest thinking and the application of his theory to practice.

What has been made clear in the discussion above is that career learning and development can occur, is needed even, at various points in an individual's educational and working life. Thus a programme of career learning and development can be offered to participants in further and higher education, to those seeking work, returning to work or wanting to develop or change occupation, and to others who are exiting from paid employment. Programmes can be tailored to support the specific needs of certain groups (with the usual warning about stereotypical labelling here); for instance this could be based on cultural expectations, additional educational needs, long-term unemployment and so on. Depending on the requirements of the group, sessions may focus on sources for locating opportunities, 'job hunting skills', self-presentation and other aspects that take into account the needs of the group, preferably through a process of consultation and negotiation rather than based on assumed needs.

Many 'adult' jobseekers can make use of readily available self-help books (e.g. Corfield, 2009a, 2009b, 2010a, 2010b). Digital technologies have a central role in helping individuals to access opportunities and can be used for career learning and development, independent of a practitioner, but for many a human interaction is preferable in order to interpret or relate the information to personal circumstances. That said, by definition, the open access of ICT increases the opportunities for inclusive practice (more will be said in the next chapter with regard to digital technologies and career counselling and coaching).

Career coaching is all about learning and development. It can help people learn to identify, develop and refine a range of competences that enable them to secure opportunities and occupations in what is an increasingly competitive job market. In a career coaching setting, clients are most likely to want to gain a job, change occupation or develop within an organisation. But the process is one of enablement rather than 'doing it for them', and career coaching acknowledges that the client has agency and the activity works towards developing and maintaining the client's autonomy. Client autonomy is not a straightforward given; some are more autonomous than others, and an effective coaching programme will be designed with this in mind – according to the capacities of the individual and within the constraints of the agreed contract. Alongside decision making, career coaching can help the client to understand the contemporary world of work, to develop job search strategies, to create a CV that can be adapted to different opportunities, to perfect presentation skills and to learn how to perform well at job interviews.

Whether a practitioner is working as a career counsellor in a school, a career educator in a range of institutions or a career coach, there is an assumption that they will have knowledge about the labour market. A prospective student applying to a career management programme at a university, to become a qualified career practitioner, may think that the course is all about occupational information (the content of different jobs and the qualifications required), plus labour market information (facts and figures on employment and unemployment trends, current industries and regional differences). How important are these aspects for careers work? The next section considers this question, but first what do you think?

Activity 12.1

So, in your view, how would you rate the points below in terms of effective careers work that leads to positive outcomes for the client? Use the following scale: 4 = essential; 3 = important; 2 = useful; 1 = less useful; 0 = not useful.

The practitioner has an extensive knowledge of:

- occupational information;
- labour market information;
- theories that underpin practice;
- skills for interacting with clients and others;
- models to frame interactions with clients;
- presentation and teaching skills;
- current recruitment practices.

I would find that activity hard. My usual response to being asked to rate aspects would be 'it depends'. I would hope that if you have worked through this book from Chapter 1 there would be none of the above viewed as 'not useful'. My expectation is that you would think they were all important and that more than one was essential. I would anticipate also that you reflected on your answers as to why you gave each aspect a particular score. Much may depend on the context that you are working in, or intend to work in, which will rate some aspects higher than others.

Knowing about the labour market

If 'careers information' is in part what defines 'careers work' then how much does a career practitioner need to know? Opinion differs. I have two colleagues who work as independent career practitioners and one thinks occupational information and knowledge of the labour market is essential, and the other disagrees. The first person thinks the client will expect this of a professional career practitioner and not to have this knowledge will weaken the service they offer. My other colleague thinks that it is the client who needs to decide what information they need as a result of the career coaching or counselling session. They make suggestions of where the client can look, but it is the client's responsibility, as an autonomous individual, to find the required information. Yates (2014) also discusses this question and says that you 'will find practitioners at every point in the scale' (2014: 156) in terms of how much is enough. My view resonates with Yates in that some knowledge is useful to ensure that important points are acknowledged and the realities of the world of work or education are considered. In the previous chapter it was emphasised that knowledge/information is shared, with caution, and as appropriate to the needs of the client.

One point worth clarifying is the difference between labour market information and labour market intelligence. As above, labour market information is about facts and figures and is, hopefully, based on objective data. 'Hopefully', as alongside the wide access to career information on the internet, the consumer of this information has to make a judgement on the reliability of the source. Labour market intelligence is the term given to labour market information that is then interpreted and can be applied by individuals for their career decision making. In a programme of career learning and development this would make the objective information 'user friendly'. For example graphs, charts and 'bald' facts need to be understood in context (and the point has been made many times now – contexts vary). Labour market information (LMI) can be gathered according to what is needed for an individual client or group of clients depending on learning level, age, abilities, cultural issues and other variables. A useful site to explore for LMI and to learn how to turn this into 'labour market intelligence', is the National Guidance Research Forum at: www2.warwick.ac.uk/fac/soc/ier/ngrf/

When I trained as a careers adviser, part of that training involved visits to 'opportunity providers', i.e. employers and also training companies and further and higher education institutions. The aim was to develop an understanding of the work, training and education market and also to develop the necessary skills for communication with those providers in order to develop networks that are useful for working with clients. When in practice it was essential that the careers adviser 'knew their patch', thus gaining local labour information was a regular feature of the work. However, for some, building networks can be easier to talk about than achieve, if what attracts people to the work is the one-to-one interactions with clients, rather than 'employer visits'. The ability to network then should not be assumed but is a skill that may need to be acquired.

Reflection point 12.2

What picture comes to your mind when you read that last sentence? Is networking something you do with ease? How would you feel about having to make 'cold' contact with and then visit a large employing organisation in order to increase your labour market intelligence? Or to visit a local plumbing and heating engineer who contacts your organisation to say she is thinking about taking on a trainee?

Networking skills

As in many things, preparation is all. Successful visits are well organised in advance, in terms of time available and setting a clear focus for the meeting. A structure is useful that has a beginning, middle and end, where the purpose of the visit is reviewed, time is discussed and both parties have room to negotiate the content of the meeting. Goals can be clarified during the meeting and action, as relevant to the aims and goals, can be agreed and then taken forward. All this should sound familiar as it is an adaptation of the three-stage model discussed in this book.

Many professionals are good at networking with colleagues in the same profession and career practitioners are no exception. But in the changing world of work, practitioners often have to market their services to others – to their secondary clients (the opportunity providers mentioned above), to organisations and individuals with whom they would like to work and, in many cases, to other professionals. In the case study below a career coach talks about developing networking skills and why he views this ability as important.

Case study 12.2: Who knows you?

Lucas used to work as a careers adviser in a service supporting disadvantaged young people, but when he was made redundant due to a cut in funding for the service, he decided to work independently as a career counsellor and coach.

'Well, it wasn't easy as we had just moved into our own flat – I had a mortgage and we wanted to start a family, so not the best time to be self-employed! But I had my qualification and experience and a bit of severance pay, although that did not amount to much. I had worked with other professionals when supporting young people but this was

(Continued)

(Continued)

different – I had to build new networks. Previously it was relatively easy – someone had been there before if you like, built the contact with the organisation, but now I was on my own. I developed a website but I had to get out there and talk to people. I had not found that easy in the past, for instance at a conference I'd prefer to talk to people I knew, rather than go and introduce myself to someone unknown. But all that had to change, so in building up my contacts I needed to get past that barrier. I asked myself what's the worst that can happen if you go up and introduce yourself or try and make contact by phone or email? I found if I was prepared, had something to say, well, nine times out of ten, it was fine, more than fine – useful. And I do have the skills to ask open questions and to listen. Most people like to talk about their jobs or their organisation, so I found ways to meet people and to get known. When I did the career guidance course, one of the tutors said, 'Forget " it's not what you know but who you know" – for successful networking, the key is *who knows you*'. Turns out, she was right! It takes some effort, but I visited medium and large organisations, schools and colleges and gradually, with my existing contacts and the website, I built up my independent practice as a career counsellor and coach. Now I get work through that networking – I don't need to advertise.'

There are other skills and competences that a practitioner can gain for their own career development, for example for service management, research and scholarly activity, training other colleagues and so on. Standards and competences for professional practice were discussed in an early chapter in the book and a list of the competences that have been identified as essential, depending on the practitioner's role, are provided in Appendix 1.

Careers work in group settings

Earlier it was suggested that learning about self and career in group settings is a valuable aspect of careers work. This has been recognised within some, but not all, training courses and programmes for career practitioners (Higgins and Westergaard, 2001). The skills are similar to, but not the same as, teaching a curriculum subject. The difference is the greater extent to which the learning can be applied to the individual and their future choices and decision making. 'Careers work in group settings' does not mean doing a 'careers interview' with four or more people. The focus in what follows is on career learning via group activities. This section will now move on and consider this in more detail. Those working as career coaches would probably say that you cannot coach a group of people;

career coaching is about working with individuals. However, career learning and development 'delivered' in group settings has many advantages that can underpin one-to-one careers work. The benefits will be discussed first before a model for structuring the work is introduced.

Aside from career learning and development programmes, it is worth noting that a critical study by Thomsen (2012) has challenged established ways of thinking about the predominance of the one-to-one 'delivery' of careers work. Her analysis suggests that it is the community rather than the individual that should be the starting context to begin the process of career guidance. In other words, Thomsen views working in a group context as more effective for many clients, of varying ages, in terms of the career learning and development achieved. She suggests that such collective and communal practice can avert the tendency to assume individuals make career and educational 'decisions', divorced from their social context.

It is not the intention of this chapter to discuss what we mean by learning, but before listing the benefits of careers work in a group setting something needs to be said about experiential learning and transformative learning. Experiential learning is a well established concept drawing on the work of Dewey (1938), Lewin (1951) and Kolb (1984). Westergaard explains:

> For learning to take place, individuals will need to reflect on the experience they have had, to make sense of it and to consider what they would do differently if they were to have a similar experience in the future. They would then act on this when the opportunity arose. (Westergaard, 2009: 20)

Learning is rooted in prior experience, but is influenced both by the old and new experience and the context within which that learning takes place. Transformative learning is a related but extended concept. Mezirow states that:

> Transformative learning may be defined as learning that transforms problematic frames of reference to make them more inclusive, discriminating, reflective, open, and emotionally able to change. (Mezirow, 2009: 22)

In discussing adult learning this suggests that rather than acting on 'assimilated belief, values, feelings, and judgements of others' (2009: 23) adults learn how to reason for themselves. Transformative learning would include recognition of the influences of power in society, structural constraints, ideology and a critical appreciation of the impact of class, gender, ethnicity and so on, the individual's life chances. All of this may seem a little removed from 'careers education' but it has already been stated that careers work should not be a 'one-off' intervention, but a learning and developmental process: could it be transformative too? Careers work in a group setting would claim to be learner-centred and not about 'telling' clients what to do. Within constraints it would aim to be democratic via negotiated content, it would wish to be inclusive and involve critical refection and be dialogical.

Transformative learning, then, pays attention to the whole person where deeply held assumptions are likely to be questioned. Yorks and Kasal (2006: 46) refer to this as 'inviting the whole person into the classroom environment', and such expressive ways of knowing mean, 'the person in fullness of being: as an affective, intuitive, thinking, physical, spiritual self'. Drawing on the work of Dirkx (2006), Taylor states:

> To successfully engage expressive ways of knowing in the classroom, edu-cators have to be prepared to work on their own holistic awareness, creating a learning environment conducive to whole person learning (for example, by adopting rituals or creating community) and modelling emphatic connec-tions of learners' experiences through expressive activities, for example, by storytelling and cooperative inquiry. (Taylor, 2009: 11)

The above lends itself to careers work and to models of practice that recognise the agency of the individual but within a social, cultural, economic and historical setting. It also highlights the links with constructivist approaches such as narrative career counselling, but applied in a group setting which takes account of social context.

On the ground of practice though, career counsellors and coaches do work within constraints – the biggest of these being time. The more democratic, inclu-sive and transformative we aim to be, the higher demand for time (Taylor, 2009), as relationship-building is key. Although there are limitations to what might be achievable, that does not mean that we shrug our shoulders and just give everyone a hand-out to read at home. So if not transformative, the primary outcomes of working in a group for career learning and development are that the group/individual has:

- greater self-awareness;
- an understanding of possibilities;
- begun to evaluate possibilities;
- recognised the decisions to be made;
- started to formulate decisions;
- thought about their information needs;
- become aware of how these needs might be met;
- begun to evaluate information;
- recognised further guidance needs.

Working in a group setting, the individual can benefit from the shared knowledge and experience of the group, which can reduce the sense of isolation and potential stress that can be involved in decision making. They can listen to the views of others and observe how they approach the topic. Being involved in group activities can increase the opportunity to learn new ideas about themselves and the world through this shared, dialogical process. Learning in group settings is co-constructed as individuals are exposed to a wider range of life experiences. It might be argued that when working with young people in a school setting the life experience is more limited, depending on the context, but that is an assumption. A group of 14-year-olds may have very different backgrounds and life experiences that if used as a resource can lead to transformative learning for the whole group. In the literature, transformative learning is usually associated with adult learners, but fostering more holistic approaches that provide space for young people to share their understandings can lead to deeper reflection for the whole group (including the facilitator), challenging existing frames of reference at both the personal and socio-cultural level. And when working with young people, my approach was always to communicate with them as young adults – never 'kids'.

There can be disadvantages. Often providing career counselling and guidance in group settings can be viewed as a cost-cutting activity to replace one-to-one interactions. My own experience, like the practitioner in Case study 12.1, is that group work is a very useful resource as part of the process, but not as a replacement for one-to-one work. Unless managed well by the facilitator, it is possible for members of the group to withdraw and not participate. Planning, preparation, negotiation, flexibility and the use of group facilitation skills are essential for group work to be successful.

Applying the three-stage model to group work

The point has been made before that a model provides a framework or structure, but should be used flexibly, according to the requirements of the client or, in this discussion, group. That said a simple three-stage model can be applied: (1) opening; (2) development; and (3) conclusion. The design of a session can be developed using these headings. Figure 12.1 outlines these stages and steps that can be used to structure a group work intervention.

With regard to group work skills, these are similar to the counselling skills used for one-to-one work. The skills involved in working with groups are required for:

- introducing the session;
- choosing the most appropriate 'teaching' or facilitation style;
- using strategies to work with individual members of the group;
- developing an appropriate climate and relationship with the group;
- structuring a beginning, maintaining and ending the session;
- recognising the dynamics of the group;
- developing strategies/options to deal with possible eventualities.

Stage 1 Openings, **allow you to:**

- introduce yourself;
- enable the group to feel comfortable;
- set the tone of the session;
- focus on the subject of the session;
- find out what group members already know;
- encourage all group members to participate;
- establish the group dynamics;
- negotiate 'ground rules' – the ways of working together;
- agree the agenda – what will happen and how.

Stage 2 Development, **provides an opportunity for the group to:**

- participate in activities;
- discuss ideas;
- develop an understanding of the topic;
- gather/share information;
- begin to relate the topic to their own situation.

Stage 3 Conclusions, **provide an opportunity to:**

- summarise
- draw the threads together;
- evaluate what has been learnt;
- enable group members to think about their own 'next steps' in relation to the topic;
- deal with any questions or omissions;
- check that the session has been useful;
- identify opportunities for further support;
- end with a shared sense that the work has been worthwhile.

Figure 12.1   The three-stage model applied to group work

The structure outlined in Figure 12.1 resonates with the Single Interaction Model (SIM, Reid and Fielding, 2007) introduced earlier in the book for one-to-one career counselling and coaching. In what follows I am going to focus on preparation, Stage 1 and contracting with groups; the latter seems to be the part of the process that those new to group work find the most difficult. A summary of key points for Stage 2 and Stage 3 will be offered after this. I am going to use a mix of 'you' and 'we': the use of 'you' often sounds like telling the reader – not my intention, but the more inclusive 'we' seems to work less well here.

Stage 1: Openings

In your preparation you will have decided on an aim, objectives and the desired outcomes for the session which can be evaluated. You will have prepared for the session with some knowledge of the group and how the session may be linked to a learning and development programme. At the start, you will need to introduce your session and yourself. It may be a 'getting to know you' time on both sides if you have not worked with the group before. Then you will want to share with them what the session is about and in what way it might be relevant to their needs. On this last point, it is essential that the group is able to identify the relevance for them and have an opportunity to do this. There needs to be room for flexibility on the part of the practitioner in the case where adaptations may be needed. All of the above involves rapport building to create a good working relationship. There is the checking of expectations and agreeing which of those might be met as well as those which cannot; in other words, negotiating the contract. Using icebreakers and warm-up exercises can help to achieve this as a shared process.

Icebreakers

A brief activity used to break the ice and animate the group. It does not have to be related to the topic of the session (although it is helpful if there is a link) and is used frequently where the group has not met before, or is going to meet on a number of occasions. Icebreakers are usually very simple, not very detailed and lasting just a few minutes to get everyone joining in. There are many icebreaking games; quite often they are name games to get everyone to know each other with the added bonus of allowing the practitioner to know each participant's name. But a word of caution here, they can take longer than you think.

Warm-up exercises

In the context of careers work in a group setting, a warm-up as an activity introduces the topic of the session and leads to the main body of the session. As such warm-ups are usually longer than icebreakers, though not necessarily so, and they are related to the topic under consideration. Warm-ups can be short, fun activities and everyone should be involved, so to an extent there is an overlap with icebreakers. In some ways warm-ups can serve as both ice breakers and as a lead into the work of the session. Participants should be able to see a clear link between the warm-up and the main session, and the activity should help them to identify the relevance of the session. Warm-ups help to build a positive climate by inviting participation from all members at the beginning of the session. They may also be useful in helping to initiate discussion. They are likely to be most useful when you have a very limited amount of time, as it enables the group to get involved with the topic to be covered from the outset. You will be able to find examples of various icebreakers and warm-up exercises that you can use with groups in various resource materials and books on group work. Having engaged the group to think about the topic to be worked on, then the next step will be much easier and a good working climate should be established.

To complete this introductory stage (Stage 1) we need to check out the group's expectations and agree the limitations and possibilities of what you have to offer them in this session. To do this, as in one-to-one work, we need to contract with the group. This is essential so that we can identify and meet their needs, make the time spent as relevant to these as is possible and to avoid imposing on the group what we think they want to know or ought to know.

Contracting with groups

Although contracting appears to be a simple concept and one already discussed in the context of one-to-one work, people do tend to find it confusing, especially in relation to groups. One difficulty might be the worry that you can only negotiate a contract with one person at a time. Another confusion about contracting is the idea that you are negotiating what the session will be about in terms of subject area, e.g. would the group prefer to have a session about decision making or self-assessment or something completely different from what you have prepared. This is not what contracting with groups is about.

It is though about negotiating, within a relatively broad framework of the subject you have planned, what will be most relevant for you to cover and focus on for the group as a whole, so that you are meeting their needs and expectations as far as possible. For example, in simple terms, in a group session on self-assessment, we will need to know what the group is expecting it to be about, and what they think they need to know about self-assessment, so that they are sure the session is of value to them. Gathering this information will help a group facilitator to focus on the points and ideas that the group feels are most relevant to them. In this way we are less likely to go over what they already know, or miss out on some very basic but important points, because we have assumed that they have this knowledge already. As above, this can lead to imposing what we think they should know instead.

Contracting with a group is a very similar process to contracting with individuals. In the one-to-one situation it is an interview that is on offer, and we negotiate within that purpose/framework what the client's needs are, and do our best to meet them. At the same time we make it clear to the client what we cannot offer in this situation and possibly discuss how their other needs could be met in other ways: so it is with group contracting. Contracting with the group in this early stage is also a way of negotiating and then establishing the norms of behaviour for working together – which can be returned to later if necessary. Just the same as individual contracts, contracts with groups lead to much greater client satisfaction for two reasons:

1. you are able to meet their needs much more successfully if you know what they are;
2. if you have made it clear what you cannot do within the session, the individuals are less likely to go away feeling dissatisfied about unmet needs, as you have indicated what cannot be covered.

The latter point means that the group will be able to focus their attention on what can be done during the session, rather than wondering when you are going to get to the bit that covers their interests. Of course, you cannot negotiate with, say, 20 people in turn, so you negotiate with the group as a whole using a variety of methods. Method is the essential difference between contracting with individuals and contracting with groups.

Methods for contracting with groups

There is a range of methods that can be used to contract with groups and you will need to identify the method that will suit your topic, group size and participants best. You will also need to consider how much time you have and, if it is limited, then methods that involve just a few minutes are likely to be best. In some cases, you can adapt the contracting process so that it becomes a warm-up as well.

At this point I want to re-emphasise the importance of contracting with groups. Too often it is the bit that is left out with the excuse, 'oh, I have not got time to contract with the group', or 'that means I will have to prepare three different sessions because they will probably want to cover something I have not prepared'. These are not viable excuses and they lead to dumping what we want on the group and sessions that the participants find boring and irrelevant, sometimes leading to disruptive or withdrawn behaviour. Such an approach would not achieve the aim of person-centred career counselling and coaching and will come nowhere near transformative learning. Being effective means giving the preparation more thought, so that we can attempt to meet a range of needs by being flexible about what the session can cover. This can be worked on at the design and preparation stage. So where do you start with designing a flexible group session that will account for a range of needs that might emerge from the contracting stage?

When deciding on your aim for the session, you will think about what the needs of your target group might be, i.e. the learning objectives for the session. In doing this you make some assumptions about what these are and which needs have priority. You will think about what you hope the group will gain and apply from participation in the session – the learning outcomes once the group has experienced the session. The learning outcomes should move from the general to the specific, and then to the personal. For instance, if the session were about career options that are available, the group would want general information about what these are, specific ideas about how to evaluate these and ideas about relating the information to their individual interests and circumstances. The intended learning outcomes also need to be SMART (specific, measurable, achievable, realistic and time bound). In the planning and preparation stage the practitioner will need to keep thinking, realistically, about what can be achieved in the time available. This thinking needs to take place before the interesting exercises are developed that will take into account a range of learning styles (being aware that we often unconsciously design sessions around our own interests and dominant learning style).

Activity 12.2

Imagine you have been asked to run an interactive group work session on applying for jobs. Make a list of as many aspects of the topic that you think might be covered in a session. Think about where the group work is taking place (you decide) and consider who might be taking part, what they might want to know, the learning environment, when this would be happening and what the previous learning experiences might be like. This list can give you some useful clues as to what might arise as expectations and needs during the contracting process.

Having identified the group and the context, you could start the process by using the following headings:

- Aim of the session
- What I want to achieve
- Aspects that the participants might want to cover.

The intention of the above activity is not to frighten you into thinking there is no way you can cover all the issues that might arise. The intention is to emphasise the importance of thoughtful planning, so that the focus is clear and effective preparation takes place (i.e. making sure you will have all the materials you may need). That done and with a clear aim and intended learning outcomes, you can then design the rest of the session based on what methods will be best to achieve the desired goals. Working through your subject in this way, you are preparing a flexible approach to the session that will then be able to accommodate any needs that arise. This preparation will also help you to identify what you cannot achieve in the session. As a result you will have identified both the possibilities and the limitations of the group session. This will be the basis of your contracting exercise with the group.

Once you begin the session, having prepared your group session this way, you are not being asked to alter what you had originally planned. Hopefully you can now see what you could add or replace depending on what emerges as the main needs of the group. Their main needs will be reflected in your contracting activity, and you can then agree with the group which of these you can meet and which you cannot. One advantage from this type of preparation is that you can feel much more confident about facilitating your session and you will have thought it through thoroughly. You are, therefore, less likely to be taken by surprise and feel unequal to the situation.

Summary of Stage 1

Do not worry if you find contracting with groups difficult, as this is common even for people who are used to teaching a curriculum subject. The following may help to simplify the concept, although any simplification runs the risk of reducing the activity to a functional approach (by employing a 'checklist') which negates negotiation. So, with that word of warning, a summary of Stage 1 of the process follows.

Negotiating the contract begins from the first introductions which set the tone of the session. Checking the group's understanding of the role of the career practitioner as a facilitator, rather than teacher or presenter, establishes that the session will be interactive. A common mistake in negotiating the contract is to ask closed questions, often as a result of nerves. Closed questions are often unhelpful as they demand a yes/no response, which assumes the individual or group is confident enough to give such a definite answer. The result is often no response, as individuals are not sure of the 'right' answer and do not want to be seen giving the 'wrong' answer. Silence is the easiest response, particularly when a member of a group.

So, time needs to be invested in rapport-building in the early stages. Open questions are used to check understanding about roles; purposes of the session; relevance of the topic; previous knowledge of the topic and ways of working together. For example, having spent a little time on introductions, you might use the following questions:

- What sort of work do you think a careers practitioner (or whatever title is appropriate) does in this school (college/workplace)?
- When you came into the room, what were your expectations about the session?
- Why do you suppose I thought this topic would be useful for us at this point in time?
- Tell me, what you have done before related to this topic?
- We will be working in smaller groups and discussing the results with the whole group, what do we need to think about when working together in this way?

Or, as appropriate,

- What would you suggest would be useful ground rules for this type of session?

All of the above are questions that ask, share and negotiate and avoid telling the group. Using open questions and following up on the responses will establish the need for involvement and increase relevance. However, when asking open questions, avoid the 'what do you know about …?' approach which often misses the mark as it appears to be a test of knowledge. Your summary at the end of Stage 1 will then set the agenda, i.e. what we are going to do; why we are doing it; how we are going to do it; how much time we have: a group work contract.

A final thought before we move on: if the group responds with 'We did this last term/in another session' – do not panic. You can say, 'Great, then we can really build on that knowledge. So tell me what did you learn from what you did on that previous occasion?' You then have the opportunity to adapt your material to move through the introductory exercises quicker, and/or develop the more detailed parts or increase the time for feedback and discussion.

Stage 2: Development

In your planning you will have identified activities that the group can work on for their career learning and development. As part of the methodology for meeting the aims and working towards the intended learning outcomes, you are likely to have paired and/or small group activity with feedback to the whole group. If the group appears a little too lively, individual or paired activity can calm the group and if too quiet, then triads are useful. If the small groups are too large, then some members may not participate. It can be useful to work in pairs and then share the thinking with a larger group before discussing with the whole group. It is the role of the facilitator to monitor the engagement of the group and to make adjustments accordingly so that learning continues to take place. The basic and advanced skills discussed in the previous chapter will be used as required, and summaries are useful to review the learning before moving on to the next exercise or stage.

Stage 3: Conclusions

In the final stage it will be important that members of the group have an opportunity to reflect on how the session relates to them and their individual needs – so that the learning and the resulting action points from the session are owned by the individual. At the end of the session it is useful to conclude by reviewing what was agreed at the start. Where an aspect was not covered, this may have been because another point or activity appeared more useful as the work progressed. This is fine, this is being flexible – but at the end of the session it is helpful to discuss with the group how they might follow up that point if you are not working with them again. As with one-to-one work, it is constructive to get the group to identify what they found useful in the session, in other words ask them. Often an evaluation exercise or form is used to gather this information, but evaluation forms can be too long and boring – better if this can be kept interactive and creative.

What has not been discussed in the above is creativity in the design of group work activity for career counselling and coaching. There are many texts that provide ideas for this and an example is offered in the suggested reading. The use of digital technologies and creative approaches for one-to-one and/or group work is discussed in the following chapter, but before concluding here, I want to make a brief mention of another model that can be applied to group work settings.

The FAAST model

Jane Westergaard (2009) has written a step-by-step guide for effective group work for those working with young people in a range of contexts. Although focused on work with young people, topics covered are applicable to working with other groups, such as a discussion on learning theory, the impact on the work of group dynamics, advice on how to improve group facilitation skills and how to manage challenging behaviour. The text takes readers through the process from identifying a topic and setting objectives, to planning activities and evaluation of the outcomes once the session has ended. Westergaard frames this within what she terms the FAAST model. FAAST stands for:

- **F**ocus
- **A**im
- **A**ctivities
- **S**tructure
- **T**echniques.

She makes the point that the acronym does not indicate a short cut (fast) way for designing group work sessions and, like the discussion in this chapter, much emphasis is placed on the planning and preparation stages, to ensure that effective personal learning and development takes place for the individual group members.

In the description of the Westergaard text above, I mentioned how to manage challenging behaviour. This aspect of group work can be what practitioners, not trained as teachers, find most 'challenging' themselves. The angst this creates in students on career guidance and counselling training programmes can be palpable, but is usually out of proportion to what they will experience. However, the worry is real, so in Appendix 3 I have included an adapted handout discussed in the teaching of group work skills.

Learning in organisations

What has not been covered in this chapter is the theory and practice of working (rather than learning) in a group in an organisation. There are many texts that cover this and, as one example, the work of Charles Handy is extensive and well known (e.g. Handy, 1993, 1999). Johnson and Johnson (2012) also cover group theory and application, but in addition offer useful insights and exercises for working with groups in learning situations.

In the coaching literature Zeus and Skiffington (2000) pay particular attention to the importance of the learning environment of the organisation and state, 'Coaching individuals occurs in the context of their workplace and problems in organizations are inseparable from people and how they think and behave' (2000: 193). They go on to clarify that providing a programme of structured training that happens in a 'classroom' on its own, does not constitute organisational learning. Organisational learning includes specific processes that maintain, enhance and develop the performance of the organisation based on experience. Work production systems, in this view, are also learning systems and the latter are intrinsic to work performance where both are integrated. Zeus and Skiffington suggest that work organisations need to audit the learning and development by: looking at strengths and weaknesses; creating a profile of the opportunities for formal and informal learning; evaluating the success and effectiveness of current systems; and 'benchmarking' best practice against other similar organisations in terms of organisational learning and development. To do this, they conclude, 'organisations need transformational learning rather than just incremental learning' (ibid.). In this sense, managers also have a role as coaches; at the very least they should model the benefits of continuous learning and development. And career coaches can assist with this emotional learning work, in order to build safe learning environments for staff throughout the organisation, at all levels.

Chapter summary

This chapter has explored the term 'career learning and development' for a range of contexts and suggested that the learning can be transformative for those involved. It has considered the benefits of labour market information and labour market intelligence, and the debate about how much information a practitioner can or should know. To be effective in the current context the development of networking skills was discussed, before moving on to review the benefits of providing career counselling and coaching in group settings. A three-stage model for structuring such work was introduced, based on SIM. Finally, emphasis was placed on the importance of a policy for learning and development within organisational contexts.

Further reading

Barnes, A., Bassot, B. and Chant, A. (2011) *An Introduction to Career Learning and Development 11–19*. Abingdon: Routledge.

Bassot, B., Barnes, A. and Chant, A. (2014) *A Practical Guide to Career Learning and Development: Innovation in Careers Education 11–19*. Abingdon, UK: Routledge.

These two books achieve what the titles suggest and are a very useful resource for those involved in career learning and development in educational settings.

Johnson, D. and Johnson, F. (2012) *Joining Together: Group Theory and Group Skills* (11th edn). Harlow: Pearsons Education.

Now in its 11th edition – an indication of the usefulness and popularity of this book. I found the insights gained from this comprehensive text invaluable for understanding and practising group work. There are many creative ideas and exercises that can be adapted for careers work.

Westergaard, J. (2009) *Effective Group Work With Young People*. Maidenhead: Open University Press/McGraw-Hill.

Although focused on work with young people, this step-by-step guide can be applied in wider settings. The content moves from theory to practice, demonstrating how a practitioner can improve group facilitation skills and manage challenging behaviour. Case studies illustrate the work throughout.

13

Using digital technologies and creative approaches in careers work

This chapter will:

- discuss how the internet has changed careers work;
- provide examples of digital technologies in use;
- consider how digital technologies can be blended with 'traditional' careers work;
- offer ideas for other creative approaches.

Introduction

The internet and digital technologies have extended access to careers materials and have changed the 'face' of careers work in many sectors. Using such technologies may be a supplement and extension to other practices or may be the sole intervention, but the order in which this can take place can vary and, as argued later, blended delivery appears to be the most effective. An overview of current developments is offered here with the caveat that these are changing rapidly. One of the aims of this chapter will be to rethink how career counselling and coaching can be, and in many places is being, 'delivered'. One-to-one careers work does not have to be face-to-face and even face-to-face (an awkward term) can be achieved through digital means. As a large part of the population who may be receiving career counselling and coaching live their everyday lives through digital media, their expectation is likely to be that practitioners will interact with them in the same way.

The chapter also considers other creative methodologies as alternatives to the one-to-one 'talking' intervention. The interview is often seen as the core service in career counselling and coaching, but this is not always sustainable in terms of cost and perhaps more importantly, in terms of access – and the interview will not suit all clients in any case. If we take creative to mean something that engages the imagination, then many of the models already discussed in this book are creative. However, other approaches go further and incorporate art, drama and other imaginative methods: potentially these may be more appealing for a range of clients.

How the internet has changed careers work

Within careers work the use of digital technologies gathered pace from the 1990s after the birth of the world wide web, but utilisation of the internet did not really advance until the late 1990s, with more serious use evident from 2000 onwards. This latter period included the growth of social media. Practitioners may or may not have 'grown up' with digital technologies and they may embrace the phenomenon or wish to ignore it – but the latter position is, increasingly, untenable. The internet is a place where many go to explore and develop their career thinking and development, and career practitioners will want to know enough about what is available, even if it is not central to their particular working context.

Reflection point 13.1

In terms of careers work, on a scale of 1–10, with 1 being 'not interested and will not use digital technologies' to 10 being 'yes, all the time on every occasion' – what is your position? Why have you placed yourself at that point on the scale, what are your reasons?

This reflection point feels a bit 'confessional', so it seems fair to state my own position. I am about a six and leaning towards a seven. My reasons are that, as already stated, engagement is unavoidable and there are many benefits that are obvious to me; and yet I do not view the internet or digital technologies within careers work as offering a complete service, nor, of course, do face-to-face services. I have no doubt this is because I entered the profession interested in people and like working with them one-to-one and in groups; albeit that such work can take place online. I am also wary of how technology can instrumentalise human interactions and be reductive in terms of expecting instant solutions to complex issues. That said instrumentalisation can occur when interactions are governed by rigid criteria or the need to meet targets, whereas technology may provide an alternative for many to connect and share ideas in new ways. Thus, the internet and other digital technologies are very useful tools and, like most of us, I cannot imagine my life without them. I can go on holiday for a week or two and not look at emails, but the holiday and all arrangements will have been booked via the internet. I have a relationship with the internet; it is 'blended'; it is an important part of my life both private and professional.

In order to write this chapter I have drawn on the work of colleagues who have a deeper understanding than mine; notably I will make particular reference to the writing of Tristram Hooley and to Bill Law in the UK, but will also mention the work of others who contributed to an edition on this topic in the *Journal of the National Institute for Career Education and Counselling* (2012). All authors draw on literature sources extensively, but here I will concentrate on the main points (to learn more, the reader can follow up on the references via the original material and visit the additional websites offered at the end of the chapter).

Constructing a framework for digital career literacy

In what Hooley refers to as 'conceptual architecture' (2012: 3), he poses three questions with regard to the inter-relationship between the internet and careers work. The first question examines how the internet reshapes the context within which individuals pursue their career. Hooley outlines the development of the use of the internet for careers work from the early days, to the use of Web 2.0 in 2004, and the development of social tools such as blogs, wikis and the now widespread use of social media. With others (Hooley et al., 2010) he has charted further development, identifying how the Web 2.0/3.0 era might have an impact on the way individuals manage their career development. What becomes evident is that individuals' use of the internet, via desktop computers and now a range of mobile devices, means that 'vast amounts of personal data are now routinely available to their present and future employers' (Hooley, 2012: 4). And the rapid growth continues.

Hooley is careful to point out that whilst the expansion is rapid and the reach extensive, it should not be assumed that access is omnipresent. Within the UK there remain many who do not have access to the internet or have not developed the skills to benefit from its use (ONS, 2014). Often, but not always, these may be individuals who are already disadvantaged by other social and economic factors. Lack of access to the internet can increase their disadvantaged position in a competitive labour market and/or access to a range of supporting services. For example, for careers work the internet provides: a career resource library; a marketplace for interacting with employers and learning providers; a social space for networking to find opportunities; a place for building an individual's profile, promoting and communicating this with others (Hooley, 2012).

The second question Hooley addresses is the skills and knowledge required to develop a career through the medium of the internet. Digital literacy is the term used to describe proficiency with use of relevant technologies and Hooley extends this, thus, 'Digital career literacy is concerned with the ability to use the online environment, to search, to make contacts, to get questions answered, and to build a positive professional reputation' (2012: 5). He goes on to suggest that career practitioners who are not developing their digital career literacy will be left behind in their own careers, as well as in their ability to help clients.

In an early chapter in this book, the need for standards to be identified for professional work was argued for and it would be an out-of-date list of competences that did not include aspects of digital literacy for careers work. Whilst not ignoring the complexity of the issues involved, here I will quote what Hooley offers as a synthesis of essential aspects for the development of digital career literacy. This brings together three key concepts, information literacy, digital literacy and career management skills, into a framework for what is termed, 'The Seven Cs of digital career literacy':

- **Changing** describes the ability to understand and adapt to changing online career contexts and to learn to use new technologies for the purpose of career building.
- **Collecting** describes the ability to source, manage and retrieve career information and resources.
- **Critiquing** describes the ability to understand the nature of online career information and resources, to analyse its provenance and to consider its usefulness for a career.
- **Connecting** describes the ability to build relationships and networks online that can support career development.
- **Communicating** describes the ability to interact effectively across a range of different platforms, to understand the genre and netiquette of different interactions and to use them in the context of career.
- **Creating** describes the ability to create online content that effectively represents the individual, their interests and their career history.
- **Curating** describes the ability of the individual to reflect on and develop their digital footprint and online networks as part of their career building. (Hooley, 2012: 6)

Activity 13.1

Whilst the above framework may relate to the development of individuals' digital career literacy, career practitioners will, increasingly, need to be able to support clients in this development. So, this is an area of knowledge that practitioners will require in order to meet the expectations of their clients. Taking each element in turn, make notes about:

(Continued)

(Continued)

1. your level of experience;
2. which aspect you would like to develop further;
3. how you might begin that development.

Leading on from the above, the third question that Hooley poses relates to how career practitioners can use the internet in the delivery of their work. In broad terms, the online environment provided by the internet can be utilised for the delivery of careers information, to offer automated interactions and be used as a means of communication with clients (Hooley, 2012).

The amount of careers information available online is immense, accessible and, potentially, negates the need for books and leaflets and the space to house such material. It can also incorporate more interactive material that has wider appeal for a range of users. For example there are developers of resources who expressly wish to reframe career education programmes in schools and re-engage young people via careers resources that use rich interactive media (Manson, 2012).

The internet also has the advantage of linking sites to widen a search for information – this can be a time-saver for clients, but the value of a search will, whether in a traditional library or online, depend on the interpretation and relevance of the information found. We may think that most people are aware that not all the information online may be accurate or representative of that which it purports to describe, but this is an assumption. The need for critical assessment of the information available is a crucial skill to develop, whilst recognising the enormous potential to access current, detailed information.

Automated interactions suggest that the presence of a career practitioner may not be necessary for all interactions. When offered by career organisations they can be a kind of 'triage service' and can also provide useful matching tools as a starting point for career development, potentially freeing up time for career practitioners to engage in higher-level work with clients. There is a range of internet versions of conventional career assessment tests available online and various games and other interactive exercises are also automated, including those that may include a number of players. Accordingly Hooley states (citing Dugosija et al., 2008), 'the range of career benefits that individuals acquired from participating in online gaming, included increasing their social and professional networks' (Hooley, 2012: 8).

Of great significance in the delivery of careers work, digital technologies support communication – from email, texting, Skype and other online synchronous discussion tools, to newer forms of communication utilising one-to-one and one-to-many communication technologies. Increasingly these have evolved into the many-to-many communication channels online that practitioners and others use via social networking sites (Hooley, 2012). Each of these can provide alternative ways of engaging in career counselling. However, in the desire to communicate effectively and within whatever might be the current vogue, there is a danger that practitioners can invade spaces where they may not be welcome. When working with particular groups, for example young people, rather than increasing contact this can have the opposite, negative effect. Thus a respectful use of social media to promote careers work needs to be negotiated with the 'target audience'.

Case study 13.1: Whose online space?

Ellis works with young people who are long-term unemployed and have been categorised as NEET (not in education, employment or training). He talks here of the development of digital technologies to support his work.

'Yes, in the early days in this job, some years ago now when I first qualified, we were contacting young people using text and shorthand abbreviations that we thought they'd like – they hated it! To them, as one of them told me, it sounded like "adults getting down with kids" – embarrassing really. But we learnt from that and since then we always ask them what would work and try it out with a small group who know we are piloting the use of a particular tool. There isn't always time for detailed evaluation studies in this job, but the principle is that we ask and negotiate our access to what they see as their space. We have used Facebook in that way and that seems to work well. I am really interested in all this stuff so I have to be careful not to impose it on young people; however, the vast majority are two pages ahead of me in any case, but not all my colleagues are as keen. I do look at research and read evaluation articles and it has become my job to disseminate new developments to other colleagues, who may not be as savvy in terms of what's out there. Getting the balance right between enthusiasm and putting people off is difficult, but it is working so far. Above all else I see digital technologies as useful tools that help with our prime purpose – helping young people access education, training or work.'

Digital technologies in practice

Bill Law is an early pioneer of the potential of online careers work and his Career-learning cafe has been mentioned previously. In a comprehensive analysis of careers work and the internet (2012a) he suggests that it is no longer possible to contain the explosion of what is available online within off-line careers services.

Like Hooley, he charts the development of the web and his analysis finds varying degrees of interactivity on the sites that are available. Within education he notes that many teachers 'tend to seek clearly-bounded uses that support familiar schooling activity' (Law, 2012b: 14). Careers workers have taken a similar position, according to his analysis, and, despite many significant developments, they are, generally, wary of the use of social media technology. Law outlines the benefits and the cautions that are required in his analysis of online careers work. In the latter category, drawing on research, he includes the possibility that 'tick-and-click' activity can reduce concentration and that online interest groups can lead to enclaves that become exclusionary. He mentions also the potential harm from disclosure where protective barriers are breached and personal data is used indiscriminately for the interests of business. Use of the internet is now so ubiquitous that many users 'value the net for its ease-of-use, [but] pay little heed to who operates a site, and do not probe the credibility of sources' (Law, 2012b: 15). This warning points to the need for 'digital career literacy', as described by Hooley.

Cautions to one side, Law sees careers workers as educators who, in the way they support their clients, can enable individuals to make good use of the technologies. His detailed analysis advocates for the avoidance of over-simplistic use of the technologies that may be found in policies based on saving resources. For example, what can be characterised in current times as a tendency to view the internet as having all the answers, thus negating the need for other support from a knowledgeable professional. This view reifies the internet which is created and developed by humans; in other words the internet does not exist outside of the information that is placed on it by individuals. Educators though, and here we can include career practitioners, can be over-cautious, and while they may not need to be experts in the use of all digital technologies, they do have a role in 'enabling people to take on board other points-of-view, to take one thing with another, and to take nothing for granted' (Law, 2012b: 19).

Reflection point 13.2

What is your view about the discussion so far? Accepting that we all have different levels of use of digital technologies, what level of competence do you think is required for a career counsellor or career coach to be effective in their work with clients? And what about career services – what approach should they take, in your view?

My response is it depends on their role and the expectations of the client or service they are working with. But that avoids the question to a large degree. An enthusiast can be an expert, but there is a strong argument that to be credible a career practitioner must have a basic knowledge of the available technology, if not wishing to be an expert user. Trying to keep up with the rapid growth of new developments will be a full-time occupation for some and an everyday habit for the young – most of us could not compete with this. In terms of service delivery, the discussion so far appears to point towards the importance of a blended environment for the use of digital technologies in careers work. One such approach is described by Dyson (2012), working in a youth employability service in the south of England.

Dyson describes the approach as integrating face-to-face work with online engagement, making this then a blended approach. The service includes the more traditional offer of individual appointments, the availability of drop-in locations and home visits, telephone and text communication for keeping in touch. Alongside this, the online service includes the considered, secure and negotiated use of a social media site (Facebook). Following the initial use which proved popular with young people and the increased access and use of the service this created, a range of online tools was integrated with the site, such as 'appointments booking systems, online publication programmes and interactive quiz creators' (Dyson, 2012: 29); the latter being interactive quizzes that employ image, text and video media. Individual and group sessions used through these media were found to increase the motivation of young people, develop their career thinking and strengthen their continued engagement with the service and contact with their advisers. In support of a blended approach, Dyson states:

> Ultimately the online work enhanced the existing face-to-face [service] and provided support for young people who may not have engaged at all without the online service. Existing clients were able to access a greater level of support through the online service and some young people who had refused support, both face-to-face and online, were later able to re-engage through Facebook. (Dyson, 2012: 13)

The service continues to develop other digital technologies, keeping pace with developments as they arise, but through testing their efficacy and security for the young people they work with to provide a harmonious blend of off-line and online services.

The above example is designed for young people in particular and, often, for young people in challenging circumstances. However, technologies for digital career literacy can be used across the various groups of clients alongside whom career counsellors and coaches work. When based in learning theory, or specifically career learning theory (Innes, 2012; Law, 1996), approaches for 'service delivery' across the sector can be rooted within something substantial, based on how individuals learn about themselves, society and career. Evaluation is important to ensure that outcomes are more likely to lead to the ongoing design and adaptation of tools that are effective; albeit measuring the effectiveness of any career intervention is always difficult.

Training centres for careers work do themselves offer elearning and blended learning courses for career practitioners (Chant, 2012), for both professional development and initial training. Being on the receiving end of blended learning may be a starting point for some practitioners, but is this enough? A study by Kettunen et al. (2014) suggests the need to cultivate pre-service and in-service training for career practitioners to support and increase their competency, and that such development should be based on research that identifies the critical aspects that will lead to effective use of digital technologies. Such training, drawing on research, can be practical, 'hands on' and grounded in practice, in order to enable practitioners to use the tools available. In addition there is a need for critical reflection on the benefits and the drawbacks that the digital technologies provide. To support all-age continuing personal development for career/life decisions, perhaps a more philosophical understanding of the implications and opportunities of using web technology is also required (Dickinson and Henderson, 2012).

Activity 13.2

As a useful activity at the end of this part of the chapter, go online and search using terms that include the word career, such as: career development; career information; career advice; career guidance; career counselling; career coaching; career services and so on. As you do this think about what this is like for a client who is looking for support at an educational or career transition point, rather than someone looking for job vacancies.

I will not ask you to count the number of sites. It is more useful to ask: what does the experience suggest to you with regard to internet career support and the option of a blended approach?

Other creative approaches

Digital technologies are now such a normal part of life for so many of us that we may wonder if they can be labelled 'creative' (i.e. they engage the imagination). Innovations will continue to amaze us, however, and to succeed developers must carry on being creative, as providers come and go if they do not. Much more can be said and a whole chapter on digital technologies in careers work would be justified, but a reminder here that this book is an introduction to career counselling and coaching and more detail can be found elsewhere. So, this final part of the chapter will consider other creative approaches that exercise the imagination, including those that draw on the 'creative arts' such as drama, art, craft work and creative writing.

Before moving on it is important to remind ourselves that we all have the capacity to be creative, it is not a special gift. Prima ballerinas, portrait and landscape painters and ceramicists, for instance, have special gifts, but unless we have a disability that prevents us from doing so, we can all, however inexpertly, use craft material, draw, write a story, and maybe act. For many the request to 'be creative' may give rise to feelings of insecurity, but within a space where the relevance of the exercise is shared and where an individual can have their fears contained, creative approaches can unlock thoughts, feelings and ideas that do not usually surface, allowing unforeseen reflections and connections to be made. Emotions can be stirred too – so the facilitator needs to manage the process and use their counselling skills to gain the most from a creative approach.

It may sound trite, but creative approaches can give permission for the individual to engage with their inner child, usually suppressed once we reach our teenage years. Using coloured pens and drawing simple figures to represent time, place and interests can feel liberating. Cutting up pictures, using glue and glitter in a purposeful exercise can be fun, but also meaningful in terms of the inner world of thoughts and motivations. Activities can take varying amounts of time and resources, from a five-minute discussion with a pad of paper and a pencil to draw and discuss a career time line, to a number of workshops where a sculpture may be the end result. A few examples will be offered in what follows.

Visual tools – drawing

Whilst the talking interview is dominant in career counselling and coaching, it is widely acknowledged in other helping services that for many, thoughts, feelings and emotions may be difficult to articulate in words and alternatives are useful. Cregeen-Cook (2011) points out that the use of visual imagery is accepted in many therapeutic settings, for example in Sutherland's (2009) use of storytelling within art therapy. The use of such techniques is 'designed to promote clarity of thought, as a first step towards positive action and to put seemingly unmanageable and unsolvable problems in a new perspective' (Cregeen-Cook, 2011: 47). Such tools can be thought of as visual metaphors and it is in the discussion with others about what such metaphors can represent that an individual can gain insight and a new perspective on their core interests in relation to life/career. There has been an increased attention given to the use of metaphor as an entry point into 'seeing' and reflecting on the influences within career decision making, notably in the work of Inkson (2006). Visual extension of the place of metaphor can also be found in Law's work on storyboarding (see the Career-learning cafe). Cregeen-Cook (2011) views the use of visual tools as effective where a safe space is created, in Winnicott's language (1971), which enables the client to explore their motivations and increase their autonomy.

Drawing activities can be simple and do not rely on expensive resources or technical drawing skills. They can make use of paper worked on individually or employ a 'graffiti wall' for groups, which in most cases uses boards with poster paper, pens and/or sticky notes. In her research Cregeen-Cook used a 'crossroad tool'. A piece of paper with, placed centrally, the image of a crossroad signpost with arms pointing in different directions: this is a common metaphor when discussing 'directions' for education, training or career transitions. With few instructions, clients can be asked to place themselves at the centre, draw pathways, add words, draw symbols, include family and other people of significance to them, use coloured pens of their choosing and indicate the different directions they could take. The activity can help the individual to identify those aspects that are important to them and the priorities they see as important. Simple drawing activities, such as this, can be customised for different individuals and groups and can be adapted for interactive online use. Having said that, it is through the ensuing discussion that the deeper learning may be evident, so as an isolated activity the benefits may be less pronounced.

Visual tools – time lines

Creating a time line can be a simple pen and paper drawing, as the client wishes. In considering a career future, one approach is to ask the client to plot significant previous transitions before the present, marked with a cross. The future line can then be drawn in response to questions such as, 'Where would you like to be in two years, five years, ten years?' and so on. It may not be possible for a specific career to be identified, but general aspects can be envisaged (for example, a working environment, or being/working at home, with what type of people, doing what kinds of activity). Hindering factors can be discussed and drawn in (sometimes the line may encounter metaphoric mountains, broad rivers and the like) and a conversation can take place about resources that will help (a person as mountain guide, a boat or bridge). If used as a tool to engage a career conversation, this may be an easier route to reflection than having to articulate thoughts, feelings and future actions in words alone, and can make more visible and realistic unknown future scenarios.

Visual tools – collage

The more in-depth the activity the more alert the facilitator needs to be about the vulnerability of the client or clients. A contract of ways of working together will include being respectful and keeping discussions confidential; albeit there may be some limitations on confidentiality (depending on the age and circumstances of the individual or group – as discussed in a previous chapter). Mutual trust needs to be built and maintained for the development of a safe space for individuals to discuss openly their artefact, and access the deeper understanding that may come to the surface.

Collage is an example of a playful activity, with a serious purpose. It is an artistic technique based on composing cuttings from different materials (including paper, various images, photographs, fabric and so on) and placing this on or within a frame. The practice has ancient roots, but attained the status of an artistic technique during the twentieth century, for example via the works of artists like Pablo Picasso. The collage-maker uses objects readily available regardless of their original purpose. They use 'found' objects in the creation of something new, giving the objects, within a different frame, a new shape or 'identity' that tells a different story. Used in career counselling and coaching, the intention is that the exercise will articulate the individual's perspective through a visual representation and elicit deeper meaning. And again, the discussion of the created collage with an empathic listener is essential, before considering what this means in terms of goals and further action. It is an approach that has gained ground in qualitative research (Butler-Kisber, 2010; Gauntlett, 2007) and can be adapted for researching education, training and career options and choices. Helen, a career coach, explains how she used collage with a group of adults in the case study below.

Case study 13.2: Collage as a creative tool for career counselling

'I was asked by a medium-sized company to provide career coaching for a group of employees whose employment was at risk. The company was moving to a new location and there were individual members of staff who were unsure if they wanted to make the move, and they were worried about what else they might do in terms of alternative work. Participation was voluntary with the understanding that joining the group was not a signal to the company that they wanted to leave. In the first workshop I had eight people – I insisted that the numbers had to be small as we needed time to process the results of the activity within a 'safe' environment. It was successful and following the evaluation the company then asked me to repeat the workshop for another six participants.

I did not reveal the method before the first day as I did not want to put people off if they thought they had to be "artistic". Also I wanted a mixed group in terms of gender

(Continued)

(Continued)

and thought some men might think this was all a bit too wishy-washy, if they knew in advance what we would be doing. Of course, some women might think that too, but in the event all the participants engaged with the activity and their evaluation indicated that they got a lot out of the activity.

Anyway, it was designed as a two-hour workshop in three stages. I was also conscious that this was a difficult time for them all and we established a contract of working together in the session that paid attention to mutual trust and confidentiality issues. There is a need for flexibility in our approach, but this is what I normally do. The first thing I ask them to do is to write down the words that best describe them, paying attention to their strengths and their individual qualities. They are not asked to share what they write, but I do ask how easy or otherwise they felt about doing this. Most express some difficulty with this. So, this warm-up exercise enables them to focus on themselves and their characteristics. It also then demonstrates the enhanced and different awareness that can emerge from the creative technique we engage with next.

The second stage is the collage. I bring scissors, different types of glue, a wide range of magazines, different types and colours of paper, bits of textiles, glitter, stick-on stars, felt tip pens. These I spread out around the room – to encourage people to get up and move about. They are then asked to create a collage that represents them, their interests and the things that are important to them. No explicit link is made with a future career. I also give no further instructions but, without being patronising, answer "you decide – it's up to you". For example at the start, people will ask if the collage needs to be a certain way on the paper or can it go outside the borders, can they tear the paper and so on. I also play classical music quietly in the background, not to stop any talking but to create a relaxed atmosphere. I give an outline of the time available, so that people do not worry if someone seems to finish before them.

In the third stage, when everyone is ready I ask them to work in pairs (and never more than three) and to discuss their collage with their partner. I emphasise the importance of listening, not interrupting and asking open questions to encourage the teller to add to the story – using the simple phrase "tell me more about that". But, I also ask participants to respect any boundaries that their partner wishes to maintain – to see the signs when they do not want to say more. So, in simple terms, first I ask them to tell the story of their collage, and what they think the different parts represent; then I ask them to discuss together what it might say about their values and core interests, i.e. what is important to them at this point in time. I do not join in but I observe the groups as this is the point where emotions can emerge – not a bad thing, not harmful, but if it happens, I need to ensure these are contained for the person concerned. When all partners have done this I then get reactions from the group to express what they think they may have learnt through engaging in the activity.

In the evaluation, people say they gain a real insight into what is important for them and that they had not reached that level of insight previously from talking to others about the decisions they need to make. The activity engenders reflection of course, it should not be rushed and the atmosphere needs to be calm. People do talk to each other when making their collage, but it often feels quite studious – there's a lot of concentration and thinking going on. It would be different with a young age group maybe, but I'm not sure. Everyone seems to enjoy the activity, although of course it will not suit everyone – one person in the first group said they liked doing the collage but did not find out anything new about themselves. Other people told me later that they framed their collage and displayed it at home. Collage is one tool amongst others; in both groups there were people who would also benefit from a one-to-one interview, following a further period of reflection having gained insight from the activity. Overall the idea is to provide a means and a place for deep reflection which aids decision making and future planning.'

Creating an artefact can be done via a number of different media and might extend to textiles or perhaps even sculpture. Sculpture can involve wire mesh and papier-mâché, using three dimensional shapes – I am not suggesting Italian, Carrara marble is required! The method used will depend on the time and resources available and the purpose of the activity.

Creative writing

Creative writing can be another powerful tool for reflection and, by taking a different route for exploring self and career (different from the one-to-one interview), can be both playful and access deeper, unexpressed feelings and emotions – which may lead to more congruent education and career choices. As Celia Hunt cautions (2010) an approach that mines in the seams of emotions must be used carefully, as unexpected material may emerge for people. As in the previous example, ground rules would be agreed, but a particular emphasis is required on the building of trust and the atmosphere needs to be collaborative. Thus this is also not an approach to be rushed and a proper introduction and explanation of the purpose and possible outcomes is required. Hunt prefers to use the approach with a group that has already worked together and where a level of trust is established. In fostering reflection, the approach draws on psychodynamic thinking and the concept that there is a tendency for a splitting of the personality into different characters – 'into different and sometimes conflicting self-concepts' (Hunt, 2010: 19). Hunt suggests that the approach is best used for adults who already have work experience and who are considering a career shift.

The guidelines for the exercise are as follows:

1. Make a list of things that characterise you in your career.
2. Select two of them, preferably two that are contrasting, and write them on a piece of paper at the top of adjacent columns.
3. Add to the columns two or three metaphors for each of your chosen characteristics, starting with 'he/she is [like]...'
4. Develop these characteristics into fictional characters by answering the following questions for each of them:

    • What are his/her physical characteristics?
    • What sort of clothes does he/she wear?
    • How does he/she relate to others?
    • What does he/she do for a living?
    • What is his/her name?

5. Now that you know your characters a bit better, write down something that each of them might typically say.
6. Write a short third person narrative in which your characters meet each other, talk and eventually exchange something of value.
7. Reflect on what you learn from this exercise about your career identity.
8. The exercise can be repeated with another pair of characteristics. (Hunt, 2010: 18)

I have engaged in creative writing workshops facilitated by Celia Hunt on two occasions, some time apart and each with a different focus due to the context. As I recall, my characters in the second workshop split into a person who was pragmatic, 'grounded', tidy, liked structure and planning, and another character who liked to be spontaneous, playful, a rule-breaker and autonomous. Following step four in the workshop my two characters were then dressed and named accordingly. I invented a couple of phrases that each might use (step five). Next, I wrote a third person story and had them meet at a community event to discuss a road building project (step six – not sure why this scenario as I was not involved in such a group), where one was for the road building and one against. I developed a dialogue between them in keeping with their characters, but they moved from points of disagreement to some understanding of the other's viewpoint via the exchange.

The exercise took place at a time when a move to a different position in my organisation was possible and it was an opportunity that I felt some ambivalence towards. Engaging in the activity highlighted the areas that were important to me in terms of life/career, with life coming before career (which was better suited to my more 'playful' character). In this particular case I then listened to my own career advice and did not apply.

Simpson (2011) is another advocate for creative writing as a tool for clients to tell their unique stories when thinking about career development. Her interest evolved from in-depth autoethnographic work as part of a Master's degree, from which she is now developing this and other creative exercises for use with clients. She acknowledges the constraints in a time-bound, resource-restricted service that many career practitioners work within, but concludes:

> Moving towards professionalism calls for dynamic practice: creativity is the key if guidance practitioners are to be recognised as innovative professionals who embrace these challenging times. (Simpson, 2011: 58)

Lengelle's research on creative, expressive and reflective approaches to narrative careers work has been published in journal articles and is now available in a text that explores meaningful career conversations through the use of 'career writing' (Lengelle, 2014).

Drama

When done well drama, from the Greeks onwards, can access the emotions of the audience and simulate real-life issues and problems and, with different levels of interaction and participation, engage the audience in finding solutions to the situation being dramatised. Through the experience of a performance, an individual can 'rehearse' an issue that might arise later in their life, giving them some knowledge-at-hand. Unless already skilled in this area, a career practitioner might want to try short vignettes rather than complete performances. However, getting a group to work collaboratively, to identify a career issue that is important to them, to work on the script, to ad-lib and to direct a short piece has the potential to be transformative.

In the UK a training organisation known as CragRats offers 'Theatre-in-Education' programmes using dramatic performances and workshops, employing professional actors. The company specialises in various educational areas and has a proven track record being 'especially powerful when used in confronting hard-to-reach subjects or to challenge inflexible mindsets' (www.cragrats.com/about). Their programmes include the topics of Careers and Post-16 Options, Personal Achievement and NEET Awareness.

On a smaller scale a **role play** can be used by career counsellors and coaches in order to engage the imagination. Role-playing refers to the changing of an individual's behaviour in order to experience, to act out, a different role, to gain an insight into what it feels like 'to be' in that role, and/or to see an issue from another perspective. Role play can be a powerful approach for shifting a perspective or deepening understanding. Engaging in a role play can help a client to plan and rehearse how to act in situations in which they are not comfortable, for instance: talking to their parent who may not admire the choice they are intending to make; being interviewed for a job or college place; negotiating a change of course or job role; or having an appraisal meeting and so on.

Reflection point 13.3

As a final reflection point, look back over the alternative creative approaches in the second part of this chapter – which might you try and which would you tend to avoid and why? Thinking about why is important as it highlights our own fears, which otherwise might cause us to exclude an approach that our clients would find helpful.

Chapter summary

This chapter has discussed how the internet is changing careers work and has provided some examples of digital technologies in use. It has reflected on the implications of the increased use of such technologies and suggested that to increase effectiveness these approaches should be blended with traditional careers work. It also advocated that specific learning or training is required for practitioners to support their digital career literacy. In outlining the above, the chapter made use of the work of colleagues who have in-depth knowledge of the area. Finally, the chapter discussed a number of ideas for the inclusion of creative approaches that the career counsellor and career coach can incorporate into their practice.

Further reading:

On digital technologies and careers work:

The writing of Tristram Hooley, Bill Law and others that has informed the development of this chapter can be found in: National Institute of Careers Education and Counselling (NICEC) (2012) 'Digital technologies in career education and guidance', *Journal of the National Institute for Career Education and Counselling*, 29.

Longridge, D., Hooley, T. and Staunton, T. (2013) *Building Online Employability: A Guide for Academic Departments*. Derby: International Centre for Guidance Studies at the University of Derby. Available at: http://derby.openrepository.com/derby/bitstream/10545/294311/1/building%20online%20employability_finaljm.pdf (last accessed 13 November 2014).

This guide is designed to help academic departments support students to think about their careers and to use the online environment wisely. Academics (from any discipline) are often approached by students seeking help with their careers. The guide offers useful information for any academic and will be useful for career practitioners in their conversations with their clients when thinking about online employability.

The *British Journal of Guidance and Counselling* have published a symposium issue edited by Stephen Goss and Tristram Hooley which, aside from the editorial, carries 11 articles by different authors on 'Online practice in counselling and guidance' (volume 43, number 1, February 2015).

Two useful websites already mentioned in the book, but of note here are:
The Career-learning Cafe: www.hihohiho.com
National Guidance Research Forum: www2.warwick.ac.uk/fac/soc/ier/ngrf

Other websites that can be of interest, related to the issues raised in the chapter are as follows (with thanks to Tristram Hooley for these suggestions):
www.ces.ed.ac.uk/PDF%20Files/FinalReport.pdf
http://jca.sagepub.com/content/early/2014/05/15/1069072714535020.abstract
http://link.springer.com/article/10.1007/s10775-013-9258-7
www.tandfonline.com/doi/abs/10.1080/03069885.2014.939945#.VDf58IeE3rk

On other creative approaches:
Butler-Kisber, L. (2010) *Qualitative Inquiry: Thematic, Narrative and Arts-Informed Perspectives*. London: Sage.

This book is designed for students of qualitative research, but by opening up the world of performance and the visual, it is a valuable resource for thinking about how to use arts-based methods that can be adapted for exploring career-decision making.

CragRats Theatre can be found at: www.cragrats.com/about
Looking at the videos on their website can provide inspiration

Hunt, C. and Sampson, F. (2006) *Writing Self and Reflexivity* (3rd edn). Basingstoke: Palgrave Macmillan.

This is an excellent text for a critical understanding of both the theoretical and practical underpinnings of creative writing and for considering its use for careers work. Individual chapters link theory to practical aspects of writing, using illustrations from fiction, poetry and literary non-fiction. Examples of practical exercises are offered.

Lengelle, R. (2014) 'Career writing, creative, expressive, and reflective approaches to narrative and dialogical career guidance', published PhD thesis, Tilburg University, Tilburg, The Netherlands.

This is a PhD thesis that examines how career writing is a learning process and also a reflexive project of how we construct the self and articulate a career identity. Aside from explaining the research it gives examples of creative career writing in practice.

McMahon, M. and Watson, M. (eds) (2015) *Career Assessment: Qualitative Approaches.* Rotterdam, Netherlands: Sense Publications.

This book was mentioned previously; in addition to what is offered on assessment and the general development of theory and practice, there are a number of chapters that outline (in more detail than is offered here), creative approaches for career counselling and coaching.

14

Becoming a critically reflective practitioner

This chapter will:

- emphasise the importance of critically reflective and reflexive practice;
- outline models and practices that can be beneficial for critically reflective careers work;
- state the case for supervision of careers work;
- introduce a model that can be used with clients to aid their career thinking;
- offer vignettes of career pathways for career practitioners.

Introduction

In this final chapter the concept of the critically reflective practitioner will be discussed and models will be outlined and related to careers work. The aim is to demonstrate how reflective and reflexive practices benefit the work of career counsellors and coaches, enhancing their own professional development and the career thinking of their clients. Although supervision is evident in therapeutic counselling it is not widespread in career counselling and is less likely to be found in career coaching. However, supervision is also a reflexive practice and its particular contribution towards ethical and professional practice will be mentioned in this chapter. Moving from practitioners to clients, a model that encourages clients to reflect on and challenge their assumptions, in order to aid their career thinking, will also be introduced.

Career practitioners spend their time listening to the stories of others, but rarely have the opportunity to experience the same degree of attention to construct their own career narratives. The final section of the book will illustrate potential career pathways for career practitioners through short vignettes depicting future possibilities. It may help the new practitioner to think about the development of their own career and may suggest alternatives for others thinking about changing or developing their current role.

Critically reflective and reflexive practice

The need for reflective practice appears in many training courses in education, health and the social services. However, the depth of reflection required will vary. This may mean reflecting on an individual client 'case' in order to solve a problem and improve practice, in a cycle of reflection employing the well-known process outlined by Kolb. Kolb's (1984) four step experiential learning cycle involves Concrete Experience (describing the experience in detail), Reflective Observation (thinking about what 'I' was trying to do, why, and the consequences of the action or behaviour), Abstract Conceptualisation (how does this experience relate to what I know already, what I can learn from this, what else do I need to find out about) and Active Experimentation (what will I do next time in a similar situation, based on the analysis of this experience). A deeper process of reflection, reflexive practice, involves examining one's own thoughts, feelings and actions and their impact on both the client and on the self as the practitioner. Critical reflection requires the resource of time, and time is often squeezed by the need to meet a range of competing demands whether in work or in training. Thus reflective practice may be espoused as important for professional practice in a range of helping professions, but evidence of how this is facilitated and supported can be difficult to find.

Engaging in purposeful and critical reflection can improve practice and can also be taken into direct work with clients – the reflexive practitioner can 'practice what they preach' and support clients by creating spaces for deeper thinking about career. A reflexive practitioner is less likely to be driven by behaviour that is centred on reaching targets that are not intrinsic to the client's values. Engaging in critical reflection involves a questioning of the political forces that shape practice, albeit that is not an easy position to adopt when practitioners themselves can feel powerless within services beset by resource issues and potential redundancies. There are constraints that as practitioners we may be conscious of, but there are other 'assumptions' that we may not be aware of that a critical approach can reveal. But, lack of time cannot be a reason to ignore the benefits of reflexive processes. In careers work an 'intervention' can be a reflective space to pause, opening up the possibility for questioning assumptions to enhance more creative thinking. Before continuing, it will be useful to revisit the definition for reflectivity and reflexivity offered earlier in the book.

> A reflective practitioner is someone who is able to reach potential solutions through analysing experience and prior knowledge, in order to inform current and future practice. The internal process of reflection that is active and conscious could be described as reflectivity. Reflexivity is the process by which we are aware of our own responses to what is happening in a particular context … [i.e. a career counselling or coaching interaction] … and our reactions to people, events and the dialogue taking place. A reflexive understanding will include an

awareness of the personal, social and cultural context and its influence on both the speaker and the listener. Reflexive awareness in counselling practice, leads to a deeper understanding of how we co-construct knowledge about the world, and ways of operating within it, that are more meaningful for those involved. (Reid, 2013: 12)

Critical reflection is about an awareness of the social and political context within which career counselling and coaching take place. It is concerned with an acknowledgement of how any interaction is influenced by a range of factors – as above, not all of them conscious. We need to acknowledge that a relationship like career counselling or coaching does not take place in a vacuum, separate from what is happening in the 'outside' world. As mentioned in Chapter 3, we all bring our life scripts and social, familial and cultural influences and defences with us into the interaction. Schön was also introduced in Chapter 3 and his notion that theory and research occupy the 'high, hard ground', whilst practice resides in the 'swampy lowlands' (1983: 54). Practitioners work within the complexities of practice and the ability to reach potential solutions in the moment, through analysing experience and prior knowledge, is not easy. Munby and Russell (1989) claim that Schön's work is not sufficiently analytical as, 'The reflection that Schön is calling attention to is *in the action*, not in associated thinking about action' (1987: 73). Eraut (1994) is also critical of Schön's work, and questions the position of the reflective expert as enshrined by professional codes and the status they give. The space to engage in what Eraut prefers to call 'metacognitive' (that is, thinking about thinking) or 'deliberative' thought processes (1994: 145) is not just for new practitioners or for 'old' practitioners in new roles, but should be continuous for all practitioners. Eraut suggests that Schön fails to give sufficient attention to the variable of time when considering the reflective process and this criticism is particularly acute for hard-pressed helping services with limited resources. Action in such contexts will often proceed on the basis of rapid interpretation of the situation rather than critical reflection. In a criticism of Schön and Eraut, Ixer (1999: 513) goes further and states that in the context of 'busy practice' in the helping professions 'there is no such thing as reflection'. These criticisms suggest a requirement for a more developed use of critical reflection that moves beyond a focus on 'solving the client's problems', as if the practitioner is the objective expert operating outside of the process and not having an impact on what is taking place.

Reflexivity, then, involves inner reflection, to be aware of the impact of our behaviour on the process and entails a conscious awareness of our thoughts, feelings and imaginings. A consciousness about what is happening in our minds and bodies, what Etherington (2004) describes as the need 'to know the inner story that we tell ourselves as we listen to our clients' stories' (2004: 29). This is a deeper, metacognitive process that can lead to changes in the way we communicate with our clients. It can enhance the working alliance, the relationship with the client, acknowledging and fostering the client's agency to effect change in their lives. 'For the practitioner, it assists them to be fully conscious of and act upon the subjective influences which have an impact on their practice – it can cultivate strengths and aid the development of more informed and satisfying practice' (Reid and Bassot, 2011: 105).

Activity 14.1

It may be useful to pause at this point, before we move on to expand the discussion on criticality. To ensure that you have an understanding of the terms so far, write a short summary on the two concepts of reflective and reflexive practice.

In advocating for critical reflection, the observation has been made that this requires a separation from the immediate experience and this critical reflection can be enhanced within a conversation with others. Early writing on reflective practice can suggest practices which are somewhat sealed within a cycle which may become self absorbed and uncritical. Critical reflection is a learning process that adults can engage in if they are able, or enabled, to look back at the social norms and behaviours that were internalised uncritically as part of their socialisation in childhood. There is a contemporary trend to avoid looking back, and yet engaging with our past can, as Freud taught us, lead to a deeper understanding of the present, and in turn, reflexively, to reconfigure a sense of the possibility for the future – in all its constraints and uncertainties. To delve deeper into the concept of critical reflection to enhance reflexivity, I am going to make use of the influential work of Stephen Brookfield.

Critical reflection to enhance reflexivity

Brookfield (2005) draws extensively on the work of the critical theorists (writers such as Adorno, Gramsci, Horkheimer, Althusser, Marcuse and Habermas – see Brookfield, 2005) in order to challenge practitioners to rethink their assumptions about how adults learn about self and others. Although the work is focused on the sector for adult learning and teaching, it is highly relevant for those teaching and practising in careers work, with both young and 'older' adults. Brookfield has moved away from earlier conceptions of reflective practice that were concerned mainly in explaining general approaches rooted in humanistic psychology, which, he highlights, paid inadequate attention to social class and the underlying inequalities in Western society. In the 2005 text he also turns a critical eye on the Eurocentric approach to learning and teaching and the related reflective practices, drawing on literature that offers analyses from race and gender theorists, and from writers who challenge both (e.g. hooks, and Davis – see Brookfield, 2005). Brookfield explains that thinking critically is necessary to understand and then challenge the inequalities evident in the dominant ideology in any given society, the discourses that are seen as normal and democratic, and yet disadvantage large sections of the population. There is a conscious raising endeavour here redolent of the work of Freire (1970, 1994), which also informs his work. The point of this discussion is that ideology and discourses lead to normative behaviours and assumptions that are often not questioned. Mezirow (1991), theorizing adult learning, refers to this critical questioning as a 'systematic' critical reflection that centres on probing sociocultural distortions. Brookfield explains that critical theory derives from questioning ideological (often masquerading as 'common sense') understandings of how the world works, by stating:

1. That apparently open, Western democracies are actually highly unequal societies in which economic inequity, racism and class discrimination are empirical realities
2. That the way this state of affairs is reproduced and made to seem normal, natural and inevitable (thereby heading off potential challenges to the system) is through the dissemination of dominant ideology
3. That critical theory attempts to understand this state of affairs as a necessary prelude to changing it. (Brookfield, 2005: vii)

According to the view above, within organised social systems, which include the judiciary, policing, health, social care and education, individual 'subjects' are socialised and 'disciplined' within discourses (accepted ways of thinking and speaking) that establish which social roles are possible and impossible; that is, they set and constrain the norms in a society. In this way, discourses are based on what counts in terms of 'truth', knowledge, cultural values and socially defined norms of behaviour. A social and critical analysis challenges humanistic psychology that assumes that the individual is able to act from a politically neutral stance, outside of the operations of knowledge/power within a society (Foucault, 1980). From this perspective, social systems can become viewed as a form of surveillance. Career counselling and coaching, incorporating processes of reflection, may also be a way of disciplining individuals as 'subjects' into the prevailing capitalist economy, with its focus on neo-liberal effectiveness and the demands of the market. Reflective processes and supervision, discussed later, can be seen as confessionary practices, disciplining subjects into society's norms. Power is not just top down and all embracing, however; we resist through developing the necessary criticality around whose purposes such practices serve. The argument that it is important to acknowledge that careers work is a not a politically neutral activity has already been made in the book, alongside the need for a theoretical understanding of the models that are applied in practice. Thus, this must also include a critical questioning of the theory and models that we apply when we ask students and/or clients to engage in reflective practice; if we are to be reflexive teachers and practitioners we are not immune to critical scrutiny. Earlier in the book it was suggested that we need to pay attention to the language we use and, in advocating for critically reflective practice, we need to recognise that words can become fashionable and concepts can have their meaning 'emptied out' – words such as 'empowerment' and 'transformative' are particular examples. Critically reflective practice may be another; adding the word 'critical' without an examination of power and the politics of power does not lead to a psychosocial understanding of the concept. The terms reflective and reflexive practice do have different meanings, as defined above, but are often used interchangeably, so for the rest of the chapter, and in keeping with the arguments made above, the embracing term critically reflective practice will be used.

Reflection point 14.1

The discussion above may need to be digested before moving on. The need for a critical understanding of the influence of the social context on the individual and their thought processes has been 'rehearsed' before. Take a moment to consider if there are any terms or concepts that are not clear to you. If this is the case, use the index to look back at where these may have been covered before, or take time out perhaps to browse the internet for a further explanation.

In order for career practitioners to challenge assumptions – their own and/or their clients' – that are grounded in an unconscious and dominant ideology, it seems reasonable that we move on from theory and offer a few concrete tools. In doing so a cautionary note is required. In keeping with the tenets of critical theory, any such tools will work for some people and not others, and it is not the purpose here to suggest one way of working to engender critical reflection. The danger of moving on to tools for 'critically reflective practice' is that we put theory aside and stop thinking about the need for criticality, but move on we must.

Being critically reflective: models and practices

There are many books on reflective practice that do not take the critical approach described above. The focus is usually on what is happening within the interaction or on reflecting on the action to inform and improve further practice. Wider issues relating to power, its operation in any given society and the effects on the individual, are less likely to be considered. However, moving on from a social and political critique, which at times can feel like unrelieved pessimism, and keeping the need for criticality in mind, such models can offer useful starting points. As an introduction, I will draw on four approaches cited in Reid and Bassot (2011).

Gibbs' (1998) *reflective cycle* provides practitioners with a structure that has a focus on the affective or emotional impact of an experience. Reflective questions are:

- What happened?
- What were you thinking and feeling?
- What was good and bad about the experience?
- What sense can you make of the situation?
- What else could you have done?
- If the situation arose again, what would you do?

Our emotions often precede rational thought and paying attention to our feelings can reveal our attitudes and values, our 'world view' or 'frame of reference'. This focus can help us to reflect on how our emotions, feelings derived from our past experience, may be having an impact on the interaction, either positively or negatively.

Boud and colleagues's (1985) *model of reflection* is more detailed and examines the attitudes and values that inform our frame of reference, with an acknowledgement that we live our lives in contexts that will reinforce these. Their seven levels of reflectivity suggest we should examine our relationships with others, reflecting on the habits that we have learned through experience:

1. *Reflectivity* – becoming aware of how we see things, and how we think and act.
2. *Affective reflectivity* – becoming aware of our feelings about how we think and act.
3. *Discriminant reflectivity* – questioning whether or not our perceptions about people are accurate.
4. *Judgemental reflectivity* – becoming aware of our value judgements.
5. *Conceptual reflectivity* – questioning the way we think about other people.
6. *Psychic reflectivity* – recognising when we are quick to make judgements about people on the basis of limited information about them.
7. *Theoretical reflectivity* – becoming aware that the reasons we are quick to make judgements about people are based on cultural and psychological assumptions.

If an interaction with a client is not problematic, the chances are that we will not reflect on it, but if unsatisfying in some way it would be my expectation that a professional career practitioner would question what happened and why.

Osterman and Kottkamp's (2004) *reflective cycle* recognises that problematic experiences play a vital role in learning. Their cycle includes four phases: (a) identification of the problem: the discrepancy or gap between an ideal and a current reality, a dilemma (that by definition is not easy to solve) or a situation that resonates with our own personal experience; (b) observation and analysis: the complex step of both describing and analysing the situation. Osterman and Kottkamp (2004: 28) use the metaphor of a theatre critic to describe a process of 'watching and analyzing our own actions on stage: we become both subject and object'. Within this phase they employ the seven steps of Argyris' (1982) *Ladder of Inference*, as follows, to identify how assumptions are made:

1. I experience a situation.
2. I observe selectively. I see what I want to see.
3. I add meaning (cultural and personal).
4. I make assumptions based on the meanings I add.
5. I draw conclusions.
6. I adopt beliefs about the world.
7. I take action based on my beliefs.

Following this analysis, where assumptions are questioned and actions are critiqued, Osterman and Kottkamp suggest a third phase: (c) abstract re-conceptualisation: where new thoughts and understanding emerge. Finally, (d) active experimentation is the fourth phase, where new ideas are tested in practice.

Echoing Mezirow (1991), Lucas (1991) asserts that the development of reflective processes involves a systematic enquiry to improve and deepen one's understanding of practice. The word systematic suggests a methodical process that will require time, and the outcome can be enhanced if critical reflection can take place in a safe space, with one or more others. The need for change may emerge for the individual or the organisation and change is often challenging. As implied earlier, continuous improvement is a goal of professional practice and critical reflection has a crucial role to play in this demanding task. Before moving on, it is useful to spend a few words on thinking more about how practitioners can reflect in a systematic way.

Reflection point 14.2

Throughout the book I have asked you to reflect, and often suggested writing a response to the issue or question posed, but how, through what type of activity, do you usually reflect when you try to analyse an experience that troubled you?

I did not ask you to write down your response above as of course the way you usually reflect will depend on your previous experience, your preferred learning style and in many cases your use of current technology. Capturing your reflections in some systematic way is useful, as this will enable you to think critically and analyse and evaluate your thoughts – maybe using the models mentioned above. That process may be through writing in a reflective journal (Bassot, 2013), through using a web-based tool, audio-recording your thoughts, drawing a spider diagram, or using some other creative means – the choice is yours. The time you spend on this will also depend on the value you place on the activity. You may be some-one who prefers to discuss your thoughts with others, having spent time silently reflecting on the issue. These differences need to be reflected in teaching practices, as imposing one way of capturing reflections is not inclusive, particularly if such work is assessed. To explain what I mean, in the case study below I will describe an experience a colleague working in health care related to me.

Case study 14.1: Public or private?

'Where I trained the tutor was a strong advocate of experiential ways of learning, which I liked. What I was less keen on was the assessment of the exercise through using a journal to write about how my thinking about practice had been transformed by reflecting on my assumptions. Don't get me wrong, exploring assumptions was a useful exercise and one that I would strongly recommend, but beyond that there seemed to be a need to be dramatic and confessional in the writing, and, for me, it felt a bit like an invasion of privacy. In other words, I got the impression that those who could demon-strate some kind of significant shift and could describe this as "transformative" in their assignment, got better marks. And yet I am self aware and I do reflect, but my writing was considered not quite good enough – I got a low grade. I passed because I guessed what was wanted and glossed it up a bit, but that was rather inauthentic.'

In the case study a practice of reflecting on assumptions was seen as beneficial. The sharing of this became less helpful when what was considered as 'good' journal writing was judged via formal assessment by a teacher who had the power to set the norm for 'good' writing. The experience would suggest that reflective journals, in whatever medium, should remain private, and not be read and assessed by those who can grade a student. It is important that we do not lose sight of the very real advantages that an understanding of critically reflective theory and processes brings to the work. However, other ways of assessing a student's understanding of critically reflective practice, where this forms part of the accreditation of a course, need to be found (for example, in my institution, this takes place via a professional discussion (Reid, 2002)).

Activity 14.2

Having reached this point in the chapter, what do you see as the potential benefits of developing critically reflective practice? Can you list these?

My thoughts are included at the end of the chapter after the suggested reading.

Supervision

Working in any helping service can be challenging and practitioners working as career counsellors will experience situations where they are troubled by the work with clients. There may also be occasions when a client presents for career coaching but other issues emerge. In such circumstances 'clinical' supervision (as found in therapeutic counselling) is helpful. Supervision is also a reflexive process. It can maintain ethical work, alongside supporting the practitioner and preventing 'burn out'. I have written about supervision for career and guidance practitioners elsewhere (Reid, 2007, 2010) and for counsellors with Jane Westergaard (Reid and Westergaard, 2006, 2013). Briefly, the term can be divided into two words, 'super' and 'vision'. The experienced person looks from above (*super*) on the work of a colleague who may, or may not, be a less experienced person, and has a view (*vision*) of the work. The purpose and provision of supervision will differ according to the context in which practitioners are working and the individuals and/or groups they work with. For example, a career counsellor working with vulnerable young people will benefit from regular supervision, whereas a career coach working in an organisation with employees may not have access to supervision; albeit they may find themselves at times in challenging situations. These variations can reflect the role, the training for the role, the level of experience and whether working in private practice or within a public service. Within therapeutic counselling it is likely to be compulsory; in other roles it may be voluntary, or not available, or not viewed as a requirement.

Supervision is not therapy. To help identify what it is about, Weiner et al. (2003) describe four primary tasks of supervision:

> ... facilitating, encouraging and informing the work of the supervisee throughout the development of their professional life; attending to the dynamics of the supervisory relationship within an organisational context; ensuring competent

and ethical practice is taking place within the developmental stage of the supervisee, and, maintaining the good reputation of the profession as a whole – through attention to professional standards and governance. (Weiner et al., 2003: 4)

A well-known description of the functions of supervision within the context of counselling work is offered by Inskipp and Proctor (1993). They describe supervision as having *formative*, *normative* (which can be viewed as a monitoring function) and also *restorative* qualities. These terms focus on the benefits of supervision for the supervisee. Kadushin (1976), within the context of social work, offers something similar, but with a focus on the role of the supervisor, and uses the terms *educative, administrative* (which can be interpreted as managerial) and *supportive*. Hawkins and Shohet (2006) define the functions as *developmental*, *qualitative* and *resourcing*, and suggest that their definitions add new distinctions to a process that 'both supervisor and supervisee are engaged in' (2006: 57). They describe the *developmental* function as being concerned with 'developing the skills, understanding and capacity of the supervisees' (ibid.), via reflection and discussion of client work. Hawkins and Shohet (2006) also stress the collaborative nature of the work and emphasise the importance of encouraging a learning culture in the practice of supervision.

Harris and Brockbank (2011) pay particular attention to the place of learning theory, suggesting that supervisors need to examine the working context and their own experience of supervision. For this perspective there is a need for the supervisor to identify the learned philosophy and potential bias in their own supervisory practice. In other words, there is a need to question their assumptions about the work and the methods they use. As Harris and Brockbank state (2011: 57), without this reflexivity, 'the implicit model is passed on to the supervisee, without the supervisor being aware of it'. What is emphasised here is that supervision takes place within a learning climate where participants are prepared to learn and work collaboratively.

Reflection point 14.3

Supervision is included in this chapter because it is a reflexive process. Before you read the section above – what did the term mean for you? If you have previous knowledge or experience of clinical supervision then the above will seem partial as an explanation, which indeed it is. If not, and as an aid to reflexive practice, is this a practice that would be useful in your current or future work?

Working collaboratively in a safe space to develop critically reflective practice is a core feature of what might be described as 'good' supervision. In careers practice, working alongside the client, providing a space for reflection, avoiding an expert stance, not rushing to assumptions or action, is also fundamental to the Career Thinking Session, as described below.

Working with clients – the Career Thinking Session

In 'busy practice', particularly when time is short and targets have to be met, finding the space to 'slow down' practice can be a challenge. It is not surprising that a service will be judged on the outcomes, for example how many clients 'move on successfully' into education, employment and training, or when in work, how well they perform in a new role. An approach that spends time on providing a space for deeper reflection and less time on ensuring that the client has made a definite decision by the end of the session, will test this expectation. The Career Thinking Session (Reid and Bassot, 2011, 2013) is one such approach. Although future-focused, it advocates spending more time with the client to reflect on the current situation, and the underlying assumptions about what is possible, before identifying future goals and moving to action. In other words it facilitates greater client reflection in the belief that eventual decision making is likely to be more satisfying for the individual.

The Career Thinking Session (CTS) is adapted from the work of Kline (1999) and can be integrated into other process models (e.g. Egan, 2007), including the three-stage model described in this book (Reid and Fielding, 2007). It differs, as indicated above, on the *specific* focus of providing a space for the client to engage in deep reflection during the session, in order to question their assumptions. The practitioner (in the role of listener as the client's 'Thinking Partner') asks a limited number of questions and listens intently to what the client says. This work can feel intensive and the counsellor or coach will, as ever, work to build trust and rapport with the client in the opening stages of the session.

Once a contract has been established, the CTS has six steps:

Step 1 – 'What do you want to think about?' Here the client needs time to express the thoughts and issues they have brought to the Career Thinking Session. It is important that the Thinking Partner does not rush in with solutions but waits for the client to speak, interjecting when necessary with positive comments and supplementary open questions to encourage the client to think further about career issues. Once the client has finished speaking and has nothing else to add, they are ready to move on to Step 2.

Step 2 – 'What do you want to achieve from the rest of the session?' This is an opportunity for the client to articulate their desired outcomes in relation to the

Career Thinking Session. Again it is important that the Thinking Partner waits for the client to respond, which may take some time. Responses from clients could include such things as 'to have more clarity in relation to my future', 'to explore how I can gain more confidence in my own abilities' and 'to think strategically about my career progression, or lack of it'.

Step 3 – 'What are you assuming is stopping you from achieving your goal?' This encourages the client to think about their limiting assumptions. These could include facts such as 'I don't have the required qualifications', possible facts such as 'my family will think I'm crazy', or bedrock assumptions about self such as 'I'll never make it because I'm not good enough'.

Step 4 – 'If you knew that… what ideas would you have towards your goal?' Here the Thinking Partner asks the client to find the positive opposites to their assumptions in order to find the Incisive Question; for example, 'if you knew you could study for the required qualifications', 'if you knew your family would support you' or 'if you knew you were good enough' – '… what ideas would you have towards your goal?' This Incisive Question encourages the client to question their assumptions.

Step 5 – Writing down the Incisive Question. This emerges from Step 4 and it is important that it is written down in the client's own words, so that it is not lost. The Thinking Partner then poses the Incisive Question a number of times, until the client has voiced all their ideas in relation to their goals.

Step 6 – Sharing limiting assumptions is sensitive and demands trust and openness on both sides. Kline states (1999: 62) that 'Appreciation keeps people thinking'. This last step asks both participants to share a positive quality found in each other that they have valued during the session. (Reid and Bassot, 2011: 112–3).

Working towards the Incisive Question (step 4) needs a little more explanation, as offered in the following case study.

Case study 14.2: Waiting to hear the client's Incisive Question

In the study that helped to develop the model, the Incisive Question for one participant, Helen, became, 'how I can keep developing myself, where I am now?' Helen was in a difficult work situation with threats of redundancy on the horizon. The Incisive

(Continued)

(Continued)

Question was not arrived at quickly for Helen and it emerged via the questions posed, which presented positive opposites to her limiting assumptions.

Barbara (as the listener) thought that she knew what this question would be. Internally she thought, 'The incisive question here is going to be "should I stay or should I go?"' After further thought and discussion, Helen said, 'I think the big question really is how I can keep developing myself, where I am now?'

This question was both insightful and meaningful for Helen and the question cut through her limiting assumptions. In using Helen's Incisive Question a number of times, Barbara then enabled her to begin to think positively about the future. Barbara, as the practitioner, might have worked from the assumption that the 'big question' was 'should I stay or should I go?' and maybe used a technique that involved weighing up the alternatives of staying or leaving. Had she done so this would have 'disabled' Helen's deeper reflection and in all probability limited Helen's thinking to a fairly superficial level (Reid and Bassot, 2013).

Any 'new' model needs practice, and any model which offers a staged or step-by-step guide can appear deceptively straightforward on the page. The above can be a power-ful way of assisting the client to question their assumptions: the limiting assumptions that are preventing them from considering an option that at the current time seems unavailable because of those limiting assumptions. It is also difficult for the practi-tioner to stay with the client's thinking and not impose their own view about what the Incisive Question might be. It requires the practitioner to trust that if they live with a little uncertainty about what is going to happen next (i.e. whether or not this will work), then the 'transitional space' (Winnicott, 1971) that the CTS offers, gives the client time for deeper reflection. The practitioner will also need to resist the tempta-tion to move too soon to confirming future goals. Within the CTS identifying goals and action is not the primary aim; the aim is that the client goes on thinking and reflecting. In other words it seeks to construct a supportive space where there is room for *indecision* as a precursor to finding a way through to a career goal and action. However, a short follow-up interview, after a period of reflection, where goals are clarified and action is discussed is likely to be beneficial, in order to support the client further. Reid and Bassot (2013) include more detail on the case study, to illustrate the CTS model in practice.

Building your own career

The aim of this book was to provide an introduction to career counselling and career coaching. The hope is that the content is useful for those new to the work, those wanting to refresh or update their knowledge and to others who may be training or teaching career practitioners. Before closing, a number of vignettes are offered to illustrate where a career in careers work may take the practitioner – this is just a small sample, not an exhaustive list. It is an interesting and fulfilling career that offers the potential to work across a number of sectors with a diverse range of clients. The vignettes are based on people I know or have met. Don't worry, the names have been changed.

Case study 14.3: Vignettes

1. **Jaxson** trained as a teacher but wanted to work with young people in a different context. He considered youth work, but then had an opportunity to talk to a career counsellor and decided careers work was what he wanted to do. 'So, I registered to study full time on a Career Development programme, which, because I completed the Master's Dissertation stage, also increased my qualification level. I was then employed in a careers service where I worked with young unemployed people and with students in schools. When the service started to change its focus, my work became more concentrated on helping young people with multiple difficulties and I really enjoyed this work, even though thinking about a career was often not top of their list of priorities. When the service ended due to funding cuts, I worked for a time at the online Adult Careers Service, but I missed the ongoing contact with clients, and then a school in my area advertised for a career counsellor to work with all students from ages 15 to 18. I applied and have been there now for two years. I see a number of students who have 'problems' of one sort or another. I can offer a referral if needed, but the role has reinvigorated my interest in counselling theory, alongside the theory that underpins careers work, and I'm thinking about further training.'

2. **Ahmed** worked as a human relations professional in a large international company that was extending its reach and taking on more staff, including HR staff. 'So there was an opportunity, from the senior manager, for me to think about if there was a specialism that I wanted to develop within the role, and there was. I had always enjoyed working with colleagues on their career development within the company and I started to look for courses that would extend my knowledge and skills. I found a blended learning post-graduate course on 'career and talent matching' which I enrolled for and my company and the professional institute approved it. This was hard to complete alongside a full-time job, but has really furthered my own professional development. And of course I have increased my competency for careers work.'

3. **Janine** did not have a degree and was not expecting to be offered a place on the, then, graduate level Qualification in Career Guidance. She had worked in a voluntary

(Continued)

(Continued)

capacity with young people and had researched the work. 'The interview went well, but it was made clear to me that without a degree I might find the study difficult, so an assignment was given to me to assess my suitability. Writing it was a bit challenging but I got very good feedback and was offered a place on the course. I loved it. When I finished I found a career counselling job at a further education college, but was determined not to give up studying as my results had been good. So I completed a part-time Master's programme too and achieved a distinction. At the same time my career counselling work at the college, although secure, became less interesting as we were given very little time with clients. So, I registered for a PhD and was accepted! The PhD is taking forward the creative work I was developing in my practice. Then I applied for and was accepted for an employability adviser role in a university, but that is a short-term contract and I'm not sure what will happen next, but, who knows, perhaps my future plan involves research and an academic career.'

4. **Sonya** trained as a career adviser a number of years ago, first with young people and then as a sixth form (age 17–18) higher education specialist. She became a senior manager in the careers service, managing a number of centres. 'I loved the work when in the school and in the centres, but eventually decided I needed a change. My career biography is varied and before working in careers, I had a number of careers including running a restaurant at one time. I took the plunge and set up as a freelance career counsellor and consultant. And I also wrote self-help career books which continue to sell well. I work with individuals and organisations; this can be for in-depth one-to-one career counselling or for career coaching on, for example, presentation skills for career development.'

5. **Jack** worked in a careers service and qualified through an 'in work' vocational course and was able to exercise his interest in the development of digital technologies for careers work. 'For me this became the focus of my work and I was given, as part of my full-time contract, a role training other colleagues in the use of digital tools. I was then also used by the service as a consultant for schools and colleges, to develop their digital career tools. I would like to develop my own digital career development apps and I am working with a friend doing this, in my own time at the moment. I am still employed by the service but I'm thinking about my next step.'

6. **Anu** decided early on that she wanted to be an academic and after working as a career practitioner for two years, saw a post advertised as a research assistant at a well-known university. 'I jumped at the chance and got the job – it meant a house move for me but it was what I wanted. I am now employed as a full-time researcher in the research institute and am involved in bid writing for funding and then working on a variety of research projects – some of which have been international in their scope. Thus far I have worked on projects exploring youth unemployment, the impact of gender on career choices, and the effective development and use of labour market information.'

7. **Miriam** worked in a public employment service with unemployed adults. 'I liked the work and gained the qualification whilst I was working in the service. I have taken every opportunity to do any courses offered by my employer. These are very focused on the needs of the service and the clients, and are usually "in house" courses, although sometimes facilitated by an external trainer. For example, recently we had a large group of migrant workers who had settled in the area and the company they had been working for closed, making them jobless. I had attended a course a while back on understanding the issues that such groups face, in order that we could improve our communication with unemployed migrant workers – ultimately so that we can get them into work. The learning from that course proved invaluable working with these recent clients, and I was able to share some strategies with colleagues. I find the work very satisfying as no two days are the same.'

8. **Victor** worked in a university career service for many years and was promoted to manager of the service. 'And then as I was about to retire from the role I began wondering what I would do next. I did not what to give up work completely, although I was looking forward to having more time to enjoy some of my other interests. As it happens I seem to be busier than ever! Through a friend who was receiving hospital treatment, I found out that there was the possibility of offering specialist career counselling or coaching, depending on the individual, to oncology patients. Not something I had ever thought or heard about before, but with successful treatments these days there are many people whose lives have changed, yes, but they have a life, they have a future, and they want help thinking about what to do next. My work is voluntary, but who knows what other opportunities there may be to specialise out there, now and in the future, for voluntary or paid employment.'

Chapter summary

This chapter has focused on the importance of developing critically reflective practice, viewed as a core aspect of professional practice for career counsellors and career coaches. It has also sounded a cautionary note, in keeping with paying attention to the word 'critical'. Beyond the theoretical or philosophical discussion, it has also outlined models and practices that can be beneficial as a starting point for the development of critically reflective careers work. Within the focus on critically reflective work, supervision was discussed briefly as an area for development in careers work, noting, despite the benefits it brings, that its inclusion in practice is dependent on a range of issues. Reflection is not just for practitioners – the Career Thinking Session was also introduced as a model that assists the client to reflect, critically, on the assumptions that may be limiting the opportunities open to them as they construct their careers. Finally, the chapter offered vignettes on possible career pathways for career practitioners.

Further reading

Bassot, B. (2013) *The Reflective Journal*. Basingstoke: Palgrave Macmillan.
A useful and flexible resource to help the reader understand 'how to do' reflective practice: particularly helpful for those who like journal writing, or who wish to develop the skill as an aid to reflective practice.

Brookfield, S.D. (2005) *The Power of Critical Theory for Adult Learning and Teaching*. Maidenhead: Open University Press/McGraw-Hill.
This is an excellent resource that is very readable and yet takes a serious engagement with critical theory. For any researcher, teacher or practitioner who espouses critically reflective practice this is an essential text.

Reid, H.L. and Westergaard, J. (2013) *Effective Supervision for Counsellors: An Introduction*. Exeter: Learning Matters/Sage.
This book introduces both 'new' and 'in-training' supervisors and counsellors to the concept of supervision and its purpose within counselling. The focus is on key elements of supervision, including methods, processes, skills and policy, and the development of the supervision relationship is examined in depth.

Activity 14.2: My thoughts

My thoughts, but you may have others on your list that I have missed:

- Helps to keep us current as we question our knowledge, understanding and assumptions.
- Increases our self-awareness and attentiveness to both the conscious and unconscious processes that may be affecting our work.
- In turn, avoids the rush towards making assumptions and acting on those assumptions.
- Helps us to see 'the bigger picture' and question the discourses that are shaping policy and practice.
- Enables us to recognise cultural dissonance when our normative behaviour is not obvious to us and is imposed on others.
- Aids the agency of our clients when we listen more and slow down the process.
- Leads to supervisory practices that are normative, formative and restorative.
- Fosters continuous professional development and can be a route to constructing knowledge with others, for the benefit of both practitioners and clients.

Final words

Where careers work goes in the next 20 years is difficult to predict, but it seems impossible to imagine a world without education, training and work, and it seems inevitable that people will need career counsellors and coaches to work alongside them, in various ways, as they reflect on their interests and circumstances in order to shape their careers. In Victor's words in the final vignette, 'who knows what other opportunities there may be to specialise out there, now and in the future, for voluntary or paid employment'. We do not know what we will need to know in the future, we can only imagine. The book has advocated for continuous professional development and critically reflective practice, and stated that change, requiring innovation, is inevitable. But this can, at times, feel a bit like a treadmill. So it has also asked for a space for slowing down, for narrative, for creativity and for imaginative practice.

Appendix 1

Competence standards for career guidance and counselling – overview of competences for all types of career professionals

	Career Education Competences	Career Assessment and Information Competences	Career Counselling Competences	Career Service Management Competences	Career Systems Development Competences	Generic Professional Competences (All Roles)
Career Experts of a particular role should (additionally) be able to…	– Develop methodologies for **measuring people's career management competences** for particular target groups, based on scientific evidence and methodology – Develop strategies, curricula and training programs for **improving the career management competences of various target groups** based on recognised needs of the target group and relevant quality standards	– **Design and validate psychometric tools (tests, questionnaires, scales etc.) scientifically,** to provide a relevant and reliable diagnosis of people's career-related interests, abilities, competences, motivations and other characteristics – Design and develop **career information systems** to systemise relevant information on specific labour markets, education and training systems, and to anticipate emerging trends and issues	– **Design and validate career counselling approaches and instruments** to support clients with specific needs to solve their career-related problems – **Review the practice of career guidance counsellors and career advisors** for the development of their competence and professional self-awareness in a collaborative way, paying particular attention to intercultural and ethical aspects	– **Evaluate** the quality of techniques and program evaluation models used in career services, applying standards and expertise on innovative and effective practices – **Appraise human resources of career services** applying appropriate management approaches to **ensure the quality and sustainability of career services** provided, also in relation to funding – Implement a **quality assurance and development system** to secure relevant quality standards and improve the quality of services in a collaborative way with other stakeholders	– **Develop and implement concepts for more inclusive and effective career systems** in collaboration with employers, policy-makers and other stakeholders, based on an evaluation of the systems' ability to foster social justice, employment and the wellbeing of communities, organisations and individuals – Design **policies and strategies for the inter-sectorial and interdisciplinary coordination** in cooperation with relevant stakeholders at regional, national or international level – Devise recommendations on how to **overcome a career-related conflict,** based on the best interests of all involved stakeholders	– **Provide academic training to reach learning outcomes** according to international and national quality standards to assure the competence of all types of career professionals – **Conduct and publish original research and develop fundamental theories** on career-related topics to inform evidence-based practice, applying scientific standards rigorously – **Design and validate scientifically based concepts** (e.g. psychometric measures, quality standards, ethical guidelines) **in cooperation** with other professionals and stakeholders

(Continued)

	Career Education Competences	Career Assessment and Information Competences	Career Counselling Competences	Career Service Management Competences	Career Systems Development Competences	Generic Professional Competences (All Roles)
						– **Justify the value of interdisciplinary research and training in the field of CGC** based on the findings of various academic disciplines and empirical knowledge on the particular challenges of career services
Career Guidance Counsellors should (additionally) be able to…	– **Assess the career management competences** of clients with appropriate instruments and approaches – **Design and implement career education sessions and educational methods** to meet learning needs for the particular target group	– **Assess informational needs of clients,** regarding their interests and competences, the relevant labour market, and features of vocational and educational systems, to **confront informational problems** such as information overflow, stereotypes, disinformation, and lack of information	– **Conclude a client's main reason for seeking support** in an empathic and respectful way, based on a client-centred interview – Formulate an offer for a **counselling agreement** with a client, **specifying objectives and approaches** that suit the client's priorities and resources	– Construct appropriate **communication** channels, language and arguments to attract members of a particular target group to a particular career service offer – **Implement career services** strategically in cooperation with other relevant actors – **Produce good professional relations** with clients, colleagues and organisations to ensure quality of career services	– **Identify common interests** between the perspectives of different stakeholders in supporting a particular target group (e.g. early school leavers), **to propose how relevant cooperation structures** could be built up and maintained	– Produce a case study of a professional interaction with a client, **reviewing the client's needs, the process of professional support and their own behaviour on the basis of professional and ethical standards** for career guidance and counselling and related theories

Career Education Competences	Career Assessment and Information Competences	Career Counselling Competences	Career Service Management Competences	Career Systems Development Competences	Generic Professional Competences (All Roles)
	– Select scientifically validated methods and tools for self-assessment, as well as information sources to satisfy the clients' informational needs – Assess particular resources, interests or other relevant characteristics of an individual client using a validated career assessment approach in a collaborative way, to provide the client with personally relevant information	– Explore which psychological and external resources are available to support the client to cope with phases of stress and achieving personal growth – Assess the meaning of complex situations and different types of information together with clients, based on their interests, competences and other resources – Apply suitable models for creative problem-solving, decision-making and planning, based on the interests and preferences of clients, as well as their resources	– Review career services and their organisation on the basis of quality standards for career guidance and counselling and the needs of their specific target groups, and propose viable approaches for service enhancement, based on such an analysis	– Justify a need for support and propose a strategy in the case of an individual client in dealing with relevant stakeholders (e.g. parents, employers, public institutions) for the sake of the client's career development	

(Continued)

(Continued)

Career Advisors should be able to…	Career Education Competences	Career Assessment and Information Competences	Career Counselling Competences	Career Service Management Competences	Career Systems Development Competences	Generic Professional Competences (All Roles)
	– Explain how **to prepare applications** for jobs and training opportunities (CVs, letters, interviews) to the level of general standards – Explain how to learn about **educational and occupational options and requirements**	– Identify websites, self-assessment tools and other sources which **provide career information** for the particular target group of the client, **responding to the explicit interests, abilities, skills, competences and needs** they have formulated	– Produce a **confidential, respectful and supportive environment** for clients to speak openly about their career-related concerns and questions – Confirm the **type of career-related challenge** a client is facing, based on active listening to concerns and questions voiced by client	– **Report on the quality of career services** based on specific quality criteria and standards for career guidance and counselling – Assess **potential benefits of career services for individuals, communities and organisations** to better deal with existing and emerging challenges	– Arrange **a voluntary meeting of a client with a placement-provider**, relating to the needs formulated by the client	– **Judge when to make a referral** to a career guidance counsellor or to another professional service, based on **assessment of one's own ability** to provide the support needed by a client

Available at: www.nice-network.eu.

Appendix 2

The mentoring game

The game is designed to build relationships between mentors and mentees in a mixed group. The questions need to be adapted to suit the group and the mentoring context. It can also be used in the training of mentors before they start the work – in this situation it is important to mix the group as much as possible. The conversations around the questions should highlight (and increase understanding of) the differences and similarities in what life was like 'growing up' for the different players, in various locations and different eras. The game should be enjoyable, but it is important it is set within a contract of working together which includes confidentiality and the freedom to 'opt out' of taking part. If an individual decides the game will be upsetting for them, they can observe.

In addition to the suggestions on layout and questions in Chapter 3, questions might include:

When you were a teenager:

- Where were you living?
- Did you have any brothers or sisters?
- Did you have your own bedroom – how was it decorated?
- What was your favourite TV programme?
- Did you have a TV or computer in your bedroom?
- What were you good at in school?
- Was there a time when you thought you were a 'failure' at anything?
- Did you play any sports or belong to any clubs?
- Did you do anything slightly risky that got you into trouble?
- How old were you when you first had a mobile phone?
- What did you read?
- Who was your favourite pop star or TV/film star?
- If you tried smoking or drinking alcohol, when was the first time?
- Where did your extended family live?
- Were you expected to do any jobs at home?
- What did you do on a Saturday night?
- Were you ever in trouble at school?
- What was your first date like?
- What was the best holiday you had with your family?
- What did you save your pocket money for?

- Did you have a part-time or Saturday job?
- What was your most embarrassing moment?
- What fashions did you like?
- What was your hairstyle like?
- How far were you from the nearest town?
- What was your favourite shop?
- Did you ever do things that your parents/carers told you not to?
- What did you do on your 16th/18th birthday?

Appendix 3

Managing challenging behaviour in group settings[1]

For any session that may provoke controversy or involve the giving and receiving of feedback, it is always advisable to negotiate ground rules at the start of the session.

Behaviour	Why	What to do
1. **Overly talkative**	May be over-enthusiastic or a show off. May also be exceptionally well informed and anxious to demonstrate it, or just naturally garrulous.	Avoid sarcasm and do not embarrass them – they may be useful later. Slow them down with a difficult question. Interrupt with, 'That's an interesting point… what do other people think?' In general, involve the rest of the group as much as possible – but they will expect you to manage this.
2. **Highly argumentative**	Combative personality… professional heckler. Or may be normally good-natured but upset by other issues external to the session.	Keep your temper firmly in check and do not let the group get excited either. Don't turn a disagreement into a spectacle. Try to find some merit in one of their points. But, as above, give it back to the group, thus avoiding a combat situation between you both. This gives you time to think. Be aware of your body language. A private discussion later to find out what is wrong may help to show understanding and win their co-operation.
3. **Quick, helpful**	Really trying to help, but in fact makes it difficult as keeps others out.	Cut across tactfully by questioning others. Thank, but suggest we put others to work. Use them to summarise.
4. **Personality clashes**	Two or more members clash. Can divide your group into factions.	Emphasise agreement – minimise points of disagreement. Draw attention to the objectives of the session. Cut across with direct question on the topic. Bring another member into the discussion. Return to ground rules and remind group the discussion is about issues not personalities.

(Continued)

---

1   Drawing on the work of Johnson and Johnson (1987)

(Continued)

Behaviour	Why	What to do
5. Asks for your opinion	Trying to put you on the spot. Trying to have you support one view. May be simply looking for advice.	Generally, avoid solving their problems for them. Never take sides. Point out your view is relatively unimportant, compared with the view of the rest of the group. BUT, don't let this become a phobia – there are times when you must, and should give a direct answer. Before doing this, try to determine the reason for asking for your view. Say 'First let's get some other opinions…'
6. Obstinate	Won't budge. Prejudiced. Has missed the point.	Throw the views open to the group and let them feed back. Indicate that time is short, we need to move on, perhaps they could discuss it more later, but for now ask them to accept the group consensus on the point.
7. Griper	Has pet peeve. Professional griper. Has legitimate complaint.	Point out we cannot change the policy here; we need to look at how to operate as best we can within the system. Indicate you'll discuss the problem, later in private. Have another member of the group answer. Indicate pressure of time.
8. Side conversations	May be related to the subject. May be personal. Distracts members and you.	Don't embarrass them. Call one of them by name, ask an easy question or, restate last opinion expressed by a group member, and ask their opinion. Try stopping in mid-sentence, look at them, when they notice, smile and continue. Move around the room and saunter over and stand casually behind members who are talking. Try to do this so it is not obvious to the rest of the group. If all else fails, explain quietly that it is difficult for the group to concentrate if too many people are talking at once. Keep it pleasant, avoid alienating individual group members.

Behaviour	Why	What to do
9. Changing the subject	Not rambling, just off base.	Take the blame; 'Something I said must have led you off the subject…', or 'I obviously did not make it clear… this is what we should be looking at/discussing' and then restate the point.
10. Rambler	Talks about everything except the subject. Uses far-fetched analogies and long sentences – gets lost.	When they stop for breath thank them, re-focus their attention by restating the points and move on. Grin… tell them it's an interesting point and, in a friendly manner, indicate we are a bit off the subject. Last resort glance at a watch or clock.
11. Inarticulate	Lacks ability to put thoughts into words. Is getting the idea, but cannot convey it. Needs help.	Don't say, 'What you mean is this…' Say 'Let me try to summarise that', and then phrase it better – check you have understood their meaning. Twist the ideas as little as possible, but have them make sense.
12. Definitely wrong	Comes up with comments that are obviously incorrect. In over their head.	Must be handled delicately. Say, 'I can see how you feel', or 'That's one way of looking at it', or 'I see your point, but how can we match that with this particular situation?'
13. Won't talk	Bored. Indifferent. Feels superior. Timid. Insecure.	Your action will depend on what is (de)motivating them. Arouse their interest by asking for their opinion. Draw out the person next to them and ask the quiet one to tell them what they think of the view expressed. If the person is seated near you, ask their opinion so that they feel they are talking to you, not the whole group. If they are the 'superior' type, ask for their view, after indicating the respect held for experience (but don't overdo this, as the group will resent it). Stimulate them for a moment by tossing a provocative query. If the sensitive person won't talk, compliment them the first time they do. Be sincere.

Controversy and conflict can energise groups and avoid passivity. It is important to stress that group members should be critical of ideas, not of persons. Imputations that insult or challenge a group member's intelligence, integrity or motives should always be avoided. Combine 'unconditional positive regard', Rogers (1961), with intellectual challenge. 'I am interested in your ideas but I can not agree with you on that point...', or 'I have come to a different conclusion'.

'Do not take personally other members' disagreement and rejection of your ideas. ... (This) should be taken as an interesting situation from which something can be learned, not as a personal attack' (Johnson and Johnson, 1987: 313). Make sure the conflict is over issues not personalities.

Avoid win–lose conflict as it promotes distrust, dislike, rivalry and attempts to undermine each other's point of view. Define any conflict in the smallest and most specific terms – it will be easier to resolve. One of the most effective conflict resolution skills is to see the issue from the other person's viewpoint – practise empathy. Finally, deal with conflict; ignoring it does not make it go away.

References

Johnson, D. and Johnson, F. (1987) *Joining Together: Group Theory and Group Skills* (5th edn). Harlow: Pearsons Education.

Rogers, C. (1961) *On Becoming a Person*. Boston, MA: Houghton Mifflin.

References

Adler, A. (1956) *The Individual Psychology of Alfred Adler*. New York: Basic Books.

Alexander, G. (2006) 'Behavioural coaching', in J. Passmore (ed.), *Excellence in Coaching*. London: Kogan Page.

Alheit, P. (1995) 'Biographical learning: theoretical outline, challenges, and contradictions of a new approach in adult education', in P. Alheit, A. Bron-Wojciechowska, E. Brugger and P. Dominice (eds), *The Biographical Approach in European Adult Education*. Vienna, Austria: Verband Wiener Volksbildung, pp. 57–74.

Amundson, N. (2006) 'Active engagement and the influence of constructivism', in M. McMahon and W. Patton (eds), *Career Counselling: Constructivist Approaches*. Abingdon: Routledge.

Appadurai, A. (2007) 'The right to research', *Globalisation, Societies and Education*, 4 (2): 167–77.

Archer, M.S. (2012) *The Reflexive Imperative in Late Modernity*. Cambridge, NY: Cambridge University Press.

Arendt, H. (1997) *The Human Condition*. Chicago, IL: University of Chicago Press.

Argyris, C. (1982) *Reasoning, Learning and Action: Individual and Organizational*. San Francisco, CA: Jossey-Bass.

Arnold, J. (2004) 'The congruence problem in John Holland's theory of vocational decisions', *Journal of Occupational and Organizational Psychology*, 77: 95–113.

Arthur, M.B. and Rousseau, D.M. (eds) (1996) *The Boundaryless Career*. New York: Oxford University Press.

Arulmani, G. (2009) 'A matter of culture', *Career Guidance Today*, Institute of Career Guidance, 17 (1), March: 0–12.

Arulmani, G. (2011) 'Receive in order to give: eastern cultural values and their relevance to contemporary career counselling contexts', in H.L. Reid (ed.), *Vocation, Vocation, Vocation: Placing Meaning in the Foreground of Career Decision-Making*. Occasional Paper, Centre for Career & Personal Development, Canterbury Christ Church University, Canterbury, pp. 16–22.

Arulmani, G. (2014) 'The cultural preparation process model and career development', in G. Arulmani, A.J. Bakshi, F.T.L. Leong and A.G. Watts (eds), *Handbook of Career Development: International Perspectives*. New York: Springer.

Arulmani, G. and Nag-Arulmani, S. (2004) *Career Counselling. A Handbook*. New Delhi: Tata McGraw-Hill Publishing.

Arulmani, G., Bakshi, A.J., Leong, F.T.L. and Watts, A.G. (eds) (2014) *Handbook of Career Development: International Perspectives*. New York: Springer.

Bandura, A. (1977) *Social Learning Theory*. Englewood Cliffs, NJ: Prentice-Hall.

Barnes, A., Bassot, B. and Chant, A. (2011) *An Introduction to Career Learning and Development 11–19*. Abingdon: Routledge.

Bassot, B. (2013) *The Reflective Journal*. Basingstoke: Palgrave Macmillan.

Bassot, B., Barnes, A. and Chant, A. (2014) *A Practical Guide to Career Learning and Development: Innovation in Careers Education 11–19*. Abingdon: Routledge.

Bauman, Z. (2006) *Liquid Life: Living in an Age of Uncertainty*. Cambridge: Polity Press.

Beck, A. (1976) *Cognitive Therapy and the Emotional Disorders*. New York: International University Press.

Berne, E. (1964) *The Games People Play*. Harmondsworth: Penguin Books.

Besley, T. (2002) *Counseling Youth: Foucault, Power and the Ethics of Subjectivity*. Westport, CA: Praeger.

Biesta, G.J.J. (2006) *Beyond Learning: Democratic Education for a Human Future*. Boulder, CO: Paradigm Publishers.

Bimrose, J. (1996) 'Multiculturalism', in R. Bayne, I. Horton and J. Bimrose (eds), *New Directions in Counselling*. London: Routledge.

Bimrose, J. (2009) *Careers Guidance, Identity & Development. Beyond Current Horizons: Technology, Children, Schools & Families*. London: DCSF/Futurelab. Available at: www.beyondcurrenthorizons.org.uk/wp-content/uploads/ch4_bim rosejenny_carreersguidance20090116.pdf (last accessed 7 January 2015).

Bimrose, J. (2010) 'What do clients need and really want?' in H. Reid (ed.), *The Re-Emergence of Career: Challenges and Opportunities*. Occasional Paper, Centre for Career & Personal Development, Canterbury Christ Church University, Canterbury, pp. 9–14.

Boud, D., Keogh, R. and Walker, D. (1985) *Reflection: Turning Experience Into Learning*. London: Routledge Falmer.

Bourdieu, P. and Passeron, J.C. (1977) *Reproduction in Education: Society and Culture*. London: Sage.

Bozarth, J.D. and Fisher, R. (1990) 'Person-centred career counselling', in B. Walsh and S.H. Osipow (eds), *Career Counselling: Contemporary Topics in Vocational Psychology*. Hillside, NJ: Erlbaum.

Brookfield, S.D. (2005) *The Power of Critical Theory for Adult Learning and Teaching*. Maidenhead: Open University Press/McGraw-Hill.

Bruner, J. (1990) *Acts of Meaning*. Cambridge, MA: Harvard University Press.

Butler-Kisber, L. (2010) *Qualitative Inquiry: Thematic, Narrative and Arts-Informed Perspectives*. London: Sage.

Caldwell, B.J. and Carter, E.M.A. (eds) (1993a) 'The workplace of the 1990s', in *The Return of the Mentor: Strategies for Workplace Learning*. London: Falmer Press, pp. 1–8.

Caldwell, B.J. and Carter, E.M.A. (eds) (1993b) 'Transforming the workplace', in *The Return of the Mentor: Strategies for Workplace Learning*. London: Falmer Press, pp. 205–20.

Carruthers, J. (1993) 'The principles and practices of mentoring', in B.J. Caldwell and E.M.A. Carter (eds), *The Return of the Mentor: Strategies for Workplace Learning*. London: Falmer Press, pp. 9–24.

Castells, M. (1996) *The Information Age: Economy, Society and Culture. Vol.1: The Rise of the Network Society*. Oxford: Blackwell.

Chant, A. (2012) 'E-learning for the careers profession: what are the lessons for the use of IT in the delivery of IAG?' *Journal of the National Institute for Career Education and Counselling*, (29): 33–8.

Cochran, L. (1997) *Career Counselling: A Narrative Approach*. Thousand Oaks, CA: Sage.

Colley, H. (2003) *Mentoring for Social Inclusion: A Critical Approach to Nurturing Mentor Relationships*. London: Routledge Falmer.

Collin, A. (2000) 'Dancing to the music of time', in A. Collin and R.A. Young (eds), *The Future of Career*. Cambridge, NY: Cambridge University Press.

Collin, A. and Young, R.A. (2000) 'Introduction: framing the future of career', in A. Collin and R.A. Young (eds), *The Future of Career*. Cambridge, NY: Cambridge University Press.

Connor, M. and Pohara, J.L. (2012) *Coaching and Mentoring at Work: Developing Effective Practice* (2nd edn). Maidenhead: Open University Press.

Corfield, R. (2009a) *Preparing the Perfect Job Application* (5th edn). London: Kogan Page.

Corfield, R. (2009b) *Successful Interview Skills* (5th edn). London: Kogan Page.

Corfield, R. (2010a) *Knockout Job Interview Presentations*. London: Kogan Page.

Corfield, R. (2010b) *Preparing the Perfect CV* (5th edn). London: Kogan Page.

Cregeen-Cook, S. (2011) 'Beyond words: an explanation of the use of 'visual tools' within career guidance practice', *Journal of the National Institute for Career Education and Counselling*, 27: 47–53.

Csikszentmihalyi, M. and Beattie, O.V. (1979) 'Life themes: a theoretical and empirical investigation of their origin and effects', *Journal of Humanistic Psychology*, 19: 45–63.

Culley, S. and Bond, T. (2011) *Integrative Counselling Skills in Action* (3rd edn). London: Sage.

D'Andrea, M. and Daniels, J. (1991) 'Exploring the different levels of multicultural counselling training in counsellor education', *Journal of Counselling and Development*, 70: 78–85.

de Shazer, S., Berg, I.K., Lipchick, E., Nunnally, E., Molnar, A., Gingerih, W. and Weiner-Davis, M. (1986) 'Brief therapy: focused solution development', *Family Process*, 25: 207–21.

Dewey, J. (1938) *Experience and Education*. New York: Collier Books.

Dickinson, D. and Henderson, L. (2012) 'Orientation, navigation and engagement: a philosophy for human and digital navigation', *Journal of the National Institute for Career Education and Counselling*, 29: 52–9.

DiClemente, C.C. and Velasquez, M. (2002) 'Motivational interviewing and the stages of change', in W.R. Miller and R. Rollnick (eds), *Motivational Interviewing: Preparing People for Change* (2nd edn). New York: The Guilford Press.

Dik, B.J., Strife, S.R. and Hansen, J.C. (2010) 'The flip-side of Holland types congruence: incongruence and job satisfaction', *The Career Development Quarterly*, 58: 352–8.

Dirkx, J.M. (2006) 'Engaging emotions in adult learning: a Jungian perspective on emotion and transformative learning', in E.W. Taylor (ed.), *Teaching for Change. New Directions for Adult and Continuing Education, No. 109*. San Francisco, CA: Jossey-Bass.

Dugosija, D., Efe, V., Hackenbracht, S., Vaegs, T. and Glukhova, A. (2008) *Online Gaming as a Tool for Career Development*. Available at: www.comsys.rwth-aachen.de/fileadmin/papers/2008/2008-steg-vaegs-gaming.pdf (last accessed 11 June 2012).

Dyson, E. (2012) 'Face-to-Facebook: a blended approach to careers work', *Journal of the National Institute for Career Education and Counselling*, 29: 27–32.

Egan, G. (2007) *The Skilled Helper: A Problem-Management and Opportunity-Development Approach to Helping* (8th edn). Pacific Grove, CA: Brooks/Cole.

Egan, G. (2013) *The Skilled Helper: A Problem-Management and Opportunity-Development Approach to Helping* (10th edn). Pacific Grove, CA: Brooks/Cole.

Etherington, K. (2004) *Becoming a Reflexive Researcher*. London: Jessica Kingsley.

Eraut, M. (1994) *Developing Professional Knowledge and Competence*. London: Falmer Press.

Foucault, M. (1979) *Discipline and Punish: The Birth of the Prison* (Trans, Alan, Sheridan). Harmondsworth: Penguin Books.

Foucault, M. (1980) *Power/Knowledge: Selected Interviews and Other Writings 1972–1977*. London: Harvester Press.

Freire, P. (1970) *Pedagogy of the Oppressed*. New York: Continuum.

Freire, P. (1994) *Pedagogy of Hope*. New York: Continuum.

Frigerio, G. and McCash, P. (2013) 'Creating career coaching', *Journal of the National Institute for Career Education and Counselling*, 30: 54–8.

Gale, R. (2000) 'Rethinking social justice in schools: how will we recognize it when we see it?' *International Journal of Inclusive Education*, 4 (3): 253–69.

Gati, I. and Tal, S. (2008) 'Decision making models and career guidance', in J.A. Athanasou and R. Van Esbroek (eds), *International Handbook of Career Guidance*. Berlin: Springer.

Gati, I., Krausz, M. and Osipow, S.H. (1996) 'A taxonomy of difficulties in career decision making', *Journal of Counseling Psychology*, 43: 510–26.

Gauntlett, D. (2007) *Creative Explorations: New Approaches to Identities and Audiences*. Abingdon: Routledge.

Gergen, K.J. (1994) *Reality and Relationships: Soundings in Social Construction*. Cambridge, MA: Harvard University Press.

Gibbs, G. (1998) *Learning by Doing: A Guide to Teaching and Learning Methods*. Oxford: Further Education Unit, Oxford Polytechnic.

Giddens, A. (1999) *Runaway World*. London: Profile Books.

Ginzberg, E., Ginsburg, S.W., Axelrad, S. and Herma, J.L. (1951) *Occupational Choice: An Approach to a General Theory*. New York: Columbia University Press.

Gordon, M. M. Ogilvie (1908) *A Handbook of Employments Specially Prepared for the Use of Boys and Girls on Entering the Trades, Industries, and Professions*. Aberdeen: The Rosemount Press.

Goss, S. and Hooley, T. (eds) (2015) 'Symposium: online practice in counselling and guidance', *British Journal of Guidance & Counselling*, 43 (1): 1–7.

Gottfredson, L.S. (1981) 'Circumscription and compromise: a developmental theory of occupational aspirations', *Journal of Counseling Psychology*, 28 (6): 545–79.

Gramsci, A. (1971) *Selection From the Prison Notebooks*. New York: International Publishers.

Grant, E.M. and Johnston, J.A. (2006) 'Career narratives', in M. McMahon and W. Patton (eds), *Career Counselling Constructivist Approaches*. London: Routledge.

Guichard, J. (2009) 'Self-constructing', *Journal of Vocational Behavior*, 75: 251–8.

Handy, C. (1993) *Understanding Organizations* (4th edn). Oxford: Oxford University Press.

Handy, C. (1999) *Inside Organizations: 21 Ideas for Managers*. London: Penguin Books.

Harris, M. and Brockbank, A. (2011) *An Integrative Approach to Therapy and Supervision: A Practical Guide for Counsellors and Psychotherapists*. London: Jessica Kingsley Publishers.

Hawkins, P. and Shohet, R. (2006) *Supervision in the Helping Professions*. Maidenhead: Open University Press.

Higgins, R. and Westergaard, J. (2001) 'The role of group work in careers education and guidance programmes', *Career Research and Development*, 2: 4–17.

Hodkinson, P. and Sparkes, A.C. (1997) 'Careership: a sociological theory of career decision making', *British Journal of the Sociology of Education*, 18 (1): 29–44.

Hodkinson, P., Sparkes, A.C. and Hodkinson, H. (1996) *Triumphs and Tears: Young People, Markets and the Transition From School to Work*. London: David Fulton Publishers.

Holland, J. (1985) *Making Vocational Choices: A Theory of Vocational Personalities and Work Environments*. Englewood Cliffs, NJ: Prentice-Hall.

Holland, J. (1997) *Making Vocational Choices: A Theory of Vocational Personalities and Work Environments* (3rd edn). Odessa, FL: Psychological Assessment Resources.

Hooley, T. (2012) 'How the internet changed career: framing the relationship between career development and online technologies', *Journal of the National Institute for Career Education and Counselling*, 29: 3–12.

Hooley, T., Hutchinson, J. and Watts, A.G. (2010) *Careering Through the Web: The Potential of Web 2.0 and 3.0 Technologies for Career Development and Career Support Services*. London: UKCES.

Hopson, B. (1981) 'Response to the papers by Schlossberg, Brammer and Abrego', *Counselling Psychologist*, 9 (2): 36–9, 131, 142–4, 148, 169.

Human Rights Act (HRA) (1998) *Human Rights Act*. Available at: http://www.legis lation.gov.uk/ukpga/1998/42/contents (last accessed 25 April 2015).

Hunt, C. (2010) 'Exploring career identities through creative writing', *Career Research & Development, the NICEC Journal*, 23: 18–19.

Hunt, C. and Sampson, F. (2006) *Writing Self and Reflexivity* (3rd edn). Basingstoke: Palgrave Macmillan.

Inkson, K. (2006) *Understanding Careers: The Metaphors of Working Lives*. Thousand Oaks, CA: Sage Publications.

Innes, T. (2012) 'Using career learning theory to inform the design and evaluation of ICT based CEIG services', *Journal of the National Institute for Career Education and Counselling*, 29: 21–6.

Inskipp, F. and Proctor, B. (1993) *The Art, Craft and Tasks of Counselling Supervision, Part 1. Making the Most of Supervisors*. Twickenham: Cascade Publications.

Irving, B.A. (2005) 'Social justice: a context for career education and guidance', in B.A. Irving and B. Malik (eds), *Critical Reflections on Career Education and Guidance: Promoting Social Justice Within a Global Economy*. Abingdon: Routledge.

Irving, B.A. and Malik, B. (2005) *Critical Reflections on Career Education and Guidance: Promoting Social Justice Within a Global Economy*. Abingdon: Routledge.

Ivey, A.E., Ivey, M.B. and Simeg-Morgan, L. (1997) *Counseling and Psychotherapy: A Multicultural Perspective* (4th edn). Needham Heights, MA: Allyn & Bacon.

Ixer, G. (1999) 'There's no such thing as reflection', *British Journal of Social Work*, 29: 513–27.

Jackson, C. (2013) 'The changing shape of the career profession in the UK', *Journal of the National Institute for Career Education and Counselling*, 30: 3–12.

Johnson, D. and Johnson, F. (1987) *Joining Together: Group Theory and Group Skills* (5th edn). Harlow: Pearson Education.

Johnson, D. and Johnson, F. (2012) *Joining Together: Group Therapy and Group Skills* (11th edn). Harlow: Pearson Education

Kadushin, A. (1976) *Supervision in Social Work*. New York: Columbia University Press.

Kay, D. and Hinds, R. (2012) *A Practical Guide to Mentoring: Using Coaching and Mentoring Skills to Help Others Achieve Their Goals* (5th edn). Oxford: How to Books Ltd.

Kelly, G. (1955) *The Psychology of Personal Constructs, Volumes 1 and 2*. New York: WW Norton.

Kenny, K., Whittle, A. and Willmott, H. (2011) *Understanding Identity & Organizations*. London: Sage.

Kettunen, J., Sampson, J.P. Jr. and Vuorinen, R. (2014) 'Career practitioners' conceptions of competency for social media in career services', *British Journal of Guidance & Counselling*. doi:10.1080/03069885.2014.939945 (Accessed 4 October 2014).

Kidd, J.M. (1996) 'The career counselling interview', in A.G. Watts, B. Law, J. Killeen, J.M. Kidd and R. Hawthorne (eds), *Rethinking Careers Education and Guidance: Theory, Policy and Practice*. London: Routledge.

Kidd, J.M. (2006) *Understanding Career Counselling: Theory, Research and Practice*. London: Sage.

Kidd, J.M., Hirsh, W. and Jackson, C. (2004) 'Straight talking: the nature of effective career discussion at work', *Journal of Career Development*, 30: 231–45.

Killeen, J. (1996a) 'Career theory', in A.G. Watts, B. Law, J. Killeen, J.M. Kidd and R. Hawthorne (eds), *Rethinking Careers Education and Guidance: Theory, Policy and Practice*. London: Routledge.

Killeen, J. (1996b) 'The learning and economic outcomes of guidance', in A.G. Watts, B. Law, J. Killeen, J.M. Kidd and R. Hawthorne (eds), *Rethinking Careers Education and Guidance: Theory, Policy and Practice*. London: Routledge.

King, I. (2010) 'Disentangling professional careers: a narrative approach to embracing third-age career aspirations', in H. Reid (ed.), *The Re-Emergence of Career: Challenges and Opportunities*. Occasional Paper, Centre for Career & Personal Development, Canterbury Christ Church University, Canterbury, pp. 51–8.

Kline, N. (1999) *Time to Think*. London: Ward Lock.

Kolb, D.A. (1984) *Experiential Learning: Experience as the Source of Learning and Development*. Englewood Cliffs, NJ: Prentice Hall.

Krumboltz, J.D. (1994) 'Improving career development from a social learning perspective', in M.L. Savickas and R.W. Lent (eds), *Convergence in Career Development Theories: Implications for Science and Practice*. Palo Alto, CA: Consulting Psychologists Press.

Law, B. (1981) 'Community interaction: a 'mid-range' focus for theories of career development in young adults', *British Journal of Guidance & Counselling*, 9 (2): 142–58.

Law, B. (1996) 'A career-learning theory', in A.G. Watts, B. Law, J. Killeen, J.M. Kidd and R. Hawthorne (eds), *Rethinking Careers Education and Guidance: Theory, Policy and Practice*. London: Routledge.

Law, B. (2003) 'Guidance: too many lists, not enough stories', in A. Edwards (ed.), *Challenging Biographies: Re-Locating the Theory and Practice of Careers Work*. Southborough: Canterbury Christ Church University, pp. 25–47.

Law, B. (2012a) *On-Line Careers Work – Colonist or Inhabitant?* Available at: www.
hihohiho.com (last accessed 12 November 2012).

Law, B. (2012b) 'On-line careers work – hit and myth', *Journal of the National Institute for Career Education and Counselling*, 29: 13–20.

Law, B. and Watts, A.G. (1977) *Schools, Careers and Community*. London: Church Information Office.

Lengelle, R. (2014) 'Career writing, creative, expressive, and reflective approaches to narrative and dialogical career guidance', published PhD thesis, Tilburg University, Tilburg, The Netherlands.

Lent, R.W. and Brown, S.D. (eds) (2013) *Career Development and Counselling: Putting Theory and Research to Work* (2nd edn). Hoboken, NJ: John Wiley & Sons.

Leong, T.L. and Pearce, M. (2014) 'Indigenous models of career development and vocational psychology', in G. Arulmani, A.J. Bakshi, F.T.L. Leong and A.G. Watts (eds), *Handbook of Career Development: International Perspectives*. New York: Springer.

Levitas, R. (2005) *The Inclusive Society: Social Inclusion and New Labour* (2nd edn). Basingstoke: Palgrave Macmillan.

Lewin, K. (1951) *Resolving Social Conflicts*. Washington, DC: American Psychological Association.

Longridge, D., Hooley, T. and Staunton, T. (2013) *Building Online Employability: A Guide for Academic Departments*. Derby: International Centre for Guidance Studies at the University of Derby. Available at: http://derby.openrepository. com/derby/bitstream/10545/294311/1/building%20online%20employability_ finaljm.pdf (last accessed 13 November 2014).

Lucas, P. (1991) 'Reflection, new practices and the need for flexibility in supervising student teachers', *Journal of Further and Higher Education*, 15 (2): 84–93.

McLennan, N. (2013) *The Perfect Coach: Bringing Out the Best in Others*. London: Aria Publishing.

Manson, A. (2012) 'A developer's perspective on CEIAG', *Journal of the National Institute for Career Education and Counselling*, 29: 47–51.

Maree, K. and Molepo, M. (2006) 'The use of narratives in cross-cultural career counselling', in M. McMahon and W. Patton (eds), *Career Counselling Constructivist Approaches*. London: Routledge.

Maslow, A. (1970) *Motivation and Personality* (2nd edn). New York: Harper and Row.

McIlveen, P. and Patton, W. (2007) 'Dialogical self: author and narrator of career life themes', *International Journal for Educational and Vocational Guidance*, 7 (2): 67–80.

McLeod, J. (1997) *Narrative & Psychotherapy*. London: Sage.

McLeod, J. (2003) *An Introduction to Counselling* (3rd edn). Buckingham: Open University Press.

McLeod, J. (2009) *An Introduction to Counselling* (4th edn). Maidenhead: McGraw Hill/Open University Press.

McMahon, M. and Patton, W. (2006) *Career Counselling Constructivist Approaches*. London: Routledge.

McMahon, M. and Watson, M. (2010) 'Story telling: moving from thin stories to thick and rich stories', in K. Mare (ed.), *Career Counselling: Methods That Work*. Cape Town, South Africa: Juta.

McMahon, M. and Watson, M. (eds) (2011) *Career Counselling and Constructivism*. New York: Nova Science.

McMahon, M. and Watson, M. (eds) (2015) *Career Assessment: Qualitative Approaches*. Rotterdam, The Netherlands: Sense Publications.

McMahon, M., Watson, M., Chetty, C. and Hoelson, C.N. (2012) 'Examining process constructs of narrative career counselling: an exploratory case study', *British Journal of Guidance & Counselling*, 40 (2): 127–41.

McMahon, M., Watson, M. and Patton, W. (2013) *My System of Career Influences (MSCI): A Qualitative Career Assessment Reflection Process: Facilitator's Guide*. Samsord, Queensland: Academic Press.

Mearns, D. and Thorne, B. (2000) *Person-Centred Therapy Today*. London: Sage.

Mezirow, J. (1991) *Transformative Dimensions of Adult Learning*. San Francisco, CA: Jossey-Bass.

Mezirow, J. (2009) 'Transformative learning theory', in J. Mezirow and E.W. Taylor (eds), *Transformative Learning in Practice: Insights From Community, Workplace, and Higher Education*. San Francisco, CA: Jossey-Bass.

Miller, J. (2006) 'Using a solution-building approach in career counselling', in M. McMahon and W. Patton (eds), *Career Counselling: Constructivist Approaches*. Abingdon: Routledge.

Miller, W.R. and Rollnick, R. (2002) *Motivational Interviewing: Preparing People for Change* (2nd edn). New York: The Guilford Press.

Mills, C. (2011) *Career Coach*. Richmond, London: Trotman Publishing.

Monk, G., Winslade, J. and Sinclair, S. (2008) *New Horizons in Multicultural Counselling*. Thousand Oaks, CA: Sage Publications.

Mouffe, C. (1993) *The Return of the Political*. London: Verso.

Munby, H. and Russell, T. (1989) 'Educating the reflective teacher: an essay review of two books by Donald Schön', *Journal of Curriculum Studies*, 21: 71–80.

Nathan, R. and Hill, L. (2006) *Career Counselling* (2nd edn). London: Sage.

Nelson-Jones, R. (1997) *Practical Counselling & Helping Skills* (4th edn). London: Cassell.

Nicholson, N. (1990) 'The transition cycle: causes, outcomes, processes and forms', in S. Fischer and C.L. Cooper (eds), *On the Move: The Psychology of Change and Transition*. Chichester: Wiley.

Nicholson, N. and West, M. (1988) *Managerial Job Change: Men and Women in Transition*. Cambridge, NY: Cambridge University Press.

Norcross, J.C. and Grencavage, L.M. (1989) 'Eclecticism and integration in counselling and psychology: major themes and obstacles', *British Journal of Guidance & Counselling*, 17: 215–47.

Nota, L. and Rossier, J. (eds) (2015) *Handbook of Life Design: From Practice to Theory and From Theory to Practice*. Göttingen, Germany: Hogrefe Publishing.

O'Connell, B. (2005) *Solution-Focused Therapy* (2nd edn). London: Sage.

Office for National Statistics (ONS) (2014) *Internet Access: Households and Individuals*. Available at: www.ons.gov.uk/ons/rel/rdit2/internet-access---house holds-and-individuals/2014/stb-ia-2014.html (last accessed 13 November 2014).

Osterman, K.F. and Kottkamp, R.B. (2004) *Reflective Practice for Educators: Professional Development to Improve Student Learning*. Thousand Oaks, CA: Corwin Press.

Oxford English Dictionary (OED) (1992) *Oxford English Dictionary*. Oxford: Oxford University Press.

Oxford Latin Dictionary (OLD) (2005) *Oxford Latin Dictionary*. Oxford: Oxford University Press.

Parsons, F. (1909) *Choosing a Vocation*. Boston, MA: Houghton-Mifflin.

Patterson, C.H. (1964) 'Counselling: self-clarification and the helping relationship', in H. Borrow (ed.), *Man in a World at Work*. Boston, MA: Houghton Mifflin.

Pavlov, I.P. (1927) *Conditional Reflexes: An Investigation of the Physiological Activity of the Cerebral Cortex* (Translated and edited by G.V. Anrep). London: Oxford University Press.

Payne, M. (2006) *Narrative Therapy: An Introduction for Counsellors* (2nd edn). London: Sage.

Peavy, R.V. (1998) *Sociodynamic Counselling: A Constructivist Perspective*. Victoria, Canada: Trafford.

Peck, D. (2010) 'Profile: Maria Gordon – pioneer of the profession', *Career Guidance Today*, Institute of Career Guidance, 18 (2): 16–17.

Plant, P. (2014) 'Green guidance', in G. Arulmani, A.J. Bakshi, F.T.L. Leong and A.G. Watts (eds), *International Handbook of Career Guidance*. Dordrecht, The Netherlands: Springer.

Pryor, R.G.L and Bright, J.E.H. (2011) *The Chaos Theory of Careers*. New York/London: Routledge.

Rawls, J. (1971) *A Theory of Justice*. Cambridge, MA: Harvard University Press.

Reid, H.L. (1999) 'Barriers to inclusion for the disaffected: implications for 'preventive' careers guidance work with the under-16 age group', *British Journal of Guidance & Counselling*, 27 (2): 539–54.

Reid, H.L. (2002) 'The professional discussion as an alternative to paper-based evidence for the NVQ in guidance: avoiding "death by portfolio building!"', *Career Guidance Today*, 10 (2). Stourbridge: Institute of Career Guidance.

Reid, H.L. (2005) 'Beyond the toolbox: integrating multicultural principles into a career guidance intervention model', in B.A. Irving and B. Malik (eds), *Critical Reflections on Career Education and Guidance: Promoting Social Justice Within a Global Economy*. London: Routledge Falmer.

Reid, H.L (2007) 'The shaping of discourse positions in the development of support and supervision for personal advisers in England', *British Journal of Guidance & Counselling*, 35: 59–78.

Reid, H.L. (2010) 'Supervision to enhance educational and vocational guidance practice: a review', *International Journal for Vocational & Educational Guidance*, 10 (3): 191–205.

Reid, H.L. (2011) 'Embedding multicultural principles and skills into counselling work with young people', in H.L. Reid and J. Westergaard (eds), *Effective Counselling With Young People*. Exeter: Learning Matters.

Reid, H.L. (2013) 'What is supervision?' in H.L. Reid and J. Westergaard (eds), *Effective Supervision for Counsellors: An Introduction*. London: Learning Matters/Sage.

Reid, H. and Bassot, B. (2011) 'Reflection: a constructive space for career development', in M. McMahon and M. Watson (eds), *Career Counselling and Constructivism: Elaboration of Constructs*. New York: Nova Science.

Reid, H. and Bassot, B. (2013) 'Constructing a space for career reflection: the gift of time to think', *Australian Journal of Career Development*, 22 (2): 91–9.

Reid, H.L. and Fielding, A.J. (2007) *Providing Support to Young People: A Model for Structuring Helping Relationships*. London: Routledge.

Reid, H.L. and Scott, M. (2010) 'Narratives and career guidance: from theory into practice', in H.L. Reid (ed.), *The Re-Emergence of Career: Challenges and Opportunities*. Occasional Paper, Centre for Career and Personal Development, Canterbury Christ Church University, Canterbury.

Reid, H.L. and West, L. (2011a) 'Struggling for space: narrative methods and the crisis of professionalism in career guidance in England', *British Journal of Guidance & Counselling*: 397–410.

Reid, H.L. and West, L. (2011b) '"Telling Tales": using narrative in career guidance', *Journal of Vocational Behaviour*, 78: 174–83.

Reid, H.L. and West, L. (2014) 'Telling tales: do narrative approaches for career counselling count?' in G. Arulmani, A.J. Bakshi, F.T.L. Leong and A.G. Watts (eds), *International Handbook of Career Guidance*. Dordrecht, The Netherlands: Springer.

Reid, H.L. and Westergaard, J. (2006) *Providing Support and Supervision: An Introduction for Professionals Working With Young People*. London: Routledge.

Reid, H.L. and Westergaard, J. (2011) *Effective Counselling With Young People*. Exeter: Learning Matters.

Reid, H.L. and Westergaard, J. (2013) *Effective Supervision for Counsellors: An Introduction*. Exeter: Learning Matters/Sage.

Reynolds, H. (2006) 'Beyond reason and anxiety: how psychoanalytical ideas can inform the practice of supervision', in H.L. Reid and J. Westergaard (eds), *Providing Support and Supervision: An Introduction for Professionals Working With Young People*. Abingdon: Routledge.

Roberts, K. (1968) 'The entry into employment: an approach towards a general theory', *Sociological Review*, 16: 165–84.

Roberts, K. (1977) 'The social conditions, consequences and limitations of careers guidance', *British Journal of Guidance & Counselling*, 5 (1): 1–9.

Roberts, K. (1997) 'Prolonged transitions to uncertain destinations: the implications for careers guidance', *British Journal of Guidance & Counselling*, 25: 345–60.

Roberts, K. (2005) 'Social class, opportunity, structures and career guidance', in B.A. Irving and B. Malik (eds), *Critical Reflections on Career Education and Guidance: Promoting Social Justice Within a Global Economy*. London: RoutledgeFalmer.

Rodger, A. (1952) *The Seven-Point Plan*. London: NIIP.

Rogers, C. (1951) *Client-Centred Therapy*. Boston, MA: Houghton Mifflin.

Rogers, C. (1961) *On Becoming a Person*. Boston, MA: Houghton Mifflin.

Rogers, C. (1980) *A Way of Being*. Boston, MA: Houghton Mifflin.

Rollnick, S. and Miller, W.R. (1995) 'What is motivational interviewing?' *Behavioural & Cognitive Psychotherapy*, 23: 325–34.

Rounds, J.B. and Tracey, T.J. (1990) 'From trait-factor to person-environment fit counselling: theory and process', in W.B. Walsh and S.H. Osipow (eds), *Career Counselling: Contemporary Topics in Vocational Psychology*. Hillside, NJ: Erlbaum.

Said, E.W. (1994) *Culture & Imperialism*. London: Vintage Books.

Sampson, J.P. (2009) 'Modern and postmodern career theories: the unnecessary divorce', *The Career Development Quarterly*, 58 (1): 91–96.

Savickas, M.L. (1994) 'Donald Edwin Super: the career of a planful explorer', *Career Development Quarterly*, September: 1–28. Available at: https://www.questia.com/read/1P3-2755980 (last accessed 29 January 2015).

Savickas, M.L. (2005) 'The theory and practice of career construction', in S.D. Brown and R.W. Lent (eds), *Career Development and Counseling: Putting Theory and Research to Work*. Hoboken, NJ: John Wiley & Sons Inc, pp. 42–69.

Savickas, M.L. (2006) *Career Counseling – DVD, Series II – Specific Treatments for Specific Populations*. Washington, DC: American Psychological Association.

Savickas, M.L. (2009) *Career Counseling Over Time* (Psychotherapy in Six Sessions Video Series). Washington, DC: American Psychological Association.

Savickas, M.L. (2011) *Career Counseling*. Washington, DC: American Psychological Association.

Savickas, M.L., Nota, L., Rossier, J., Dauwalder, J.-P., Eduarda Duarte, M., Guichard, J., Soresi, S., Van Esbroeck, R. and van Vianen, A.E.M. (2009) 'Life designing: a paradigm for career construction in the 21st century', *Journal of Vocational Behavior*, 75 (3): 239–50.

Schiersmann, C., Ertelt, B.J., Katsarov, J., Mulvey, R., Reid, H. and Weber, P. (eds) (2012) *NICE Handbook for the Academic Training of Career Guidance and Counselling Professionals*. Heidelberg, Germany: Heidelberg University.

Schlossberg, N.K., Waters, E.B. and Goodman, J. (1995) *Counseling Adults in Transition: Linking Practice With Theory*. New York: Springer.

Schön, D.A. (1983) *The Reflective Practitioner*. Brookfield, WI: Basic Books Inc.

Schön, D.A. (1987) *Educating the Reflective Practitioner*. San Francisco, CA: Jossey Bass.

Sen, A. (2008) 'The idea of justice', *Journal of Human Development*, 9: 331–42.

Senge, P.M. (1990) *The Fifth Discipline: The Art and Practice of the Learning Organisation*. New York: Doubleday Currency.

Sheath, J. (2013) 'The education and training of career coaches: a psychological model', *Journal of the National Institute for Career Education and Counselling*, 30: 39–45.

Simpson, L. (2011) 'Creative writing practices in career guidance: an autoethnographical approach', *Journal of the National Institute for Career Education and Counselling*, 27: 54–60.

Skinner, B.F. (1953) *Science and Human Behaviour*. New York: Macmillan.

Starr, J. (2012) *Brilliant Coaching* (2nd edn). Harlow: Pearson Education Ltd.

Sue, D.W., Arrendondon, P. and McDavis, R.J. (1995) 'Multicultural counseling competencies and standards: a call to the profession', in J.G. Ponterotto, J.M. Casas, L.A. Suzuki and C.M. Alexander (eds), *Handbook of Multicultural Counseling*. Thousand Oaks, CA: Sage.

Sue, D.W., Allen, E.I. and Pederson, P.B. (1996) *A Theory of Multicultural Counseling and Therapy*. Pacific Grove, CA: Brooks/Cole.

Sugarman, L. (1986) *Life-span Development: Concepts, Theories and Interventions*. London: Routledge.

Sultana, R. (2011) 'Lifelong guidance, citizen rights and the state: reclaiming the social contract', *British Journal of Guidance & Counselling*, 39 (2): 179–86.

Sultana, R. (2013) 'Flexibility and security? 'Flexicurity' and its implications for lifelong guidance', *British Journal of Guidance & Counselling*, 41 (2): 145–63.

Sultana, R. (2014) 'Pessimisms of the intellect, optimism of the will? Troubling the relationship between career guidance and social justice', *International Journal of Educational and Vocational Guidance*, 14: 5–19.

Super, D.E. (1951/1957) *The Psychology of Careers*. New York: Harper & Row.

Super, D.E. (1981) 'Approaches to occupational choice and career development', in A.G. Watts, D.E. Super and J.M. Kidd (eds), *Career Development in Britain*. Cambridge, MA: Careers Research and Advisory Centre/Hobsons.

Super, D.E. (1994) 'A life span, life space perspective on convergence', in M.L. Savickas and R.W. Lent (eds), *Convergence in Career Development Theories: Implications for Science and Practice*. Palo Alto, CA: Consulting Psychologists Press.

Sutherland, M. (2009) *Draw on Your Emotions*. Milton Keynes: Speechmark.

Taylor, E.W. (2009) 'Fostering transformative learning', in J. Mezirow and E.W. Taylor (eds), *Transformative Learning in Practice: Insights From Community, Workplace, and Higher Education*. San Francisco, CA: Jossey-Bass.

Thompson, N. (2011) *Promoting Equality – Working with Diversity and Difference* (3rd edn). Basingstoke: Palgrave McMillan.

Thomsen, R. (2012) *Career Guidance in Communities*. Aarhus, Denmark: Aarhus University Press.

UDACE (Unit for the Development of Adults and Continuing Education) (1986) *The Challenge of Change*. London: UDACE.

UK Equality Act (2010) *Equality Act 2010: guidance*. Available at: www.gov.uk/equality-act-2010-guidance (last accessed 22 April 2014).

Watson, J.B. (1919) *Psychology from the Standpoint of a Behaviourist*. Philadelphia, PA: J. B. Lippincott.

Watson, M.B. (2006) 'Career counselling theory, culture and constructivism', in M. McMahon and W. Patton (eds), *Career Counselling: Constructivist Approaches*. Abingdon: Routledge.

Watson, M. (2013) 'Deconstruction, reconstruction, co-construction: career construction theory in a developing world context', *Indian Journal of Career and Livelihood Planning*, 2 (1): 3–14.

Watts, A.G. (2001) 'Career guidance and social inclusion: a cautionary tale', *British Journal of Guidance & Counselling*, 29 (2): 157–76.

Watts, A.G. (2010) 'National all-age career guidance services: evidence and issues', *British Journal of Guidance & Counselling*, 38 (1): 31–44.

Watts, A.G. (2013) 'False dawns, bleak sunset: the coalition government's policies on career guidance', *British Journal of Guidance and Counselling*, 41 (4): 442–53.

Watts, A.G. and Sultana, R.G. (2004) *Career Guidance Policies in 37 Countries: Contrasts and Common Themes*. Thessaloniki, Greece: CEDEFOP.

Weiner, J., Mizen, R. and Duckham, J. (eds) (2003) *Supervision and Being Supervised: A Practice in Search of a Theory*. Basingstoke: Palgrave Macmillan.

Westergaard, J. (2009) *Effective Group Work With Young People*. Maidenhead: Open University Press/McGraw-Hill.

Westergaard, J. (2011a) 'Exploring person-centred principles and developing counselling skills', in H.L. Reid and J. Westergaard (eds), *Effective Counselling With Young People*. Exeter: Learning Matters.

Westergaard, J. (2011b) 'Understanding how cognitive behavioural approaches can inform counselling practice with young people', in H.L. Reid and J. Westergaard (eds), *Effective Counselling With Young People*. Exeter: Learning Matters.

Westergaard, J. (2011c) 'Using transactional analysis to develop effective communication in counselling young people', in H.L. Reid and J. Westergaard (eds), *Effective Counselling With Young People*. Exeter: Learning Matters.

White, M. (1989) 'The externalisation of the problem and the re-authoring of relationships', in M. White (ed.), *Selected Papers*. Adelaide, South Australia: Dulwich Centre Publications.

White, M. and Epston, D. (1990) *Narrative Means to Therapeutic Ends*. New York, NY: Norton.

Whitmore, J. (2002) *Coaching for Performance*. London: Nicholas Brealey.

Whitmore, J. (2009) *Coaching for Performance: Growing Human Potential and Purpose* (4th edn). London: Nicholas Brealey.

Williamson, H. and Middlemiss, R. (1999) 'The Emperor has no clothes: cycles of delusion in community interventions with 'disaffected' young men', *Youth and Policy*, 63: 13–25.

Winnicott, D. (1971) *Playing and Reality*. London: Routledge.

Winslade, J. and Monk, G. (2007) *Narrative Counselling in Schools: Powerful and Brief* (2nd edn). Thousand Oaks, CA: Corwin Press.

Wright Mills, C. (1959/1970) *The Sociological Imagination*. Oxford: Oxford University Press.

Yates, J. (2011) 'Career coaching: what exactly is it?' *Career Guidance Today*, 19 (3): 16–18.

Yates, J. (2013) 'A positive approach to career coaching', *Journal of the National Institute for Career Education and Counselling*, 30: 46–53.

Yates, J. (2014) *The Career Coaching Handbook*. Abingdon: Routledge.

Yorks, L. and Kasal, E. (2006) 'I know more than I can say: a taxonomy for using expressive ways of knowing to foster transformative learning', *Journal of Transformative Education*, 4: 43–64.

Young, R.A., Vallach, L. and Collin, A. (2002) 'A contextualist explanation of career', in D. Brown and Associates (eds), *Career Choice and Development* (4th edn). San Francisco, CA: Jossey-Bass, pp. 206–52.

Zeus, P. and Skiffington, S. (2000) *The Complete Guide to Coaching at Work*. North Ryde, Australia: McGraw-Hill.

General websites

The career learning cafe: www.hihohiho.com (last accessed 28 August 2014).

National Guidance Research Forum: www2.warwick.ac.uk/fac/soc/ier/ngrf (last accessed 28 August 2014).

Network for Innovation in Career Guidance and Counselling in Europe: www.nice-network.eu (last accessed 22 December 2014).

Index

adaptability, 9
Adler, A., 110–111
adult careers work
   assessment in, 151–154
   group settings in, 220
   realism and resilience in, 144–145, 147–151
   role of practitioner in, 145–147
agency, 56, 65, 105
Amundson, N., 92
anti-oppressive practice, 131–134, 140–141
anxiety, 74–75
Appadurai, A., 179
approach, definition of, 62
Archer, M.S., 154–155
Arendt, H., 138
Argyris, C., 248
Arnold, J., 50–51
Arulmani, G., 23, 99, 130–131, 164, 179, 180
ashramas, 99
assessment, 82–83, 151–154
attending, 184–185

balance sheets, 196–197
Bandura, A., 71
Barnes, A., 14, 201
Bassot, B., 203
Bauman, Z., 130, 154
Beattie, O.V., 111
Beck, A., 71
behaviourist psychology, 71–72, 178–179
Berne, E., 76–78
Bimrose, J., 12, 87, 134–135
biographicity, 105–106, 110
body language. *See* non-verbal communication
Bond, T., 177
Boud, D., 247–248
Bourdieu, P., 56
Bozarth, J.D., 69–70
Bright, J.E.H., 101
Brockbank, A., 251
Brookfield, S.D., 244–245

Caldwell, B.J., 33
career
   as changing concept, 19–20
   context and, 18–19

career *cont.*
   definition of, 6–11
   Western values and beliefs and, 22–24
career arch, 54–55
career coaching
   vs. career guidance, 25–30
   vs. career mentoring, 34
   definition of, 16–18
   training for, 29–30
career construction theory, 111
career counselling, 11, *12*, 14–16
career decision making theories
   career development theories, 47, 51–55
   integration of, 60
   person–environment fit theories, 47–51
   problems with, 59–60
   role of, 41–46
   structural theories, 47, 55–59
career development theories, 47, 51–55
career education, 11, *12*, 13–14, 15
career guidance, 11–13, 15–16, 25–30
career guidance theories and approaches
   boundaries and, 81–82
   chaos theory of careers, 101
   cognitive-behavioural approaches, 71–73
   constructivism and social constructionism, 85–88
   green guidance, 98–101
   motivational interviewing, 94–98, *96*
   multicultural counselling, 82, 134–137
   person-centred theory, 9, 64–70
   psychodynamic therapy, 73–76
   role of, 63
   solution-focused approaches, 89–94, 197
   systems theory, 101
   transactional analysis, 76–81, *78–79*
career identity, 105–106
career inventories, 82
career learning and development
   benefits of, 200–205
   definition of, 14
   labour market intelligence and information and,
      200, 205–207
   networking skills, 207–208
career mentoring, 31–39
career rainbow, 54–55
Career Thinking Session (CTS), 252–254

careers work
  assessment in, 82–83, 151–154
  core competences and training for, 20–22,
    261–264
  definition of, 6, 8–9
  paradigm shift in, 87–89
  techniques for, 194–198
  transitions in, 154–160, *156*, 161–163
  vignettes, 254–257
  See also career coaching; career counselling
Carruthers, J., 33
Carter, E.M.A., 33
Castells, M., 20
challenging, 191–194
chaos theory of careers, 101
client-centred therapy, 9, 63
closed questions, 186, 217
Cochran, L., 160
cognitive-behavioural therapy (CBT), 16, 71–73
cognitive psychology, 71–72
collage, 232–235
Colley, H., 32, 33
Collin, A., 10, 19–20
community interaction theory, 203
congruence, 66–67, 184
congruence theory of vocational choice, 47–48
Connexions service, 32
Conservative government (1979–1990), 10
constructivism, 86–87, 88
contrast technique, 195
counselling skills
  attending and listening, 184–185
  challenging, 191–194
  networking skills, 207–208
  non-verbal communication and, 182–184,
    182–183, 185
  questioning skills, 185–187
  rapport building, 187–188
  summarising, 187–189
  use of information, 189–190
  use of silence, 187
counter-transference, 75–76
CragRats, 237
creative methodologies
  creative writing, 235–237
  drama, 237–238
  imagination and, 230–231
  vs. interviews, 222
  visual tools, 231–235
creative writing, 235–237
Cregeen-Cook, S., 231, 232

cross-cultural awakening, 135
cross-cultural skills and competences, 137–140
crossroad tool, 232
Csikszentmihalyi, M., 111
Culley, S., 177
cultural integrity, 136

D'Andrea, M., 135
Daniels, J., 135
DASIE lifeskills model, 177
defensiveness, 74–75
developmental psychology, 51
Dewey, J., 209
DiClemente, C.C., 96
digital career literacy, 224–227
digital technologies, 204, 222–230
Dik, B.J., 148
direct discrimination, 125
Dirkx, J.M., 210
Disability Discrimination Act (1995), 127
discrimination, 125
diversity
  anti-oppressive practice and, 131–134, 140–141
  case study, 23–24
  cross-cultural skills and competences and,
    137–140
  equal opportunity and, 124, 126–127
  equality of opportunity and, 124–126
  language of, 124–125
  multicultural approach and, 134–137
  practical activities for practitioners and,
    140–142
  social justice and, 127–131
DOTS model, 161–163, 203
double questions, 186
drama, 237–238
drama triangle, 78–81
drawing, 231–232
Dyson, E., 229

Egan, G., 113, 164, *165*, 166, 169
ego state theory, 76–78
empathy, 66–67, 138, 184
employability skills, 9
Epston, D., 108–109
equal opportunity, 124, 126–127
Equality Act (2010), 125, 127
equality of opportunity, 124–126, 145–146
equity, 126. *See also* equality of opportunity
Eraut, M., 243
Etherington, K., 243

European Convention on Human Rights, 127
evidence-based practice, 112
exceptions questions, 91
experiential learning, 209, 242

FAAST model, 219
fair equality of opportunity, 125, 126, 145–146
Fielding, A.J., 82, 186
Fisher, R., 69–70
flexicurity, 18–19
force-field analysis, 197
formal equality of opportunity, 125
Foucault, M., 107, 109
Freire, P., 245
Freud, S., 73, 76

gaining figure-ground perspective, 195–196
game playing, 76, 78–81
Gati, I. and Tal, S., 59
Gergen, K.J., 86
Gibbs, G., 247
goal setting questions, 91
Gordon, M., 46–47
Gramsci, A., 130
green careers, 130
green guidance, 98–101
Grencavage, L.M., 60
group settings
    advantages and disadvantages of, 208–211
    challenging behaviour in, **267–269**, 270
    FAAST model in, 219
    in organisations, 220
    Single Interaction Model in, 211–219, **212**
GROW model, 178–179

Handy, C., 220
Harris, M., 251
Hawkins, P., 251
hierarchy of needs, 176
Hill, L., 112, 178
Hinds, R., 34–35
Holland, J., 11–12, 47, 48–50
Hooley, T., 224–228
Hopson, B., 156–157, *156*
Human Rights Act (1998), 127
humanistic-existential philosophy, 65
Hunt, C., 235–237
hypothetical questions, 186

icebreakers, 213
identity, 146–147, 154–155

imagine technique, 195
immediacy, 81, 192–194
inclusion, 32, 128
indirect discrimination, 125
information, 189–190
infusion, 136
Inkson, K., 231
Inskipp, F., 251
internet. *See* digital technologies
Irving, B.A., 128–129
Ivey, A.E., 134–135
Ixer, G., 243

Jackson, C., 29–30
job, use of term, 8
Johnson, D., 220, 270
Johnson, F., 220, 270

Kadushin, A., 251
Kasal, E., 210
Kay, D., 34–35
Kelly, G., 71
Kenny, K., 147
Kettunen, J., 230
Kidd, J.M., 45, 49, 60, 70, 82, 146, 152–153
Kline, N., 252–253
Kolb, D.A., 209, 242
Kottkamp, R.B., 248
Krumboltz, J.D., 203

labour market intelligence and information, 200,
    205–207
late modernity, 86, 154
Law, B., 203–204, 224, 227–228, 231–232
leading questions, 186
learning mentors, 32
Leong, T.L., 136–137
Lewin, K., 209
life coaching, 16
'Life Design' approach, 88
life lines, 110–111
life scripts, 76, 78–81
'life-span, life-space' theory, 53–55
life themes, 110–111, 119–120
liquid modernity, 86, 154, 159
listening, 184–185
livelihood, use of term, 8
Lucas, P., 248

Macmillan, H., 51
Malik, B., 128–129

Maslow, A., 176
McLeod, J., 76
McMahon, M., 82, 88, 101
mentoring, 31–39
mentoring game, 265–266
Mezirow, J., 209, 245, 248
Middlemiss, R., 32
Miller, J., 91
Miller, W.R., 95–97
Mills, C., 16, 45–46, 129
miracle questions, 90, 91, 195
model, definition of, 62
Monk, G., 86, 108–109, 134–135
motivational interviewing, 94–98, *96*
multicultural counselling, 82, 134–137
multiple questions, 186
Munby, H., 243

Nag-Arulmani, S., 99, 131, 164, 179, 180
narrative career counselling
    appeal of narrative and, 106–108
    biographicity and, 105–106, 110
    interview structure for, 113–118
    overview, 109–113
    usefulness of, 118–121
narrative therapy, 108–109
Nathan, R., 112, 178
National Careers Service, 29
needs, 176
NEET (Not in Education, Employment or Training),
    32–33
Negative Automatic Thoughts (NATs), 71, 73
Nelson-Jones, R., 177
neoliberalism, 10
network society, 20
networking skills, 207–208
NICE (Network for Innovation in Career Guidance
    and Counselling in Europe), 20–22
Nicholson, N., 158
non-discrimination, 125
non-verbal communication, 182–184, **182–183**, 185
non-verbal following, 185
Norcross, J.C., 60
Nota, L., 88

occupation, use of term, 8
O'Connell, B., 92
open questions, 186, 217–218
organisations. *See* adult careers work
Osterman, K.F., 248

paradigm shift, 87–89
Parsons, F., 11–12, 47, 50, 124
Patterson, C.H., 69
Pearce, M., 136–137
person-centred theory, 9, 64–70
person–environment fit theories, 47–51
perspective, definition of, 62
Plant, P., 98–101
positivist psychology, 201
postmodernism, 85–86
poststructuralism, 85–86
posture, 185
Proctor, B., 251
profession, use of term, 8
professional networks, 30–31
professionalism, 22
Pryor, R.G.L., 101
psychodynamic therapy, 73–76
psychometric tests, 82

questioning skills, 185–187

Race Relations Act (1976), 127
rapport building skills, 187–188, 217–218
Rawls, J., 126, 127–128
realism, 144–145, 147–149
reflective and reflexive practice
    Career Thinking Session and, 252–254
    definition of, 242–243
    models and practices for, 246–250
    narrative career counselling and, 110
    overview, 36–39, 241–246
    supervision and, 241, 250–252
reflexive imperative, 154–155
Reid, H.L., 37, 82, 137–138, 186
resilience, 9, 144–145, 149–151
restatement, 187
RIASEC model, 49–50
Roberts, K., 56–59
Rodger, A., 48, 50, 60
Rogers, C., 9, 63, 65–66, 70, 164, 270
role play, 237–238
Rollnick, R., 95–97
Rossier, J., 88
Russell, T., 243

Sampson, J.P., 88
Savickas, M.L.
    on career construction theory, 15, 45
    on career services, 10–12, 41

Savickas, M.L. *cont.*
  on middle class, 51
  on narrative careers work, 110–112, 113,
     114–117, 119
  social constructionism and, 88
scaling questions, 90, 91
Schlossberg, N.K., 159
Schön, D.A., 45–46, 243
scientific matching approach, 47
self-helpfulness questions, 91
self-presentation, 187
Sen, A., 130
Sex Discrimination Act (1975), 127
Shohet, R., 251
silence, 187
Simpson, L., 237
Single Interaction Model (SIM)
  alternatives to, 177–180
  application of, 165–169, 176–177
  in group settings, 211–219, **212**
  overview, 163–164, *165*
  three-stage model of helping in, *167*, 169–176
Skiffington, S., 16–17, 70, 89, 220
social constructionism, 85–88
social inclusion, 32, 128–129
social justice, 127–131, 145–146
solution-focused approaches, 89–94, 197
Starr, J., 89–90
structural theories, 47, 55–59
structuralism, 86
substantive equality of opportunity, 125
Sue, D.W., 134–135, 137
Sultana, R., 19, 126, 130, 145
summarizing skills, 187–189
Super, D., 10, 52–54
supervision, 241, 250–252
supplementary questions, 187
systems theory, 101

talent matching, 145
Taylor, E.W., 210
Thatcher, M., 10
Theatre-in-Education programmes, 237
theory, definition of, 62
Thomsen, R., 209
time lines, 232
transactional analysis, 76–81, *78–79*

transference, 75–76
transformative learning, 209–211
transitions, 154–160, *156*, 161–163
transtheoretical model of intentional human
    behavioural change (TTM), 96–98, *96*

unconditional positive regard (UPR), 66–67, 135,
    184, 187

Velasquez, M., 96
verbal following, 185
visual tools, 231–235
vocation, use of term, 8
vocational choice theory, 46–51. *See also* career
    decision making theories
vocational guidance, *12*

Watson, M., 82, 87, 88, 131–132, 141–142
Watts, A.G., 145
Weiner, J., 250–251
West, L., 112
West, M., 158
Westergaard, J., 66, 71, 76, 137, 191, 219, 250
wheel of change, 96–98, *96*
White, M., 108–109
Whitmore, J., 70
Williamson, H., 32
Winnicott, D., 110, 232
Winslade, J., 108–109
Wolff, Dr, 46
women, 51, 53
work-books, 16–17
work, use of term, 7–8

Yates, J.
  on career decision making, 59
  on career guidance and career coaching, 28
  on GROW model, 178–179
  on job satisfaction, 147
  on labour market intelligence and information, 206
  on motivational interviewing, 96
  narrative career counselling and, 112
  on solution-focused approaches, 89
Yorks, L., 210
Young, R.A., 10, 19–20

Zeus, P., 16–17, 70, 89, 220